Dave
Hope you can find
my book informative.
Richie

W9-BYG-277

MONEY MATTERS
AND
PERSONAL FINANCE

MONEY MATTERS
AND
PERSONAL FINANCE

Information You Should Have Been Taught in School

RICHARD E. MARINACCIO

iUniverse, Inc.
Bloomington

Money Matters and Personal Finance
Information You Should Have Been Taught in School

iUniverse books may be ordered through booksellers or by contacting:

iUniverse
1663 Liberty Drive
Bloomington, IN 47403
www.iuniverse.com
1-800-Authors (1-800-288-4677)

ISBN: 978-1-4620-0523-9 (sc)
ISBN: 978-1-4620-0524-6 (hc)

Library of Congress Control Number: 2011913274

Printed in the United States of America

iUniverse rev. date: 11/19/2011

To my three children, Richard Jr., Kristin, and Jennifer, and to my grandson, Ryan Swisher.

Contents

Illustrations

Tables

Preface

This book grew out of financial information that I put together for my children after I retired. It contains information on a number of topics about money and money matters that I consider important for adults, young and old, to understand. Unfortunately our school system, for whatever reason, fails to teach most people the financial information necessary to successfully make their way in our society. People are left to learn the hard way, mostly through trial and error. Many never learn, and they suffer sometimes disastrous consequences. The present financial distress in the United States and other developed societies is at least partly a result of this.

It has been my hope to educate my children and provide them with enough financial knowledge so they can avoid financial pitfalls and can prosper. Since it has been difficult to get my children to listen to all my talks, and since as I've told them many times I will not be around forever, and, finally, at the urging of my wife, I decided to put my financial knowledge on paper.

A major objective was to put the information in one easily read document of moderate length. If it were too long and difficult to read, not many (including my children) would read it. Much of the information can be obtained from books and papers that have been written on the various topics. Much time and effort, however, is required to learn the subject matter by studying an array of written material, and few actually do it. The information provided won't make the reader an expert on any of the topics, but hopefully it will provide a good foundation.

Although my degree is in electrical engineering and most of my work experience is in system engineering and management, I've always been interested in money and financial matters. During my life, I have accumulated a fundamental understanding of a broad range of financial topics, both from formal financial courses and through self-study and experience. Particularly since none of my children have financial backgrounds, I have tried hard to make the information understandable to nonfinancial people. Following the advice of Will Durant, author of *The Story of Civilization*, who said "Let us before we die, gather up our heritage, and offer it to our children," I have gathered up my financial knowledge and offer it to my children and other interested readers.

Acknowledgments

First, I would like to thank my wife Pat for urging me to write down the information I wanted her and my children to know about financial matters, since it provided the motivation for writing the book. She also reviewed several chapters to help determine if they would be understandable to nonfinancial people, and this was most helpful.

A number of other family members and friends reviewed some or all of the manuscript, and I would like to thank them for their efforts and helpful comments and suggestions. Particular thanks go to Kevin O'leary, owner of a fishing business in Alaska; my nephew, Joe Dyer, a partner in a Washington DC law-firm; and my niece, Jackie Dyer, a graduate of the Harvard Business School and now a full-time mother, for their review of the entire manuscript. Jackie also provided some needed editing. Thanks also go to Neville Cramer, author of the successful book *Immigration Chaos*, for his review of the chapter on identity theft and his helpful suggestions on publishing; Jon Klesner, my State Farm Insurance agent, for his review of the chapter on insurance; Mike Ford for his review of much of the chapter on debt; and to two friends since childhood, Richard Ross, a retired IRS estate tax attorney, and William Pascucci, a partner in a Norwalk, Connecticut, law-firm engaged in estate planning, for their review of the chapter on estate planning. Finally, I would like to thank Dan McCallum for our discussions about the valuation process he went through before selling his small trucking business.

Introduction

This is a book about money, its management, accumulation, preservation, and transfer to heirs. Money matters. While some may think that money is the root of all evil, money is actually the source of much good in the world, and without it civilization wouldn't have advanced very far. Money has many benefits, and it's easier to be happy with it than without it. Money can, for example, provide economic security and allow you to ride out tough economic times, let you live where and how you like, and if invested earn more money, provide jobs for others, and help develop ideas and products that benefit society.

Money creates opportunities and choices. Unfortunately, one can make bad choices` as well as good choices. If you have money, you can elect to live simply or lavishly; you can elect to do nothing or to pursue a satisfying career of some kind, whether in education, health-care, business, the arts, politics, or another area. The more money you have, the more choices that are available to you, even the choice of your mate. Since money has such an influence on our lives, we should all want to know as much about money as possible.

Good management of your money is essential if you are to accumulate any significant amount or preserve what you already have. Most Americans work hard for their money, but many spend it unnecessarily. As a result, they don't accumulate much, and some borrow excessively. For most people, money accumulation requires disciplined saving, smart investments, and time. Minimizing taxes and finance charges makes it much easier, and avoiding financial pitfalls and setbacks allows you to preserve what you have accumulated. Insurance provides protection for many of life's downside financial risks, and retirement and estate planning make it more likely that you will be able to enjoy your latter years and to transfer more of your wealth to intended heirs when you die, if that's your desire.

Topics for the book were selected to provide the reader with a basic understanding of the financial information needed to successfully navigate life in our society. Chapter 1 discusses money in general terms, including a brief history, creation by the banking system, purchasing power, earnings power, and time value. Chapter 2 discusses net worth, and shows how to calculate personal net worth. Chapters 3 through 8 cover things you can and should do to increase your net worth: management of household finances and control of spending, various types of debt and taxes and some ways to minimize them, disciplined savings, retirement planning, and investing. Chapter 9 shows how to value various types of assets. Chapter 10 discusses the various types of insurance needed to protect you and your family against potential loss of your assets and earnings power, due to various calamities. Chapter 11 deals with identity theft protection, and chapter 12 covers the essence of estate planning. Chapter 13 provides a brief summary and general financial guidance and recommendations. Appendices show how to capitalize an earnings' stream, and how you can relate the value of a company (or its stock) to its book value and the amount of capital invested in it. Chapter 9, on asset valuation, might be difficult for some. It was originally to be an appendix, but because of its importance, I decided to include it in the body of the book.

This book should be helpful to people of all ages but particularly useful to young adults, since they have had an appalling lack of financial content in their education. Hopefully, it will help start them on the right path. Since money accumulation takes time, the earlier you begin the better. Also, the more you understand about what it takes, the easier it will be to actually achieve.

Mathematical formulations have been minimized, and most have been placed in appendices. While each chapter basically stands alone, an understanding of the concepts of present and future value, presented in the first chapter, is important for a more complete understanding of several of the other chapters.

Chapter 1

Money

Money takes many forms, performs many functions, and has many interesting aspects. There is a lot to understand about money. We are all familiar with coin and currency as money, but checking accounts, savings accounts, and certificates of deposit are also considered money.[1] Money is first of all a medium of exchange; it can be used to purchase goods and services and to pay bills and debts. It is also a measure of value; asset and liability values are measured in money terms. Additionally, money is a store of value; it can be saved for later use.

Money is created and the supply controlled by the banking system. Money has earnings power and when loaned or invested can earn more money; when accumulated in various forms, it becomes wealth. The value of money, however, is not constant. Its purchasing power can change—decreasing during inflationary times and increasing during deflationary periods. Because of its earnings power, money, independent of the change in its purchasing power, has a time value; the money you now have has a future value, and money you expect to receive in the future has a present value.

To better understand money, a little history might be helpful. Money replaced barter as a way to more easily trade or exchange goods and services, and many different items have been used as money. For most of recorded history, a precious metal of some kind—mostly gold, silver,

---

[1]   A broader definition includes other assets that can be quickly converted to cash, such as Treasury securities and corporate notes.

or copper—made into coins was used as money. Some of the American colonies tried shells or wampum for a period. Maryland used tobacco for about 150 years and Virginia for nearly two hundred years. Tobacco had a brief return in World War II prison camps and in Germany after the war, in the form of cigarettes.

Paper money is a relatively recent creation and in the Western world began as notes issued by banks, first in Europe and then in the American colonies. Later American colonial governments issued their own notes. Notes circulated together with gold and silver coins. Banknotes and government notes, at least initially, were fully convertible into gold or silver, although the amount of gold and silver available for conversion was often insufficient. Government notes had the added feature that they were declared legal tender, and thus valid for payment of debts. Eventually national governments and their central banks became the sole issuers of circulating currency. Banks and other institutions still issue notes, known as commercial paper, but these notes are short-term debt and are not part of the circulating currency.

A major concern of those who have money is uncertainty about its future purchasing power. Gold and silver tend to hold their value, but paper money is different. The concern with paper money was and still is that it might be issued in excessive quantities, increasing the money supply beyond that required for economic expansion, and devaluing it. Convertibility into gold and silver provided some protection against this possibility and was the basis of the gold standard, the monetary system that prevailed throughout the world for many years. Eventually the world, including the United States, abandoned the gold standard. The United States stopped conversion during the Great Depression, primarily because the money supply was shrinking as people converted currency into gold, removing it from the treasury and the banking system, and reducing reserves. The United States not only stopped converting currency into gold, but it also actually called in the gold held by citizens. The United States returned to the gold standard in the mid-'30s but only for international transactions. It completely abandoned the gold standard in the early '70s, when it stopped using gold to settle international transactions. Shortly thereafter, US citizens were again legally permitted to hold gold, and this continues to be allowed.

Although we are no longer on the gold standard, our money continues to have value because of its general acceptability both in this country and the world. The US dollar at this writing continues to be the world's reserve currency,[2] and the debts of the United States are generally denominated in dollars. Also, oil and many other commodities are currently priced in dollars on world markets. Our currency is designated as Federal Reserve Notes, and it has been declared legal tender by the government for the payment of all debts, both public and private (you can confirm this by checking the printing on a dollar bill). It is what's called a "fiat currency," a currency by declaration of the government. Treasury issued securities—notes, bills, and bonds—are backed by the US government, and some other parts of the US money supply—checking accounts, bank accounts, and certificates of deposit—are guaranteed by the Federal Deposit Insurance Corporation (FDIC) but only up to a certain amount.

Money Creation

Money creation is performed by the banking system. Here I'm not talking about the ability of a government's central bank to print new currency, but rather the expansion of the money supply through deposit creation, a brief description of which follows. Money creation is simply the result of fractional reserve banking, the system used in the United States and around the world almost from the beginning of banking.

With fractional reserve banking, banks are only required to hold a fraction of the money deposited with them in reserve; they are free to lend the remainder. Reserves held over and above the reserve requirement are known as excess reserves. When someone deposits currency or a check into his account or opens a new account at a bank, the money received becomes an asset on the bank's accounting books and the deposit becomes a liability. The deposit is, of course, an asset of the depositor. By law the bank must keep a portion of the new deposit as reserves, but it can lend the remainder, since these are excess reserves. Assuming the reserve requirement is 10%, the bank can lend the other 90%. Unlike a single bank, the banking system can create substantial amounts of new money. Here's basically how it works. The 90% that is lent will eventually find its way to other banks, where it will be deposited. When deposited,

---

[2]   Because of the amount and growth of US debt, several countries have recently suggested that this be changed. Some are beginning to diversify their reserves out of dollars and into other currencies, gold, and other natural resources.

it increases the assets and deposits at these other banks. They must also maintain 10% as reserves, but they can lend the remaining 90%. This 90% when lent will again be deposited in still other banks, and these banks will likewise be allowed to lend 90% of the new money deposited with them. The process continues, with the result that the banking system can theoretically lend many times the original deposit made at the first bank. In general, when the banking system gains new reserves, it can create new deposits by some multiple of the reserves. The multiple is the inverse of the reserve requirement, e.g., if the reserve requirement is 10%, as above, the multiple is ten. If the reserve requirement is 20%, the multiple is only five.

The Federal Reserve, the US central bank, influences the US money supply and interest rates by exercising control over the quantity of reserves held by the banking system. It has various ways to accomplish this. The primary method is through the purchase or sale of securities (normally short-term Treasury securities). When the Federal Reserve purchases securities, it supplies money to the banking system, increasing reserves. If it sells securities, it reduces reserves. A change in bank reserves can expand (or contract) the money supply by a multiple of the change, as described in the previous paragraph.

The response of the banking system to a change in reserves, however, may be less than the theoretical multiple. Banks, for example, may decide to limit their lending for fear of not being paid back and keep excess reserves. This happened during the Great Depression. Something similar happened as a result of the financial crisis of 2008/9. In this instance, investments of the banks deteriorated, reducing their assets and ability and willingness to make loans. The Federal Reserve responded by buying securities from the banks, increasing their reserves in an effort to restore lending.[3]

Fractional reserve banking was also the cause of a serious problem. If everyone that had deposits at a bank came for their money at the same time, they couldn't all get it. The result was the so-called run on the bank, and runs happened when people became concerned they might not get

---

[3]　In a program called quantitative easing, the Federal Reserve took the unusual step of buying a considerable amount of agency debt and agency mortgage-backed securities, in addition to Treasury securities, to increase bank reserves.

their money. This banking problem was essentially solved by the creation of the FDIC, which guaranteed deposits up to a certain amount.

Earnings Power

Most people need to work to earn money to support their lifestyle. If, however, you have sufficient money or capital, you don't need to work. You may want to but you don't need to. Your money and other assets have earnings power and can work for you. Earnings come in the form of interest, dividends, rent, royalties, private business income, or simply the gain or appreciation in the market value of an asset. Net earnings, or earnings after deducting expenses, are the earnings that count.

Interest is the fee that you are paid to allow someone else, e.g., a bank, corporation, or government, to use your money. The interest rate is usually high enough to cover inflation and provide a fee for use of your money. The fee is in part determined by the riskiness of the loan. Interest rates paid on US Treasury securities, considered risk-free investments, are generally lower than those paid on corporate bonds, which have various types of risk associated with them.

Dividends are payments made by many corporations or businesses to their shareholders. They can be made in the form of cash, stock, or other property. Dividends are usually paid out of the earnings of the company and vary considerably from company to company. The dividend rate, or yield, is the dividend expressed as a percentage of the market price of the stock.

Rent is a fee charged for allowing someone to use your property or assets. Rents vary considerably and depend on the property and its location.

Royalties are payments, usually a share or percentage of the amount of product sold, made to the owner of a right (like a patent on an invention or a copyright on a book) for permission to use it.

Private business income is the net income of a sole proprietorship, or a person's share of the net income of a business partnership in which they have an interest. The net income is either paid out or reinvested in the business. The return on investment is the net income provided to the individual divided by the capital he or she has invested.

The gain, or appreciation, in the market value of an asset compared to its cost basis is a capital gain. An asset can appreciate in value for many reasons. For example, the asset may simply have been undervalued when it was acquired, the earnings prospects of the asset may have improved, or the demand for the asset may have increased.

The total return on an asset, a stock, for example, includes dividends or interest earned plus the appreciation in the value of the asset. The rate is the total return expressed as a percentage of the original market value of the asset. Total return is the most important measure of earnings.

Purchasing Power

In 1848, the economist and philosopher John Stuart Mill provided an explanation of what determines the purchasing power of money (Galbraith 1975, 20). He basically said that the purchasing power of money was dependent on supply and demand—the supply being all the money in circulation and the demand consisting of all the goods and services offered for sale. This was the original quantity theory of money and was accepted for many years in that form. Inflation could thus be caused by a money supply greater than demand and deflation by a supply shortage. This explanation, however, was not entirely correct, because, as was later discovered, even though the money supply might be adequate, money might not be spent. Modifications have since been made to Mill's explanation. The primary one was provided by Irving Fisher, the Yale economist, who made prices dependent not just on the quantity of money but also on the rate at which it is spent, the so-called velocity of money (Galbraith 1975, 208). Too great a supply of money can indeed result in inflation but only if it has sufficient velocity. If money is not spent fast enough, on the other hand, the result can be deflation, no matter how large the money supply. Complications arise in trying to control the money supply, and thus the purchasing power of money, because there is no single definition of the money supply and because the velocity of money depends on many factors, many of which are psychological.

Whatever the cause, the purchasing power of money changes with time. A dollar today generally buys less than it did in previous years because of inflation. During deflationary times it can temporarily buy more. Economists talk about current dollars and constant dollars. Current dollars are the ones you have in your pocket at any time, and they have the purchasing power that the dollar has when you buy something. Goods and services are bought with current dollars, although the bill may be paid with dollars of different purchasing power. Constant dollars are hypothetical. They are dollars that have been adjusted for inflation and deflation to try to maintain the purchasing power constant from one date to another.

Because the purchasing power of the dollar changes over time, it's natural to want to measure this change. Economists use price indices to measure how prices change over time. The Consumer Price Index (CPI) is used to measure the change in the average price of a basket of goods and services that a typical American household buys. The Bureau of Labor Statistics compiles and publishes the CPI data. Another index, the Gross Domestic Product (GDP) deflator, measures the change in the average price of all the goods and services produced in the country in a given year, not just those bought by consumers. The GDP is measured both in current dollars and constant dollars. The current dollar GDP is referred to as nominal GDP, and the constant dollar GDP is referred to as the "real" GDP. The Bureau of Economic Analysis compiles and publishes GDP data, and it determines the GDP deflator.

Inflation

Inflation is a general rise in price levels and a loss in the purchasing power of money. The average level of consumer prices in the United States, as measured by the CPI published on the website of the Bureau of Labor Statistics, has risen nearly every year the past hundred years or so, with the notable exception of 1921, 1922, the years 1926 through 1932 that encompassed the Great Depression, 1938, 1939, 1949, and 2009. Inflation as measured by the CPI increased by more than twenty times (2000%) between 1913 and 2008, and the purchasing power of the US dollar in 2008 was only about 5% of what it was in 1913. Because almost all our experience has been with inflation (not many people that experienced the Great Depression are alive today), we have come to expect, at least until very recently, that the US dollar will lose purchasing power over time.

Inflation hurts people living on fixed incomes, the elderly, for example, and those whose incomes rise less quickly than inflation. It hurts lenders and those that have their savings in longer-term fixed-income type investments. Inflation benefits borrowers, particularly those with significant amounts of debt, like the typical home owner and most governments, and it also helps those with investments in tangible assets such as commodities and real estate.

If most of your income comes from a pension that's not indexed to inflation (most private pensions are not indexed) and/or from investments like long-term bonds with fixed interest payments, your income is either fixed or nearly so, but inflation will cause your expenses to increase due to rising prices. People in this type of situation are big losers, particularly if inflation persists. If your assets are in long-term bonds with fixed coupon payments you can get hurt two ways: not only are the fixed payments worth less, but if you sell the bond prior to maturity, you lose principal as interest rates rise from those that prevailed when you originally purchased the bonds. The market value of a bond is inversely related to interest rates, as discussed in chapters 8 and 9, and the longer the duration of the bond the greater the loss. If your savings are in short-maturity fixed-income investments, you can roll them over to higher interest rate instruments as interest rates rise, offsetting some of the effects of inflation. Inflation also generally hurts all buyers of goods and services, since prices tend to rise faster than incomes.

Inflation benefits those who own tangible assets such as commodities and real estate, the values of which increase in dollar terms. Borrowers, particularly those with large amounts of debt, gain because they can pay off their debts with cheaper money. Home owners with mortgages are big winners, and they can gain two ways: first, home values rise, increasing their wealth; and second, if they have fixed-rate mortgages, their debt payments can decrease as a percentage of income, if their wages increase because of inflation. Businesses with pricing power generally gain, since they can increase prices faster than their costs rise.

Many people, particularly those who benefit, believe that some inflation is a good thing, in that it makes people feel good and in that it stimulates economic activity. Since it is virtually impossible to have perfectly stable prices, a little inflation is certainly preferable to deflation, which is much more difficult to stop once started. Most would agree, however, that a high level of inflation, like we had in the United States from 1973 to 1981, is bad, and that if not stopped it can feed on itself, get out of control, and do serious damage to the economy and society in general. The hyperinflation that occurred in Germany after World War I is an example of inflation that got completely out of control. Prices rose without limit, and the German currency ended up being worthless.

Germans to this day are wary of inflation and are more inclined to try to prevent or limit it than most other countries. While it is not clear whether inflation actually increases the size of the real economic pie, it does produce clear winners and losers. Inflation effectively transfers wealth from creditors to debtors, and it benefits those that own tangible assets.

Deflation

Deflation, the opposite of inflation, refers to the general decline in price levels and to the increase in the purchasing power of money. During the Great Depression, consumer prices in the United States dropped about 25%. Those with money assets and little or no debt benefit from deflation. Those with debt and tangible assets get hurt. The prices of tangible assets—houses, commodities, etc.—generally decline. If you manage to retain your job or your pension, you benefit, because prices tend to drop faster than wages. If you have lots of debt and your salary declines, or you lose your job and you don't have other money sources, you're in trouble. You can, for example, easily lose your house because you can't make the payments. In contrast to inflation, which can stimulate, deflation depresses people and economic activity, and it can lead to an actual depression, in which the economy shrinks significantly and unemployment reaches very high levels. Unemployment during the Great Depression rose to about 25%. Unlike a recession, which is a relatively small, temporary decline in economic activity, a depression is a large, longer lasting decline, and once it takes hold it is very difficult to recover from. During the Great Depression, real Gross National Product (GNP) in the United States fell by about 30%, and current dollar GNP declined by almost 50%. (Wonnacott 1986, 140).

The Great Depression of the 1930s may have been an extreme, but it took many years for the economy to recover. The government increased spending significantly beginning in 1930, and it managed to decrease unemployment somewhat. It, however, took the Second World War, which put most of the remaining unemployed to work and forced people to sacrifice and save and delay spending, to set the stage for a full recovery. The pent-up demand for consumer goods, together with the large amount of personal savings accumulated during the war years, provided the basis for the economic recovery that followed the end of the war.

9

Time Value of Money

The time value of money is perhaps the single most important concept to understand about money. It is well known that inflation erodes the purchasing power of money and that deflation enhances it. However, even with no inflation or deflation, the value of money is still a function of time. The "future value" is an estimate of how much the money you have today could be worth at some time in the future. The "present value," in contrast, is the value of money that you expect to receive at some time in the future discounted back to the present.

Future Value

The "future value" of money is the result of its earnings power coupled with the compounding effect. Because money you have today has the power to earn more money, its "future value" is greater than its present value. Compounding enhances the earnings power. Money allowed to grow compounded can have a future value substantially greater than its value today. The future value of money is a projection, based on expected future earnings rates and the number of compounding periods in the time interval of interest.

Earnings, or return, is the principal amount multiplied by the rate of return. If funds are not withdrawn but remain invested, and if earnings are allowed to accumulate and are reinvested, then interest, or return, is earned on both the original principal and also on the reinvested earnings. This is called compounding. Many people have described the compounding effect as a miracle, since it can result in tremendous gains over time. Taxes, however, can reduce the gains substantially and lessen the miracle. If taxes can be deferred or avoided entirely, the gains can be truly miraculous. If compounded over N periods, the future value equals the original principle multiplied by the compounding factor, $(1+R)^N$. The earnings rate, R, and the number of compounding periods, N, must be consistent. If compounded yearly, R is the annual rate; if compounded monthly, R is the monthly rate; or if compounded daily, R is the daily rate.

Figure 1-1 shows the miracle of compounding. It shows the future value of one dollar that you have today earning the stipulated rate of return, R, compounded on an annual basis. R is that annual rate of return that must be earned each and every year to achieve the result. As can be seen, the growth of your money can be quite substantial if allowed to accumulate for many years. After forty years, for example, a single dollar earning 10%, compounded annually, would be worth about $45 (if no taxes had to be paid). If the funds were in a tax-deferred account and withdrawn at that point and taxes paid at a 20% rate, for example, you would end up with about $36. If you had to pay taxes on the earnings each year, you would end up with less.

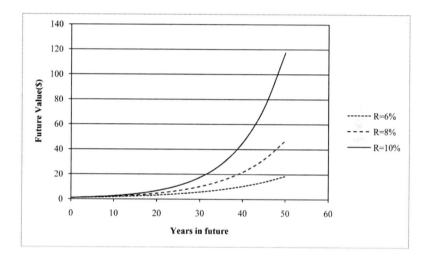

Figure 1-1, Future value of a $1 investment

Present Value

Money that you expect to get in the future, a pension or inheritance, for example, has a "present value" that is less than the amount you will actually receive in the future. Funds you expect to receive in the future get discounted to bring them back to the present. The "present value" is what you would expect to get today, if you sold your future interest in something; it is also what you would expect to pay now, if you were to buy a future interest in something. The present value of a lump sum future amount, for example, is given by the future amount multiplied by the factor $1/(1+D)^N$. The term $1/(1+D)^N$ is the discount factor and D the discount rate. Discounting is the reverse of compounding, and the discount factor is the inverse of the compounding factor. Discounting is necessary to bring money back to the present, because if you had the money today it could earn a return. As usual, the values of D and N must be consistent.

Figure 1-2 plots the present value of $1,000 as a function of the number of years in the future that the money will be received, for different discount rates. As can be seen, the present value is significantly less than the $1,000. Even if the discount rate is only 4%, the $1,000 you expect to receive thirty years in the future is worth only a little more than $300 today.

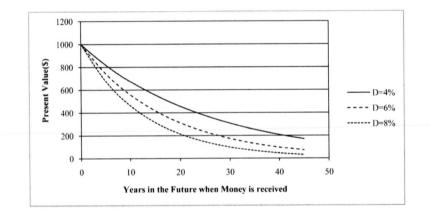

Figure 1-2, Present value of $1,000 received in the future

The discount rate used to determine the present value is basically the rate of return that you could expect to earn on the money assuming you had it today. While this is related to expected future inflation, it is not the same as the inflation rate. The discount rate is generally greater than the expected inflation rate.

In addition to calculating the present value of a lump sum future amount, one can also calculate the present value of a series of income payments. If you know or can estimate the series of income payments, these future payments can be converted into a present lump sum amount of capital. This is called income capitalization, and the general approach for doing this is called discounted cash flow (DCF). To calculate the present value of any income stream, the present value of each element of the stream is calculated by multiplying by the appropriate discount factor, and all the present values are added together to obtain the present lump sum value. Any measurable income stream can be capitalized. The income stream might be a series of interest payments, property rents, dividends, corporate earnings, or free cash flow, to name some of the more common forms. Many income streams can continue for a long time and have many elements. To capitalize these, the present value of each element must be calculated and summed. The present lump sum value of many income streams of interest, however, can be calculated with simple equations. Appendix I shows the mathematics of income capitalization and provides derivations for several of these equations.

Discounted cash flow analysis is used to determine the present value of many different types of income-producing assets. It is used, for example, to determine the lump sum value of pensions and annuities, the "rational value" of bonds in the secondary market, the "intrinsic value" of businesses and their stocks, and the investment value of income-producing real estate. Chapter 9 shows how to value these types of assets. Present value calculations are estimates. If, however, everyone agrees on the discount rate and the elements of the income stream, everyone will calculate the same value.

Chapter 2

Net Worth

Net worth is a measure of wealth. It can be your personal net worth, or it can be the net worth of your household, if you have a family. It is simply the financial value of your remaining assets after subtracting all your liabilities or debt. The greater your net worth, the wealthier you are. Calculating your personal net worth is similar to the calculation of shareholders' equity for a corporation or owners' equity for a private business. You are simply preparing a personal financial balance sheet.

A business balance sheet or balance statement presents the assets, liabilities, and owners' equity of a business entity at a given point in time. It is typically prepared on a monthly basis, and for a publicly owned company it is published quarterly. Similar to that for a business entity, your personal net worth is a snapshot of your wealth at a point in time. It is smart to measure your personal financial wealth or net worth periodically; I recommend doing it on a monthly basis.

To prepare your own personal or household balance sheet, you need to know your assets and liabilities and their current values. The following pages discuss assets and liabilities in general terms and should help you identify your own assets and liabilities and how to value them.

If you prepare your own balance statement and update it periodically, you can analyze your financial performance much like a corporation's performance is analyzed. You can, for example, calculate the growth rate of your assets and your net worth. If you are to accumulate wealth, your assets and personal net worth need to increase significantly with time. You should set goals for how much you want these to increase. Some things you should do to increase your net worth are discussed at the end of this chapter and are elaborated on in subsequent chapters.

Assets

Economic assets are things or resources owned, in whole or in part, by a person or entity, the value of which can be quantified or measured in money terms. A common characteristic of all economic assets is their potential to provide a cash benefit to the owner. The cash benefit can be immediate or sometime in the future.

Assets can be tangible or intangible. Tangible assets are things like real estate and motor vehicles. Intangible assets include financial assets, intellectual property, and goodwill. Intangible assets of households are mostly financial.

A list of commonly held household assets is given below.

<u>Tangible</u>
Real estate
Motor vehicles
Personal items
Precious metals
<u>Financial</u>
Cash and cash equivalents
Time deposits (CDs)
Insurance policy cash values
Insurance policy dividends
Retirement accounts
Stocks and bonds
Money owed to you
Tax rebate due
Private business equity

Some assets are preferable to others, but which are to be preferred at any given time depends on economic conditions. As mentioned in chapter 1, the nominal value of tangible assets increases during inflationary times and decreases during deflationary times. The value of real estate, for example, increases during inflationary times. The value of precious metals, gold coins, for example, increases during times of inflation and/or financial uncertainty. Because of interest rates, the value of certain financial assets, such as bonds, declines during inflationary times and increases during deflationary times. Cash, or currency, however, is more valuable during deflationary times.

The quality of all assets is not the same. Many assets such as bonds, money you might have loaned to others, even your pension, are debts or liabilities of others, and their value depends on the ability of the debtor to pay.

The liquidity of assets, how quickly they can be converted to cash, also differs. Some assets, such as checking account balances, bank accounts, or US Treasury bills, are highly liquid and are called cash equivalents. Publicly traded stocks and bonds are also highly liquid. Real estate, on the other hand, is not very liquid; it can take a long time to sell a property.

Asset values change with time, and for valuation purposes you should use the present market value where possible. In financial accounting, tangible assets are generally recorded at their original cost and depreciated over time. The depreciated value (original cost less accumulated depreciation) is called the book value. The actual market value may be more or less than the book value of an asset. The market value is more accurate, but it is not generally used in accounting because not everyone necessarily agrees on the market value. It is only well known when you buy or sell something. At other times it must be estimated, and different people can make different estimates.

Many financial assets, such as stocks and bonds, are valued at market prices. Stock in a publicly traded company, for example, even though it may fluctuate considerably over time, has a known market value at any point in time determined by its price on a stock exchange. The same thing is true for publicly traded bonds.

While most assets have markets where they are bought or sold, others do not. I know of no market for defined benefit pensions or Social Security retirement benefits, both of which are future economic benefits. If you are vested in a defined benefit pension plan, you've earned a certain monthly pension, payable for life beginning at your normal retirement age. The same is true for Social Security. These future monthly cash inflows are assets; their present value can be estimated, even though you are generally not able to convert these assets into immediate cash. Some companies will permit you to take your retirement benefits as a lump sum payment when you retire or if you leave the company prior to retirement for some reason. Defined benefit pensions also, typically, have some type of survivorship benefit. The present value of a defined benefit retirement plan can be calculated if you know the retirement date and the monthly benefit amount. To do this, an estimate of life expectancy after retirement is needed, together with the current discount rate for determining lump sum payouts. Chapter 9 on asset valuation explains how to do this. You should only capitalize the monthly benefit that you've earned to date, not a projection of the amount you might be entitled to if you continue working until retirement.

A similar thing can be done for any Social Security benefits you've earned to date. Social Security, however, is different; when you die the benefit paid to your estate is only $255. Your spouse's benefit, if you have one, however, may increase. Because it all may essentially disappear when you die, Social Security is not ordinarily included in personal net worth calculations.

The market value of personal items can also be estimated, and it is generally considerably less than what you paid to acquire them.

It might interest some readers to know that there is even a market for life insurance policies. If you no longer want to continue a life insurance policy you own, your insurance company will normally allow you to surrender the policy and, in exchange, receive the cash surrender value. However, if you are older than about seventy, you likely can receive a greater amount through a life settlement with a company in that business.

Perhaps your most valuable asset is your ability to earn money in the future. These future earnings can be also be capitalized, or converted to a present lump sum value, and this will be done in chapter 10, where the amount of life insurance a family bread-earner might need is discussed. The present value of your future earnings can be a very large number. Future earnings, however, are not normally considered part of your financial net worth. There is generally no guarantee of the amount of future earnings or whether you will even live to earn any money. Future earnings only have a potential value. For those individuals with guaranteed employment contracts, such as certain athletes, it might be a different story, depending on the specifics of the contract.

Asset valuation is an extremely important subject, and chapter 9 shows how to estimate the value of several different types of assets.

Liabilities

Liabilities are debts or financial obligations incurred but not yet paid. Examples are shown below. As with assets, one should use the current value of the liability.

Car loans
Credit card balances
Personal loans
Mortgage balance
Equity loan balance
Tax liabilities

Mortgage debt, for example, is the current loan balance, not the sum of all your future payments. The current mortgage balance is, in fact, the discounted present value of all those scheduled future payments, both principal and interest, with your current interest rate used as the discount rate.

The value of credit card debt is also the current balance. For people that only make minimal payments, however, it is revealing to calculate the present value of credit card debt assuming a schedule of payments, including interest payments, more representative of how the debtor might actually pay. Credit card debt carries a very high interest rate. Since this rate is much higher than any earnings rate the debtor might reasonably expect to earn on the money (if they had it today), the present value of credit card debt to the debtor would be much higher than the current balance. If the debtor was aware of this, he or she might be more inclined to pay it off quickly or might be less inclined to incur it in the first place.

Tax liabilities include any current year underpayment and any deferred taxes. Deferred taxes result from deferred income, such as regular IRAs, 401(k)s, and pensions, you might have. Deferring taxes is a good thing, but taxes cannot be deferred forever. The government wants to be paid eventually. As with other liabilities, you should use the present value of deferred taxes. Unlike credit card debt, the present value of deferred taxes will be less than the actual amount of deferred taxes you might owe. Deferred taxes will be paid in the future, possibly far into the future, and they carry no interest charges. To bring the amount back to the present, it must be discounted. To do this you need to estimate when the future distributions will be taken, the taxes paid, and to determine an appropriate discount rate.

Hypothetical Net Worth Calculation

A hypothetical personal net worth calculation is shown below in table 2-1. The example was selected to demonstrate several of the valuation calculations discussed previously.

The hypothetical individual, a single female age 35, owns a condo, for which she originally paid $160,000, with a current mortgage balance of $140,000. She owns a car, on which she still owes $5,000. She is vested in a defined benefit pension plan with a previous employer, and she will be entitled to receive benefits of $600 per month at her full retirement age of sixty-five. She also has a 401(k) with her new employer and has worked enough quarters to entitle her to Social Security benefits when she is old enough.

FINANCIAL ASSETS			
CASH	$	200	
BANK ACCOUNT	$	7,000	
CHECKING ACCOUNT	$	1,000	
401(k) RETIREMENT ACCOUNT	$	10,000	
PENSION	$	20,451	
TOTAL FINANCIAL ASSETS			$ 38,651
TANGIBLE ASSETS			
HOME@MARKET	$	200,000	
CAR @ MARKET	$	15,000	
PERSONAL ITEMS	$	4,200	
TOTAL TANGIBLE ASSETS			$ 219,200
TOTAL ASSETS			$ 257,851
LIABILITIES			
CREDIT CARDS	$	5,000	
CAR LOAN	$	5,000	
MORTGAGE BALANCE	$	140,000	
DEFERRED TAXES@20%	$	6,000	
TOTAL LIABILITIES			$ 156,000
NET WORTH			$ 101,851

Table 2-1, Hypothetical net worth statement

Let's look at the assets first. She has cash and cash equivalents (assets that can be converted into cash relatively quickly) of $8,200, as shown. Her car, for which she originally paid $20,000, is currently worth about $15,000, based on the blue book value. Her condo is currently worth about $200,000, based on the fact that several similar units in her complex have recently sold for that amount. Next let's look at her retirement accounts. Her regular 401(k) is currently worth $10,000. She plans to continue contributing at a rate of 6% so she can get the full benefit of her employer's match. Even though she will not receive any payments from her pension and Social Security for many years, these future payments can be capitalized and reflected back to the present with assumptions of retirement age and discount rate. Let's do this for her pension first. She has earned pension benefits of $7,200 a year ($600 per month) at her full retirement age of sixty-five. Her life expectancy at sixty-five is about 19.5 years. If she begins collecting at age sixty-five, as currently planned, she can expect to receive monthly pension checks for about 19.5 years. Using an annual discount rate of 5%, the lump sum value of her currently earned pension when she is sixty-five will be $88,388. To bring this number back to the present, you must divide by $(1+0.05)^{30}$ giving $20,451 for the present value of her pension benefits. The annual discount factor is raised to the 30th power, since it will be thirty years before she begins collecting this pension.

Although not included in her net worth shown above, the present value of her Social Security benefits can be calculated in a similar way. Based on information received from Social Security, she is currently entitled to yearly payments of $8,400 ($700 per month), if she begins collecting at sixty-two. Assuming she begins at sixty-two, she can expect to collect checks for about twenty-two years. Using an annual discount rate of 5% gives a lump sum value of $110,569 at sixty-two. To reflect this amount back to the present, we divide by $(1+0.05)^{27}$ and get a present value for her Social Security benefits of $29,616. Here the discount factor is only raised to the 27th power, because it will be twenty-seven years before she begins collecting Social Security.

Her liabilities consist of credit card debt of $5,000, a car loan of $5,000, a mortgage balance of $140,000, and deferred taxes on her deferred income retirement accounts, payable when she takes distributions. If she pays off her credit card debt promptly, she will only owe the $5,000. If she decides on paying only a minimal amount per month until it is paid off, it will cost her considerably more. Her credit card statement contains a section that provides an estimate of how much it will cost and how long it will take to pay off the current balance if she makes only the minimum payment each month and also if she pays a certain fixed amount each month. These amounts are the sum of all the payments (both interest and principal) over the time it takes to pay the balance off. If we assume the interest rate on her unpaid balance is 1.5% per month (18% per year), not an unreasonable assumption, and she pays only $100 per month, it will take her about ninety-three months to pay off the $5,000 balance. During that time, she will have paid a total of about $9,300 in payments. The present value of all the individual payments made over the ninety-three months discounted at 5% is about $7,700.[4]

Her 401(k) and the pension she has earned are deferred income, and she will likely have to pay taxes on these when she takes distributions. The amount of taxes she will have to pay in the future depends on her total income, the portion of her income that comes from Social Security, and the tax bracket she's in at that time. If most of her retirement income comes from Social Security, she may not have to pay any taxes on this deferred income (see chapter 6 on retirement planning for an example). Assuming, however, that this income will be taxed at 20%, the present value of her deferred taxes would be about $6,000.

There are numerous websites that provide worksheets for calculating net worth. Some sites will even do the calculations for you, if you input the necessary data. Keep in mind, however, that if you input the data, the site will have most of your personal financial information. A better alternative might be to create your own worksheet, using pencil and paper or a personal computer.

Net Worth of US Households

It may interest the reader to know that the net worth of US households (actually the combined net worth of US households and nonprofit

---

[4]   You can use the formula function (NPER) to determine the number of periods in a loan with Excel on your PC or Numbers on a Mac. When you use this function it is important to pay attention to the sign conventions. You can also use the PV function to determine the present value of all your future payments.

organizations) at the end of 2010, according to the March 2011 release by the Federal Reserve on its website, was a little less than $57 trillion (later releases likely will revise this data somewhat). This was down more than $7 trillion from the prerecession peak, reached in 2007, but up about $8 trillion from the recession low. The value of assets was slightly less than $71 trillion and the value of liabilities a little less than $14 trillion. The assets consisted of more than $23 trillion of tangible assets, valued at market prices, and nearly $48 trillion of financial assets. Nearly $16.5 trillion of the tangible assets were household real estate. The financial assets included about $8 trillion of deposits of one kind or another, nearly $4.5 trillion of various credit market instruments, such as corporate bonds and treasury and municipal securities, somewhat more than $13 trillion of stocks and mutual funds, about $14 trillion of pension and life insurance assets, and nearly $6.5 trillion of equity in noncorporate businesses. The liabilities contained about $10 trillion of home mortgage debt and about $2.5 trillion of consumer credit debt.

Increasing Your Personal Net Worth

Clearly you increase your net worth and your wealth by increasing your assets and/or by reducing your liabilities. Sometimes, however, you can increase your net worth by taking on more debt and increasing your liabilities. This happens, for example, when you use debt to buy an asset, such as a house, which normally appreciates in value. On the other hand, if you use debt to buy consumables or a rapidly depreciating asset, your net worth will likely decline.

Besides making more money, there are certain fundamental things you can and should do to accumulate more wealth. First, you need to manage your personal finances carefully. To ensure that spending doesn't get out of hand, you need to take positive steps to control it. Without spending control, you can't save much; in fact, your savings might actually be negative. You need a budget to control spending, and you need to monitor your spending often to ensure that it doesn't exceed the budget. Household finances and things you can do to control spending are discussed in chapter 3.

Avoiding nonessential debt and minimizing finance charges is an important part of spending control. The more debt you have, the more you pay in finance charges, and the less money you have for savings and investment. Debt is discussed in chapter 4.

Additionally, you should minimize taxes. You should take advantage of all the deductions and credits available to you and defer as much income and hence taxes as possible to the distant future. Minimizing taxes can free up considerable sums for savings and investment. Taxes and some ways to minimize them are discussed in chapter 5.

The retirement phase of your life, if it's to be enjoyable, requires significant financial resources. Planning for retirements is in part planning how to accumulate wealth. It is discussed in chapter 6.

Savings are essential to wealth accumulation. Without savings there can be no investment and no increase in wealth. You need a disciplined approach to savings. You need to decide how much you're going to save and take it off the top so it's not available for spending. The best way to do this is to have money withheld from your paycheck and invested. Ways to save are discussed in chapter 7.

To grow your wealth, savings need to be invested and the earnings reinvested, but you need to make wise investments. You can invest in stocks, bonds, real estate, commodities, precious metals, or private equity, to name the most common asset classes, but you need to be very selective. The keys are to be disciplined about saving (save as much as you can, and do it every pay period) and to achieve consistent annual returns. Also, the earlier you begin the better. Ways to save are discussed in chapter 7, and investing is discussed in chapter 8.

Finally, you need patience to allow time and the miracle of compounding to turn your savings into actual wealth. To provide some idea of what consistent savings, investment, and time can do for wealth accumulation, the accumulated future value of an annual investment of $5,000, earning various annual returns, is plotted in figure 2-1 as a function of the number of years of investing.

As can be seen, the accumulated value after thirty years, if you earn 8% per year, is more than $600,000. After forty years, it's about $1.4 million. If you can achieve an annualized return of 10%, the accumulated future value is more than $900,000 after thirty years and about $2.4 million after forty years. If you were a great long-term investor (like Warren Buffett, for example) and could achieve a 20% annualized return, the accumulated future value would be more than $7 million after thirty years and more than $44 million after forty years. If you invest $10,000 per year, the accumulated values would double. All values are before taxes. You can use the formula function FV (future value) in Excel on a PC or Numbers on a Mac to calculate future values.

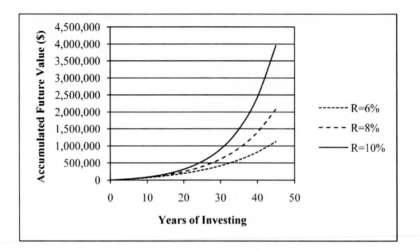

Figure 2-1, Future value of a $5,000 annual investment

Chapter 3

Household Finances and
Control of Spending

Of major importance is management of your household finances. The money coming in is used for consumption expenditures, the payment of taxes, and the payment of interest, or it is saved and invested. Consumption is used here in the broadest sense and includes expenditures for most consumer items and services.[5] An automobile expenditure is generally considered consumption spending. Gifts you make are considered consumption expenditures. Purchase of real estate, even the home you live in, is considered investment.

To save, the total outflow (the sum of consumption expenditures, taxes, and interest payments) must be less than the money coming in. The excess or savings can then be invested, and if invested wisely, can grow on a compound basis. Consumption expenditures are generally for near-term needs and enjoyment, while savings and investment are for the future, and there should be a balance between the two.

Everyone should track and analyze his or her household finances. This basically involves identifying how much money comes in during a period of time (inflow), where it comes from, and where it goes (outflow). Inflow

---

[5] The definitions used here are consistent with those used by the Bureau of Economic Analysis in maintaining the Nation's Economic Accounts. It might interest the reader to know that in these accounts education spending is considered consumption not investment. In your own accounting you can, of course, define it as investment.

and outflow are also called sources and uses, respectively. This is called a funds flow analysis. Inflow includes funds of different types, even one time sources like the sale of an asset, not just regular income. Outflow can include both spending and savings and investment.

If outflow exceeds inflow, there is a deficit for the period, and either savings must be used or money borrowed to fund the deficit. Borrowing increases debt. Alternately, inflow and outflow can be made to balance by including all borrowing in inflow.

Households should prepare a budget; the budget provides a plan for future spending. Data on past expenditures is extremely helpful in preparing a budget. Actually, two budgets should be prepared: one for the year and another for the pay period. Some expenditures may occur only quarterly or once a year, and your budgeting should take these into account. If you get paid weekly, the second budget should be for a week; if monthly, it should be for a month. Spending should be tracked and compared to the budget to see how you are doing. Writing the budget down and referring to it frequently makes it much easier to adhere to.

Funds Flow Analysis

The funds flow analysis is done over a period of time: a month or a year, for example. You can utilize cash accounting, accrual accounting, or a combination of the two for the funds flow analysis.[6] With pure cash accounting, an inflow of funds is recorded when the funds are received, and an outflow is recorded only when funds are actually disbursed or paid out. With accrual accounting, income is counted when earned, and spending is counted when the financial commitments are made (even though payment may be delayed). If you use pure cash accounting for your household finances, expenditures made with credit cards wouldn't count as outflow; only the payments actually made would be counted, since that's when an outflow of actual cash occurs. Any unpaid amount would, of course, be debt and appear as a liability on your personal balance sheet. The pure cash approach, while providing a true measure of the inflow and outflow of cash, can be misleading and cause problems for many people.

---

[6] Public companies actually use both types of accounting and prepare an income statement using accrual accounting and a cash flow statement using cash accounting.

It can lead people to the view that if they can handle their payments, all is well. Individuals that view their spending this way tend to overspend, and many get into financial trouble. If most of your spending is paid for with cash, either actual cash, checks, or debit cards, and if your credit card balances are paid in full each month, then there is no problem. The best way to do your personal accounting is to use a mixture of cash and accrual accounting, in which income, or inflow, is counted when received and spending, or outflow, is counted when the financial commitment is made. Many personal money management tools are set up to use this mixed type of accounting.

It is extremely important to know where your money comes from and where it goes. The amount of income you expect in a given period of time should set an upper limit on your spending. You can't spend more than your income or live beyond your means for any length of time. Keeping track of your spending is essential to serious efforts to control it. Past spending history provides the data necessary for efforts to identify items for reduction or elimination. Reductions can always be identified. There are various ways to keep track of your spending. If you use credit cards, debit cards, and checks for most of your spending, you have a record. If you use cash, you should keep all your receipts. It's best to maintain complete records of your spending. If you can't, you should at least record significant spending. Once you have the data, you can separate your spending into different categories to better understand where your money goes. Various software tools are available to help track spending and manage your household finances. These tools will automatically categorize most of your spending. Tools are discussed in a general way at the end of this chapter.

The lists below identify many sources and uses of money. Savings and investment is shown as a use of money. These funds could be shown as a surplus with savings, and investments as a use of the surplus. I've chosen to show savings and investment as a use of money. It's a good idea to put money into investments like a 401(k), IRA, or other savings as part of your budget, rather than waiting to see what's left after consumption expenditures are made. Many people will spend whatever money they have, if not more. To help prevent this, make savings and investment a priority, and put the money away before it can be spent. Make savings and investment a habit.

INFLOW (SOURCES)

Wages or salary
Bonus
Interest and dividends
Tax rebates
Sales of personal items
Sales of assets
Trust fund distributions
Gifts
Loans or borrowing

OUTFLOW (USES)

Living expenses
Insurance
Education expenses
Taxes
Entertainment
Gifts
Car payment
Mortgage payment
Other loan payments
Savings and investments

Table 3-1 shows a yearly funds flow analysis for the same person for whom the net worth calculation was done in chapter 2. The sources of funds total $50,950, made up of salary, interest on savings, and the sale of some used personal items on eBay. She currently spends $46,915, leaving a little more than $4,000 for savings. Savings includes a $3,000 contribution to a 401(k) at work, since she made savings and investment a priority and put the money away by having it deducted from her paycheck before she could spend it. The details of each of the elements of her spending (uses of money other than savings) are shown in table 3-2 in the next section. The largest element, $27,210, is for living expenses, which includes car payments of $3,000 and mortgage payments of $12,000. The mortgage payment includes interest, principal, and provision for property taxes. The principal portion is actually savings and technically should be broken out separately, but in this case the principal payments are very small, since she hasn't had the mortgage very long. Including FICA, federal and state withholding, and tax payments she made with her return in April of the current year, she paid a total of $10,705. Her tax payments are substantially higher than they need to be, because I've assumed that she uses the standard deduction, although she can and should itemize her deductions.

SOURCES OF MONEY	
SALARY	$50,000
INTETEST	$350
SALES ON E-BAY	$600
TOTAL	$50,950
USES OF MONEY	
Savings & Investment	
401(k) CONTRIBUTIO	$3,000
OTHER	$1,035
SUBTOTAL	$4,035
Spending	
LIVING EXPENSES	$27,210
INSURANCE	$3,000
ENTERTAINMENT	$5,000
GIFTS	$1,000
FICA	$3,825
FEDERAL TAXES	$5,680
STATE TAXES	$1,200
SUBTOTAL	$46,915
TOTAL	$50,950

Table 3-1, Hypothetical funds flow analysis

Spending Analysis and Next Year's Budget

Our society encourages spending. We are bombarded constantly by advertising in magazines, newspapers, on television, and now on the Internet. We also suffer from the need to keep up with others and are frequently encouraged by politicians, even presidents, to spend. Consumer spending is about 70% of gross domestic product (GDP) in the United States. Increasing consumer spending generally increases economic growth. As a nation we are addicted to economic growth. Slow or no economic growth would be suicide for most politicians; they might get blamed and not be reelected. It would also be bad for corporate America and workers, since their bonuses and wages might not grow or in some cases might actually decline. So advertising and politicians encourage spending, and Americans continue to spend and to take on more debt. While increased spending may be good for the economy as a whole (unless it's driven by unsustainable debt levels), it is not necessarily good for you as an individual. Unless your spending is controlled, you will never accumulate any money and never give yourself the chance to accumulate wealth, and you likely will end up in financial trouble.

The funds flow analysis shows you where your money comes from and where it goes. Once you know where your money goes, you can begin to analyze your spending habits. One-way of doing this is to separate the spending into two categories: one for required spending and the other for discretionary spending. This should be done carefully. Much of the spending people consider required is actually discretionary. How you categorize your spending depends on your own situation. You might categorize certain spending (clothes and personal grooming, for example) as required, because of your social circle or work environment and the need to fit in or stand out, whereas another person might consider the same expenditures as discretionary. Economic conditions will certainly influence your decisions.

Next, look at the discretionary spending. Are there items that can be reduced or, better yet, eliminated? Eating out, for example. It costs more to eat out than to eat at home; spending to eat out can usually be reduced, and it's generally healthier to eat at home. Gas for your automobile is another item that can be reduced. Do you drive too much or unnecessarily? How far do you commute back and forth to work? If commuting mileage is high, think about carpooling. Better yet, find a comparable job near your residence or relocate near your job. Reducing mileage not only reduces gasoline expenditures, it also reduces wear and tear on your car and, hence, maintenance expense, and also how frequently you need to replace your vehicle.

Another category is taxes. You should try to defer or avoid taxes as much as possible. There are many ways to do this legally. Learn something about taxes, so you can take full advantage of the tax laws. Become familiar with adjustments to income; itemize deductions if you can rather than taking the standard deduction; and learn about the tax credits that are available. Defer income if you can. If your company has a 401(k) program, enroll in it. The taxes on money put in a 401(k) program are deferred until you take distributions. If you already participate in a 401(k), think about increasing your contributions. Also, start an IRA for yourself and, if married, your spouse. Taxes are discussed in some detail in chapter 5.

Table 3-2 below shows an analysis of the spending for our favorite female. Let's look at her spending. She has two phones. She surely can get by with only one, so I've put her home phone in the discretionary category. She currently spends $2,500 on clothing, perhaps not an excessive expenditure for a single female; however, I've put $1,500 of it into the discretionary category. She currently spends $1,200 per year ($100 per month) on gasoline for her car, but she usually drives when she goes out with her friends, so I've moved $200 to the discretionary category. She also spends $100 per month on hair styling; I've moved $1,000 to the discretionary category. If all this discretionary spending were eliminated, her living expenses could be reduced by about $3,000.

	SPENDING ($)	REQ'D ($	DISCRETIONARY ($)
LIVING EXPENSES			
MORTGAGE	12000	12,000	0
FOOD	2600	2600	0
PHONE	360	0	360
CELL/INTERNET	600	600	0
GAS/ELECTRIC	2400	2,400	0
WATER	400	400	0
CLOTHING	2500	1,000	1,500
MED/DENTAL	500	500	0
CAR REG	200	200	0
CAR GAS	1200	1,000	200
CAR MAINTN	250	250	0
HAIR STYLING	1200	200	1000
CAR PAYMENT	3000	3,000	0
SUBTOTAL	27210	24,150	3060
INSURANCE			
HEALTH	1200	1,200	0
CAR	900	900	0
LIFE	600	600	0
HOME	300	300	0
SUBTOTAL	3000	3,000	0
ENTERTAINMENT			
VACATIONS	1500	0	1500
EATING OUT	3000	0	3,000
SHOWS	500	0	500
SUBTOTAL	5000	0	5000
GIFTS			
XMAS	500	300	200
BIRTHDAYS/OTHEI	500	250	250
SUBTOTAL	1000	550	450
TAXES			
FICA	3825	3825	0
FEDERAL	5680	3210	2470
STATE	1200	700	500
SUBTOTAL	10705	7735	2970
TOTALS	46915	35435	11480

Table 3-2, Spending analysis

The insurance expenditures were left alone; they are all reasonable and necessary. Next, look at her entertainment expenses. She spends $1,500 per year on vacations; it's all discretionary spending. She currently spends $3,000 per year on eating out, drinks at the bar with friends, and coffee at her favorite café before work each morning. She drinks expensive coffee. She pays $4 per cup and has one cup a day five days a week. That's $20 a week, or more than $1,000 per year for coffee. That's a lot of money for most people. She also spends $500 per year on shows. All entertainment is discretionary. Some, however, may be needed for mental health. Nonetheless, I've put it all in the discretionary category. Gifts are at least partly discretionary; some may be necessary. I've moved a little less than half to the discretionary category.

The final area of spending is taxes. You can't do anything about FICA; it's the payroll tax for Social Security and Medicare. Federal income taxes, however, can be reduced substantially. She currently takes the standard deduction, when she should itemize deductions. If she were to itemize, she could easily have $12,500 in deductions, made up of $9,000 in interest on her mortgage, $2,000 in property taxes, $1,200 in state income taxes, and a little in charitable contributions. Itemizing could save her about $1,420 in taxes. Next, if she were to put $4,000 into a traditional IRA, she could save $600 in current federal taxes, and if she would increase her contribution to her 401(k) from the current level of $3,000 to $6,000, she could reduce her current taxes another $450. If she does these things, she also reduces her state income tax by about $500. Total discretionary spending adds up to $11,480 (including taxes of $2,970 she could save), more than enough to fund the increase in her 401(k) and the new IRA contribution, which total $7,000.

Having done a money flow and spending analysis for the current year, preparing a budget for the following year is relatively simple. To do this, you estimate your expected income for the year and decide what your spending will be. She used the previous year's spending analysis to help decide on spending for next year. A budget is a plan for spending. If you're serious about meeting your plan, you need to control your spending in accordance with the plan. To ensure that this happens, spending needs to be tracked and compared to the budget periodically, preferably on at least a monthly basis. If spending exceeds the plan, reductions should be made for future months to get back on plan for the year.

Our hypothetical female expects her salary for next year to be the same as that for the current year. She doesn't expect to sell anything on eBay, and since she paid off her credit card balance with money from her savings account, she only has a little more than $2,000 left in the bank and will earn very little in interest. Thus, she expects her money inflow for the coming year to be about $50,000. After carefully looking at last year's spending analysis, she decided to increase her 401(k) contribution to $6,000 and to open a traditional IRA, to which she plans to contribute $4,000. She decided to budget about $38,500 for all other spending (about $3,000 more than required spending of $35,435), leaving her with a surplus for contingencies or additional savings of about $1,500.

Software Tools

There are a number of software tools available to help manage your household finances. Most banking institutions provide free online tools that keep track of the inflow and outflow of funds that move through accounts you have with them. Programs such as Wells Fargo's "Budget Watch" will track and automatically categorize spending done with their credit and debit cards and any electronic payments you make. Unfortunately, these programs do not categorize spending done with a checking account. They simply provide a total for checks. The programs also allow you to create a monthly budget, utilizing either past spending or inputs you provide. These programs make it easy to monitor actual spending and to compare spending to your budget. They work best if you do all your financial transactions with the same institution and all your spending with their credit and debit cards and electronic payments.

If you use multiple financial institutions or credit cards from several institutions, programs such as "Quicken," an Intuit product, provide similar capabilities, but they bring all your accounts from different institutions together in one site. Quicken is said to connect to more than 5,000 financial institutions. With their deluxe version, brokerage accounts can also be included together with linkage to "TurboTax," Intuit's tax preparation software.

Chapter 4

Debt Both Good and Bad

Debt is an amount owed or financial obligation you have. When you borrow money or buy something on credit, you acquire debt and are a debtor. Lenders are creditors, and for every debtor there is a creditor. Creditors charge debtors interest for use of their money, and the debtor has the legal obligation to pay the interest charges and to repay the principal. The magnitude of the interest rate is generally related to the riskiness of the loan, and for some types of loans, rates can be very high.

Debt plays a vital role in our economy. It allows creation and expansion of businesses that would be impossible because of lack of capital, and it has made the widespread ownership of homes possible. It allows both businesses and individuals to purchase goods and services before they have accumulated sufficient funds to do so. Debt is a powerful stimulant to economic growth. If used wisely, debt can be quite beneficial; if used for the wrong purpose or excessively, it can be very dangerous to your financial health. Both companies and individuals, even governments, can go bankrupt because they cannot pay their debts. Current debt and financial obligations for US households, government, and some business sectors are very high and problematic.

There are two general categories of loans: secured and unsecured. Secured loans are those in which the borrower puts up some type of collateral; unsecured loans have no collateral backing them. Collateral is intended to secure or assure repayment of the loan. Unsecured loans are granted based on the ability and legal obligation of the borrower to repay. Unsecured loans are more risky for the lender, and they generally carry higher interest rates. Credit card debt is an example of an unsecured loan.

Secured loans can either be recourse or nonrecourse loans. A recourse loan is one that in the event of default by the borrower, the lender is permitted by law to bring legal action to try to collect the full amount owed (known as a deficiency judgment). If you default on a recourse loan, the lender can, in addition to taking the collateral, legally go after your other assets. With a nonrecourse loan, on the other hand, the lender only gets the collateral put up to secure the loan. A number of states, however, have laws (known as antideficiency laws) that prohibit lenders from suing to collect more than the collateral. Antideficiency laws most often apply to loans used to purchase residences.

The interest on some types of debt is tax deductible if you itemize rather than take the standard deduction. The tax deductibility feature effectively reduces the interest rate. Interest on home mortgages and some home equity loans, for example, is currently tax deductible; credit card interest and interest on most other types of loans is currently not.

There is good debt and bad debt. Use of debt to buy generally appreciating assets like real estate, for example, is a good thing if you don't overpay and can afford to make the payments. Most things, or assets, you buy, however, depreciate, or decline in value, over time or are consumed. If you utilize debt to buy consumables or depreciating assets, the asset may be valueless before you pay off the debt. This is bad financially and a bad use of debt. Use of a credit card is all right if you don't buy more than you need, and you pay the balance off monthly without paying any finance charges.

Ideally, debt should only be utilized to buy assets that will not decline in value or that have a reasonable expectation of increasing in value over time. Under these conditions, as you pay down the debt, you will be building up your net assets, or equity, and thus your wealth. Although desirable, this approach will not be possible for many people; most, for example, need to borrow to purchase a car, a depreciating asset. They should, however, pay off the debt as quickly as possible.

Some people, because of their debt load, have total finance charges that are a large portion of their income and a huge financial burden. They have made bad choices. Many make purchasing decisions based solely on whether they can make the monthly payment; they essentially ignore the magnitude of the finance charges. They may be able to get by when economic conditions are good, but times change, and the debt burden can easily become impossible, especially when the economy deteriorates. If you function this way, you will never be able to accumulate any wealth and likely will end up in some type of financial trouble. Don't take on too much debt. Live within your means. Better yet, live well within your means.

Education Loans

A college education is an investment in your future, an investment of your time as well as a financial investment. These days a college education is expensive. According to an article in the *Wall Street Journal* (Banchero 2010), costs for tuition and fees averaged more than $7,500 per year at public institutions and more than $27,000 per year at private colleges in the 2010/11 school year. Room and board was additional. While many parents pay for their children's education, some can't afford to or simply don't, and the burden may fall on the student either partially or completely. Various types of financial assistance, however, are available, including scholarships, grants, and student loans. Also, numerous education tax breaks help offset qualified expenses, paid either by the parent or the student. Additionally, there are tax-advantaged Education Savings Plans.

Scholarships are generally given to athletically and academically gifted individuals, and grants are generally made based on financial need. Student loans, however, are available to most students who require them. Since neither grants nor scholarships have to be repaid, individuals should make every effort to obtain them first.

Various grant programs are available. Perhaps the best known is the Federal Pell Grant Program. It provides needy undergraduate students, and certain others enrolled in post-bachelor-degree programs that lead to teacher certification, with government grants provided through participating institutions.

Federal education loans account for most of the financial aid to students. A large percentage of college students (both graduate and undergraduate) borrow money using these programs every year. Federal student loans generally have relatively low interest rates and don't usually need to be repaid until after the student completes his or her education. Interest paid on these loans, up to a certain limit, is deductible as an adjustment to income on the federal return, but only by the person who paid it.

Until recently, the federal student loan program had two major elements: the William D. Ford Direct Loan (DL) program and the Federal Family Education Loan (FFEL) program. They utilized different sources of capital but made the same basic types of loans.

The federal government provides the money for the DL program and owns the loans, although the loans may be originated and administered by schools or contractors that work for the government. Private lenders, mostly large financial institutions, provided the capital and originated the loans for the FFEL program, but the federal government guaranteed the loans against loss for various reasons, including default. Recent legislation eliminated the government guarantee for the private lending program. The federal government will in the future provide all student loans directly, without using the private sector middlemen. Individuals may still be able to get loans from private lending institutions, but since the government no longer guarantees the loan, rates will be higher, perhaps much higher.

The government provides a third student loan program called the Federal Perkins Loan program. This program provides low-interest loans for needy students. These loans can be forgiven for those employed in certain public, military, or teaching service jobs. The amount of money the federal government provides for this program is relatively small.

For most people, a college education is a good investment. College graduates earn substantially more than those that only graduate from high school. Also, the knowledge you gain can make your life more interesting and enjoyable. Even if you need a loan to obtain the education, it's still a smart investment for most people.

Home Mortgage Loans

A mortgage is necessary for most people to purchase a home. Since real estate values generally increase over time, buying a home can be a good way to help acquire wealth. Since you generally must pay rent to live somewhere (unless you live with your parents or someone else rent free), it might not cost you much additional money to buy. Further, the interest on the loan is currently tax deductible, if you itemize deductions on your tax return. There are, however, limitations. If the mortgage debt is categorized as acquisition debt (debt used to buy, build, or improve), the interest is fully tax deductible as long as the debt doesn't exceed $1 million for married couples filing joint returns. For single filers the debt limit is $500K. For equity type loans (loans for which the money is used for purposes other than the purchase, building, or improvement of a home), the limits are generally much lower. As long as you *can afford the payments*, both now and in the future, and you *don't overpay* for the property, a mortgage loan is good debt.

There are many different types of home mortgage loans: fixed rate, adjustable rate mortgages (ARMs), interest only, and negative amortization loans. Interest only and negative amortization loans, hopefully, are a thing of the past. Mortgage loans can have different durations: the two most popular are the fifteen-year and the thirty-year mortgage. With a fixed-rate mortgage, you lock in the interest rate for the duration of the loan. Because interest is by far the largest part of the payment, you can be fairly certain of what your payments will be for the duration. They can still vary some, because property taxes and insurance costs can change, but these generally don't vary much.

Private lending institutions, typically, want a 20% down payment. If you put less than this down, you will be charged for private mortgage insurance (PMI). PMI can be expensive. Mortgage loans are secured loans, with the property providing the security to the lender. If you default, the mortgage company can take the property, sell it, and in many states sue you for the additional money you owe. PMI protects the lender in the case of default but only up to the amount of insurance provided. PMI generally allows the lender to sell the mortgage to Federal Mortgage entities.

With an ARM (as the name implies), the rate can vary. The rate is usually tied to some type of index that varies with the general level of interest rates in the economy. With an ARM, you can't be sure what your payments will be in the future. While there are limits on how much and how often the rates can change, the variation can be considerable. If you use an ARM to buy a house when the mortgage rates are low, be careful; you're likely to see your mortgage payments increase substantially in the future. If you can't make the higher payments, you very likely will lose the house and any equity you have in it. When rates are high, an ARM can be a good idea if you believe that rates are going to decrease in the future. They could, however, go up further; ARMs are risky.

Interest rate only mortgages are just that. With this type of loan, you pay no principal and hence never pay off the loan.

Negative amortization loans allow you to pay less interest than the loan actually requires, and the loan balance increases accordingly. At some point the payments increase to cover the larger loan that you now have. These loans are bad for most people, and they can be disastrous for some, as evidenced by the financial crisis of 2008/9.

Interest rates on fixed-rate home mortgages are generally not too much higher than the corresponding treasury rate, if your credit quality is good. They are generally lower for fifteen-year mortgages than for thirty-year mortgages. Most mortgage loans have a provision that lets you pay the loan off with no penalty. *Make sure your mortgage has this provision before you sign the contract.* Having this provision allows you to refinance without paying a penalty. When you refinance, you generally have to pay closing costs again, but if the new rates are significantly lower, it can be cost effective.

For those people whose credit is not too good, there are subprime mortgages, and here the interest rates can be very high. These types of loans can be very risky. When things go bad, default rates can get very high.

Home mortgage loans have closing costs. Closing costs include an assortment of charges and fees due at closing. Costs can include a property appraisal, credit check, property inspection, property survey, recording fees, title search, title insurance, advance payment of property taxes, and possibly a loan origination fee. There are two types of title insurance: insurance to protect the lender, which is usually mandatory, and insurance to protect the buyer, which is optional (see chapter 10 on insurance). The loan origination fee, also referred to as origination points, is an upfront charge the lender may impose for granting the loan. Other types of points, known as discount points, reduce the interest rate on the mortgage. One point is 1% of the loan value and should reduce the interest rate on the loan accordingly. Since points are considered interest charges, they are generally deductible on your tax return, but the deduction may have to be spread over the life of the loan. Closing costs can be substantial, and the magnitude often surprises the borrower.

If you think of a home purchase as an investment, the loan provides leverage. Leverage is the use of debt or borrowed money to increase investment return. Leverage is basically a multiplier and can be good or bad. Leverage works like this. Assume you buy a $250K condo and you pay 20% or $50K as a down payment. Now, say the property price appreciates

100% in twenty years to $500K. You now have a gain of $250K on your investment of only $50K, or a gain of 500%. Now to be clear, you've made sizable interest payments over this time period, and you have had to pay property taxes and insurance premiums as well. If, however, the total cost of these is not much different than what you would have had to pay in rent, then you can argue that they don't reduce your gain. The 500% return over twenty years is about 8.4% per year, compounded annually. That's a nice annual return, even if a significant portion may have been due to inflation.

Leverage, of course works both ways. Let's assume you bought at the peak of the real estate market, and the value, instead of increasing, drops to $200K. Further, let's assume that you need to sell. Since you paid $250K to purchase the property, you just lost $50K, the entire amount of your down payment, or investment. That's a 100% loss.

For many years, even though real estate values declined from time to time in various localities, they didn't decline on a national level. This led many to believe that real estate values not only never decline but also that they always increase. While it is true that property values generally increase over time (mostly due to inflation), and can increase significantly in desirable locations with limited supplies of new building land and growing populations, there can be periods of time when values not only don't increase but actually fall, sometimes precipitously.

Home Equity Loans

Home equity loans are loans that allow the home owner to borrow money on the equity they have in their homes. Equity loans, like home mortgages, are secured by the home. They are, however, basically second mortgages, and the lender of the first mortgage has first claim on the property in the event of default. Equity loans are generally only made up to a maximum amount equal to the difference between the market value of the home and any current mortgage amount. In recent years, however, some lenders have allowed loans that exceed this amount. Equity loans are of two basic types: fixed loans and equity lines of credit. The fixed type is similar to a fixed-rate home mortgage. As the name implies, the loans are for a fixed amount and have fixed interest rates. Rates are generally somewhat higher than for first mortgages. Like mortgages, they have closing costs or origination fees, but these may be waived.

Equity line of credit loans allow the borrower to draw funds from the lender at his or her convenience up to the maximum amount of credit provided by the loan. Interest is charged only on the amount actually borrowed. Line of credit loans carry a variable interest rate tied to an index, typically the prime rate; the actual rate is the prime plus a margin. The margin charged is a function of credit quality of the borrower. The interest rate can change every billing cycle. The draw period for equity line of credit loans has a limited duration, usually ten years, after which time the balance converts to a fixed-rate loan (unless the period is extended by the lender). When the loan converts, the interest rate likely increases but is fixed for the duration of the new loan. Settlement or closing costs, including a loan origination fee, are usually waived. However, if the loan is cancelled at any time within the first few years, typically three years, you are charged the loan origination fee. Also the loans usually have a maintenance charge that is generally waived if the loan balance is greater than a certain amount.

Because equity in homes increased significantly as home prices appreciated during the real estate bubble, many home owners used equity loans to take money out of their homes to provide funds for various things, including home improvements, education expenses, vacations, credit card debt payments, furniture, and living expenses. While using the equity loan for some of these things might be a good idea, it is most definitely not for some of the others. Using equity loans to supplement spending is generally a bad idea and can be costly. It is much better for your financial health to reduce spending.

Auto Loans

Most people need to borrow to purchase a car. Car companies offer loans through their dealers for convenience to their customers, and banks and other lending institutions also make car loans. Most new cars depreciate quickly; the car is worth a lot less once you put some mileage on it. The purchased car provides collateral for the loan. A down payment is generally required, so if the buyer defaults the dealer minimizes any losses.

Interest charges for car loans are generally higher than those for home mortgages and home equity loans. They can be very high for people with poor credit quality, if they can get a loan at all. Car dealers in recent years have offered substantial discounts to get buyers to purchase their cars. As an alternative, they also offer low interest or no interest rate loans as an enticement. If you need to borrow to purchase a car, you should look at the various alternatives you have. It might be to your benefit, for example, to take the price discount and use a home equity loan to obtain the funds. Interest on the home equity loan might be less, and the interest on the equity loan can be tax deductible, while interest on car loans is not.

Credit Card Debt

Credit cards provide a convenient way to buy things. They provide a record of your spending and allow you to defer payment for twenty to twenty-five days after the closing date for the month without incurring any interest charges. That means you can effectively get an interest-free loan for items you buy for about fifty days (if you buy something on the first day of the charging period and don't pay until the due date). Most provide a rewards program of some type: from points that can be used to purchase goods and services to actual cash back. If used wisely, credit cards can be a good thing. In my opinion this means not charging more than you need, and paying off the full balance each month so you avoid any finance charges.

Unfortunately credit cards make spending too easy, and they make it difficult for many people to be responsible spenders. It's much easier to hand over the plastic card than to write a check or fork over cash. For one thing you may not have the cash or the necessary funds in your checking account. So you effectively borrow money from the credit card company. It's very easy, and you may or may not be aware of the magnitude of the finance charge you are required to pay. The plastic card makes it easy to spend more than you need to or should and to run up unnecessary debt. If the monthly balance is not paid in full by the due date, you incur a finance charge of typically around 1.25% per month. While that may not sound like a lot of interest, it's 15% on an annual basis. Additionally, interest on credit card debt is not tax deductible.

Credit card companies also allow you to borrow cash with your card. When you borrow cash, the interest rate is about 10% higher, and there is no grace period. Further, interest is generally charged at the higher rate starting the day you borrow the cash. It's not a good idea to borrow cash on your credit card.

If you have a balance and only make the minimum payment the credit card company requires, it will take a long time to pay off the debt, and if you continue to charge more items, the balance will build up. The credit card companies love people who only make minimum payments; they make large profits this way. That's why they continue to send out unsolicited applications. If you don't make the minimum payment on time, you'll be charged a late payment penalty or fee. The credit card company may also report the late payment to the credit card rating agencies. These fees add to your balance, and you pay interest on the full balance.

Many people max out their cards and are never able to pay off their balance, and they continue to incur finance charges, effectively forever or until they default. Credit cards can be a good thing if used responsibly; if used irresponsibly, they can be disastrous. Many people should avoid the use of credit cards entirely, and they should destroy the ones they have.

Margin Accounts

Margin accounts allow you to borrow money from your broker to buy securities. The securities you purchase provide collateral for the loan. Borrowing money to buy stocks provides leverage, similar to that described in an earlier section on mortgage loans. Leverage can multiply your investment returns, but it can also magnify your investment losses. Margin trading can be very risky.

The Federal Reserve Board and the stock exchanges have established rules for margin trading. Brokers, however, might impose additional rules. There are limits as to how much you can borrow when you purchase the securities, called the initial margin, and requirements for how much equity you must maintain in your account, called the maintenance margin. If the equity falls below the maintenance margin because of changes in the market price of the securities, you are generally required to deposit more funds to restore the equity to the maintenance margin. If you are unable to comply, the brokerage house has the right to, and most likely will, sell securities in your account to increase the equity to the required level.

When you open a margin account, you sign a margin account agreement. The agreement defines the rules and explains the terms and conditions. As with any contract, you should make sure you understand it before signing. Interest rates vary from brokerage house to brokerage house and can be high. They generally vary with the amount you borrow.

Buying stock on margin or with borrowed money is risky business, and it is clearly not a good idea for the average investor. If you do it, you should be a very knowledgeable investor and fully understand the risks

Other Types of Debt

There are many other types of loans and debt: payday and tax-refund loans, debt consolidation loans, reverse mortgages, and deferred taxes, to name some. Payday and tax-refund loans are short term and offer customers advances on their paychecks and tax refunds. Rates for these loans, particularly payday loans, are very high on an annualized basis. Various laws have been introduced to limit the interest rates charged on payday loans.

Debt consolidation loans combine all your debt, and they offer the convenience of a single monthly payment. They can reduce monthly payments, but payments may go down simply because the time duration of the loan is extended. To get the lowest rates, you will need to provide some kind of security or collateral, likely your home. Before accepting a debt consolidation loan, you should make sure that the total interest payments are actually less than for the loans being replaced and that the rate is not a teaser rate that will go up in the future. It's also important to make sure original creditors are actually being paid, and you're not being scammed.

Reverse mortgages, also sometimes called home equity conversion loans, allow the elderly to borrow some of the equity they have in their homes. Reverse mortgages are discussed in chapter 9 on retirement planning. As said in that chapter, a reverse mortgage should only be used as a last resort.

Deferred taxes are, in effect, interest-free loans from the government. They are good loans and are an important part of helping build your wealth. The advantages of tax deferral are discussed in chapter 5 on taxes.

Debt of Businesses, Households, and Government

There are many sectors of the domestic economy, but all fall into one of three categories: businesses, households, and government. All have debt and other financial liabilities, and if the amounts for all sectors are summed, the total as of the end of 2010 was in excess of $50 trillion and perhaps in excess of $100 trillion (not everyone agrees on which amounts to include). Regardless of which number one accepts, the United States is clearly a nation of debt. We have been living beyond our means for quite a while, and although we are still a nation of considerable financial means and resources, we cannot continue living this way without serious consequences to our economic future.

The business sector is often divided into two major sectors, financial and nonfinancial. The financial sector, the solvency of which is essential to the American economy, was in deep trouble after the real estate bubble burst. Institutions had made too many risky loans, had too many bad or underperforming assets on their books, and were generally overleveraged. The federal government provided considerable financial assistance to many institutions and helped prevent a complete collapse. A number of companies have vanished, some going bankrupt and others being absorbed by more solvent organizations. Many of the remaining institutions have raised additional capital in the private markets, written off some bad assets, and, at this writing, have less leverage and much improved balance sheets. Debt of the financial sector at the end of 2010, according to the March 2011 release of the Federal Reserve, was a little more than $14 trillion. Many institutions have completely paid back the funds loaned to them by the government. Because many assets have not been marked to market (valued at markets prices), a number of experts question the realism of some financial institution balance sheets.

The nonfinancial business sector, by contrast, is in good shape. Fortunately, domestic nonfinancial businesses were relatively conservative and didn't take on too much debt and other financial obligations in the last decade. According to the March 2011 release of the Federal Reserve on its website, nonfinancial businesses (corporate and noncorporate) as a group had debt of about $11 trillion and total liabilities of more than $19 trillion at the end of 2010, but also had assets in excess of $37 trillion. While some individual businesses will go bankrupt because they can't meet their debt obligations, most businesses generate operating profits sufficient to service their debt several times over.

At the end of 2010, according to the same Federal Reserve release cited above, US households had outstanding debt of about $13.4 trillion and total liabilities of about $14 trillion. Most is home mortgage debt, including home equity loans. While many people have lost their homes and many others are currently unable to pay their mortgages, most households continue to service their mortgages and other debts. Household liabilities are nearly equal to the GDP of the nation, not a particularly good situation but still at a level that can be handled. Data from the National Income and Product Accounts of the US, provided by the Bureau of Economic Analysis on its website, shows that annual expenditures for housing (both rental and owner occupied), including utilities, plus interest payments on other household debt, was less than 20% of disposable personal income for the nation as a whole. Additionally, the recession has actually caused households to reduce their debt and increase savings.

Government debt and financial obligations, however, are a more serious concern. According to the Bureau of Public Debt website, the debt of the federal government (referred to as the total public debt outstanding) at the end of 2010 was about $13.8 trillion. Of this, about $4.5 trillion was intragovernment debt (mostly money borrowed from the Social Security and Medicare trust funds when they were running surpluses and spent for other government activities) and about $9.3 trillion was what's called debt held by the public. The debt held by the public is basically the sum of all US Treasury securities (bills, notes, and bonds) held by individuals, corporations, and state, local, and foreign governments. About half of the debt held by the public is actually owned by foreigners. The total debt of the federal government (including intragovernment debt) at the end of 2010 was more than 90% of GDP, and the portion held by the public was more than 60% of GDP. These percentages are projected to increase substantially in the future because of the continuing large annual budget deficits the federal government is expected to run. The deficit was about $1.3 trillion for 2010 and about $1.5 trillion for 2011. Deficits are financed by borrowing and add to the debt, and unless spending is reduced or tax revenues increase, the debt level will continue to increase at a rapid rate. It will exceed $15 trillion by the end of 2011.

In addition to the above debt, there is also debt issued by government-sponsored enterprises (GSEs) and certain unfunded future obligations of the federal government. GSE issued debt is substantial but technically is not guaranteed by the federal government. It only carries an implicit government guarantee not an explicit one like Treasury securities. There are unfunded financial obligations for the Social Security, Medicare, and Medicaid programs and for some government pension programs. Only those associated with the Social Security and Medicare programs are discussed here.

According to data provided in the Social Security and Medicare Trustees 2010 annual reports, the present value of the unfunded obligations of the Social Security and Medicare programs over the next seventy-five years is nearly $30 trillion (perhaps much higher).[7] Future benefits are paid from future revenues, and projected revenues are insufficient to cover these obligations. To balance these, revenues will need to be increased or benefits curtailed in some way.

State and local governments also have financial problems. Nearly all state governments have a legal requirement, either constitutional, statutory, or both, to balance their budgets. Balancing requirements differ from state to state, but they generally apply to operating budgets not capital budgets. Capital expenditures, i.e., spending for buildings, bridges, sewer systems, etc., are routinely financed by issuing municipal bonds, and the outstanding value of these bonds is nearly $2.5 trillion. However, because these governments increased spending substantially during the good times and the recession caused revenues to decline significantly, many are now facing serious operating budget deficits. Additionally, like Social Security and Medicare, state and local pensions are underfunded, and future obligations will require increased state and local government revenues. Estimates of the present value of these future

---

[7] Social Security is funded by the Social Security tax, and the hospital insurance (HI) portion of Medicare (Part A) is funded by the Medicare tax. Looked at over the next seventy-five years, the present values of the unfunded obligations of these programs are $5.4 trillion (about the same as the previous year) and $2.4 trillion (substantially less than the previous year estimate of $13.4 trillion due to projected lower payments to health care providers, which the report considers unlikely to happen), respectively. Medicare Supplemental Medical Insurance, parts B and D, are funded in part (about 25%) by monthly premiums paid by the enrollees and in part (about 75%) by funds from the general revenues of the federal government and technically are considered fully funded. The present value of the portion not funded by the monthly premiums of enrollees, however, over the seventy-five-year period is more than $20 trillion. Looked at over the unlimited future (called the infinite horizon in the trustee reports), the portion of the Social Security and Medicare programs not currently funded by specific program taxes and premiums is nearly $54 trillion (it was much higher in the previous year's report). All these numbers are estimates and change each year.

unfunded obligations range from $1 trillion to more than $3 trillion. Increases to Medicaid, mandated by the 2010 health-care legislation, will add to these obligations.

Government revenues can be increased and the deficits reduced by either growing the economy or perhaps by increasing tax rates. Economic growth solves many problems. It increases tax revenues and can reduce future deficits and make debt levels more manageable without the need to increase tax rates. Economic growth, however, generally requires increased consumer spending, business investment, or an increase of exports relative to imports brought on by a dollar that's weaker compared to the currencies of our trading partners.

Government spending might stimulate economic activity, but if it requires increased borrowing, interest rates could rise, and economic activity might actually be reduced. Borrowing to fund current consumption is seldom a good idea either for individuals or governments. Tax increases can reduce the need for borrowing, but they likely would negatively affect the economy. A better solution would be to reduce government spending, but this is very difficult for politicians to do. Unfortunately, it's easier to borrow (as long as interest rates remain low) than to reduce spending or increase taxes, but excessive borrowing is a prescription for trouble.

Domestic investment is the lifeblood of the economy, and it is needed to both replace aging assets and expand the capital base. Investment comes from savings. Domestic savings comes from households, businesses, and governments. When domestic savings are insufficient to fund domestic investment, we borrow from foreigners to cover the shortfall. Government deficits (negative savings) reduce domestic savings and make it more difficult to fund domestic investment. Because domestic savings are currently significantly less than domestic investment, large net amounts are borrowed each year from foreigners. If foreigners reduce their willingness to lend to us in the large amounts we need, interest rates will almost certainly increase. If this happens, domestic investment will most likely decline, negatively affecting the economy.

Chapter 5

Taxes and Ways to Minimize Them

Local, state, and federal governments impose taxes. Taxes come in many forms: there are taxes on items you buy, property you own, and income you have. There may also be taxes on your estate when you die and on gifts you make during your lifetime.

Most items you buy are subject to a sales tax, which is added to the purchase price of items you buy. The state, the county or district, or the local government can impose the sales tax.

State and local governments impose an annual tax on property you own, the most common being the one on real estate. Some states also impose an annual tax on personal property.

The tax most people are familiar with is the federal personal income tax. All income, except that specifically exempted by law, is subject to this tax. Most states and some local governments also impose taxes on income.

Another tax people are familiar with is the payroll tax. The payroll tax is levied on wages and is made up of two parts: the Social Security tax and the Medicare tax. These taxes are also levied on the net earnings of the self-employed; here they are called the self-employment tax.

Estate taxes are imposed on estates valued over a certain amount, and gift taxes are imposed on gifts over a certain amount. The primary estate tax is the federal estate tax, but states also impose these taxes. More will be said about estate and gift taxes in chapter 12 on estate planning.

Taxes are a necessary burden imposed on most people. Taxes can, however, be legally delayed or in some cases avoided entirely. Minimizing your taxes can be a major contributor to building and preserving wealth and passing it on to your heirs. Everyone should have a basic understanding of the various types of taxes and the ways to legally defer or avoid them. The information that follows is intended to help in that regard. Tax laws change, however, and one should always make sure to check the current rules before taking action.

Sales Taxes

The sales tax is basically a consumption tax on goods and services. It is a flat tax, with the rate the same regardless of how much you buy. The more you spend, the more you pay in sales taxes. Sales taxes are not usually imposed on food bought for home consumption or on prescription drugs. The tax can be levied by the state, county, or the local government and generally is. Sales taxes vary considerably from state to state. The seller collects sales taxes, and the seller is responsible for paying the state or other taxing authority.

Some few states—Alaska, Delaware, Montana, New Hampshire, and Oregon as of this writing—impose no sales tax. Sales taxes vary considerably from state to state and even within states. When comparing state sales taxes, any sales tax imposed by the county and the local governments should also be considered. Where I live in Arizona, for example, in addition to the sales tax imposed by the state, there is also a county sales tax and a local sales tax, and the total sales tax is considerably higher than the so-called "state" sales tax.

There are also excise taxes. These are taxes on the purchase of specific products, such as gasoline and cigarettes, for example. Excise taxes are included in the price of the product.

Federal Personal Income Taxes

While the US income tax code is very complicated and voluminous, the basic method for determining personal taxes is straightforward and relatively simple. This section provides a brief overview of the method and discusses some of the particulars.

Prior to calculating your taxes, you need to determine the number of exemptions you are entitled to and your filing status. Each exemption exempts, or removes, a certain amount of income from taxes. You are entitled to an exemption for yourself and your spouse and one for each qualifying dependent. Filing status determines tax brackets, tax rates, and the magnitude of certain deductions you are allowed. There are five filing statuses: (1) single, (2) married filing jointly, (3) married filing separately, (4) head of household, and (5) qualifying widow(er) with dependent child.

Figure 5-1 shows the basic elements in the computation of personal income taxes. The first step in calculating your tax is to determine total or gross income. Total income is worldwide compensation of all types including money, property, or services that you may receive, except that specifically excluded by law. There are two basic types of income for tax purposes: earned and unearned. Earned income is for labor and work performed and includes wages, tips, commissions, and business income. Income earned by capital, such as interest, dividends, and capital gains is considered unearned. Pensions, alimony, and unemployment compensation also are considered unearned. Certain types of income, such as welfare benefits and child support, are legally exempt from taxes.

TOTAL INCOME
-Adjustments to Income
ADJUSTED GROSS INCOME
-Exemption Deductions
-Standard or Itemized Deduction
TAXABLE INCOME

TAX on TAXABLE INCOME
-Non-refundable Credits
+Other Taxes
TOTAL TAXES
-Tax Payments Already Made
-Refundable Credits
TAXES or REFUND DUE

Figure 5-1, Basic flow for personal income tax computation

There are currently three categories of subtractions from income (other than the many expense deductions in determining net income from a business, farm, or real estate property): adjustments, exemption deductions, and either the standard or itemized deduction. Adjustments are specific deductions allowed whether or not you itemize. Some of the current adjustment deductions are contributions to traditional IRAs, contributions to Health Savings Accounts, and interest on student loans. Subtracting adjustments from gross income gives adjusted gross income (AGI).

The exemption deduction is the number of exemptions multiplied by the amount allowed per exemption for that year. For tax year 2010, the amount allowed per exemption was $3,650; for 2011, the amount increases to $3,700.

The next deduction can be taken either as the standard deduction, a fixed amount determined by your filing status, or as an itemized deduction. You get to choose the larger of the two methods. For 2010 the standard deduction was $5,700 for a single filer and $11,400 for a married couple filing jointly. For 2011, the amounts increase to $5,800 and $11,600, respectively. It's more if you or your spouse is blind or over sixty-five. To determine the standard deduction you're entitled to, the instructions for form 1040 should be followed very carefully. Some of the categories of things that can currently be itemized include: medical and dental expenses (currently only the amount over 7.5% of AGI), certain taxes you paid to state and local governments, certain interest payments (home mortgages interest, for example), and charitable contributions. Subtracting the exemption deduction and either the standard or itemized deduction from AGI gives taxable income.

Taxes are determined from your taxable income, either using the tax tables or the tax rate schedule, and depend on your filing status. The maximum tax rate is currently 35%, and it is expected to remain at that level for at least two more years (through the 2012 tax year).

Tax credits reduce the amount of tax you are required to pay. There are many different tax credits. They can result in substantial refunds, particularly for taxpayers with children. Credits are of two types: nonrefundable and refundable. Nonrefundable credits can reduce your tax to zero, while refundable credits can result in a refund even if no taxes were withheld. Some of the current nonrefundable credits include education credits, the foreign tax credit, retirement savings contribution credits, child and dependent care credits, and credits for the elderly and disabled. The nonrefundable credits are subtracted from your taxes, and other taxes are added to determine total taxes. Other taxes include taxes like the self-employment tax (actually the Social Security and Medicare taxes for the self-employed), Social Security and Medicare taxes on income not reported to your employer (tip income, for example), any advanced earned income payments received, and any household employment taxes due.

Next, tax payments already made and refundable tax credits are subtracted. Tax payments include estimated tax payments and any taxes withheld from wages or other income. Refundable credits are treated like tax payments, and include such credits as the earned income credit and additional child tax credit. The earned income credit is particularly valuable to low-wage earners with children.

Because some taxpayers with high incomes could take advantage of large deductions and credits to significantly reduce their tax liability, Congress instituted the alternative minimum tax (AMT). A modified set of rules is used in calculating the AMT. These rules reduce or eliminate many of the deductions and credits normally allowed. Taxes need to be calculated with both the normal rules and the AMT rules, and the approach that results in the higher taxes used. While the AMT was designed for higher-income taxpayers, increasing numbers of middle-income taxpayers have become liable because of inflation. To lessen the impact, the Congress generally increases the AMT exemption amount each year. At some point the Congress will come up with a permanent solution, but it hasn't happened yet.

Many people pay professionals to do their federal and state personal income taxes because they believe that taxes are too complicated to do themselves. Some, however, prepare their own returns, and increasing numbers use tax preparation software. Since user friendly and inexpensive personal tax preparation software packages are readily available, many others could take advantage of this approach and save money.

Federal personal income tax law revisions are once again (summer 2011) under discussion in the congress. Changes are unlikely to affect the overall method for computing these taxes but might change or limit, in some way, adjustments to income, itemized deductions, the AMT, and possibly even tax credits.

State and Local Personal Income Taxes

Most states and some local governments have personal income taxes. Tax laws vary considerably from state to state. Eight states at this writing impose no tax on the income of individuals. These states are: Alaska, Florida, Nevada, South Dakota, Texas, Washington, and Wyoming. Some others tax only interest and dividends. Local income taxes are usually a specified fraction of the state tax. Because some people move from one state to another during the year, states have part-year returns and full-year returns. They also have nonresident returns, since individuals may live in one state but have some taxable income in another. Thus, depending on your situation, you may have to file more than one state return.

The calculation of state income taxes is generally similar to that on the federal personal income tax return. State taxes differ in the specifics. Filing status choices are similar, but some states limit the choices. Arizona, for example, does not have the qualifying widow(er) status. Qualifying dependents on the federal return are generally qualifying dependents on the state return. Some states allow additional specific exemptions.

Calculations on most returns begin with the adjusted gross income, AGI, from the federal return, and make additions and subtractions to determine state AGI. Most states do not tax Social Security benefits. Many also exempt at least a portion of pension income from tax. Some few states do not allow the federal deduction for IRA contributions, and any contribution must be added to the Federal AGI. Some states also exempt special types of wages. Arizona, for example, exempts the wages of Native Americans earned on the reservation if the earner is an enrolled tribal member and lives on the reservation.

After computing the AGI for the state, exemption amounts and either the itemized or standard deduction are deducted to determine taxable income. Personal exemption amounts differ considerably, but most are less than the federal allowance. Some, however, are higher. Most states allow use of the itemized deductions from the federal return but with some adjustments. Arizona, for example, allows the full amount of medical and dental expenses to be deducted. Standard deductions allowed are for the most part less than the federal standard deduction.

Taxes are determined from taxable income, either from tax tables or a tax rate schedule. Tax rates are much less than federal rates, and they vary considerably from state to state. Most states have graduated rates, but some few have flat rates.

Tax credits are state specific and much different than those granted on the federal return.

Payroll Taxes

Payroll taxes fund the Social Security program, a forced contribution social insurance program. It was signed into law in 1935 during the Great Depression, when there was high unemployment and high poverty. The original act provided benefits to both retirees and the unemployed. It no longer provides unemployment benefits. Now, however, it provides retirement income, certain health care benefits (Medicare was added in 1965), survivor benefits, and disability benefits. More will be said about benefits in the section on retirement planning.

Two separate payroll taxes are currently imposed: the Social Security tax and the Medicare tax. Currently the Social Security tax is 12.4% of gross wages (including tips) up to the maximum wage limit, called the Social Security wage base. The wage base for 2010 was $106,800, and it will remain at that level for 2011. It may increase in the future because of inflation. The employee and the employer each pay half of the tax, or 6.2%.[8] The Medicare tax is currently 2.9% of gross wages, with no upper limit. Again, half of this, or 1.45%, is paid by the employee, and the other half is paid by the employer. The self-employed pay both halves of both taxes on their net income. The tax rate when Social Security began was 2% of the first $3,000 of wages. Since then, both the tax rate and the amount of wages subject to the tax have been increased many times.

During the early years, Congress increased benefits and also the number of people eligible for benefits. By the late 1970s reality began to take hold. Financial projections showed large, long-term deficits in the program. Life expectancies were increasing, and the ratio of the number of people paying into the system to those collecting benefits was declining and was projected to continue to decline. Since then amendments have generally increased taxes and reduced benefits. As discussed in the previous

---

[8]   The tax legislation extending the Bush tax cuts through 2012 also reduces the Social Security tax paid by an employee to 4.2% for tax year 2011.

chapter, both the Social Security and Medicare programs have very large future financial obligations that are currently underfunded.

When Social Security was started, life expectancies for both males and females were close to sixty-five. Since the retirement age was sixty-five, a high percentage of people died before they were eligible to collect benefits. This is no longer the case. Life expectancies are now in the high seventies and continuing to increase. A major change occurred in 1983 as a result of the Greenspan commission. The change included, among other things, increasing the full retirement age gradually to sixty-seven and subjecting a portion of one's Social Security benefits to income taxes (the portion of Social Security benefits potentially subject to the income tax is now 85%). These changes allowed the Social Security system to generate large annual surpluses for a number of years. These surpluses, because of the unified budget, offset other government spending. The Social Security Trust Funds, in exchange for the surplus funds provided to the Treasury, are given a special series of government bonds that, unlike other government bonds, cannot be traded on the open market.

Because the number of retirees has increased compared to the number of people paying into the system, these annual surpluses have essentially disappeared, and both Social Security and Medicare now run deficits. Social Security began running a deficit in 2009, earlier than previously expected, due to the recession. It may temporarily return to a surplus if the economy recovers quickly, but only for a few years. When deficits exist, general revenues are used to buy back the bonds to provide funds to maintain benefit levels. Because future Social Security and Medicare deficits are projected to be very large, maintaining the current level of benefits in the future will require some combination of tax increases and other government spending reductions.

Property Taxes

Property taxes are of two types: a tax on real property and a tax on personal property. The tax on real property is basically a tax on real estate. The tax on personal property is mainly a tax on business personal property, although some taxing authorities tax certain personal property of individuals.

The county or local government typically imposes the real estate property tax. The tax helps provide funding for public schools; community colleges; town, city, and county governments; and certain special taxing authorities. The specific taxing authorities are usually listed on your annual tax bill or tax statement. Your property taxes are determined by multiplying the assessed value of the property by the tax rate. There are a number of elements to your property taxes. Your town and county typically have several taxing authorities, including school boards, city or town councils, and other special tax boards. Each of these determines their budget, gets it approved, and determines the property tax funding required. Your property tax is the sum of your amount for each of the several taxing authorities.

The assessor's office determines the assessed value of real estate property on a periodic basis. When property values were increasing at a rapid rate, more and more municipalities began assessing property on an annual basis. You should receive a property valuation notice early in the year. You usually have a right to appeal the valuation if you disagree with it by petitioning the assessor's office within a certain limited time period.

The property tax rate is generally determined by dividing the budget or required spending by the total assessed value of all the property in the community. The different spending authorities can have different tax rates, since they have different budgets. Property tax rates are generally set to generate the required revenue for the various spending authorities within the municipality. The tax rate is often quoted as the amount per $100 of valuation or as a percentage of assessed value. Sometimes a mill rate is used; one mill is $1 per $1,000 of assessed value.

States usually impose a tax on personal property, like motor vehicles, boats, and aircraft. Some also tax intangible assets, such as stocks or bonds and the personal property of businesses. Arizona, for example, taxes the personal property of businesses and has what amounts to a personal property tax on motor vehicles, called a vehicle license tax.

Reducing and Avoiding Taxes

Minimizing taxes is one of the most important ways to accumulate wealth. You probably pay a lot more than you realize in taxes. Tax receipts (from all sources) for the nation in recent years, despite lower levels due to the recession, have been more than 30% of National Income. Considering only federal and state income taxes and the Medicare tax, for which there is no upper wage limit, marginal tax rates for many in the upper tax bracket can currently approach 50%. You can save a lot of money by reducing your taxes. Some examples are discussed below.

You can reduce your current taxes by itemizing rather than taking the standard deduction. Itemizing is usually advantageous if you are a home owner and pay a significant amount of mortgage interest, if you have large medical and dental expenses, or if you've made sizable charitable contributions. Charitable contributions can be either cash or property. Instead of throwing away used clothing or other articles, contribute them to charity. You might be surprised at their value, if they are in good condition. Use the software package called "It's Deductible" that comes with the "TurboTax" tax preparation software to determine the value of your contributions. Even if medical and dental expenses don't exceed the excluded amount and thus cannot be deducted on your federal return, they may be deductible on your state return. Also, make sure you take maximum advantage of all adjustments to income that are available. Adjustments can be taken even if you don't itemize.

You pay taxes on gains you have on the sale of property, stock, or real estate, for example. If you hold an asset for less than a year, you pay the ordinary income tax rate. However, if you hold it for longer than a year, the gain becomes a long-term capital gain; the maximum tax rate on long-term capital gains is currently significantly less than the rate on ordinary income. If you sell a home, you are currently entitled to a $250,000 exclusion on any gain if you're single or a $500,000 exclusion if you're married and file a joint return. To qualify for this exclusion, you must have owned and lived in the property as your main home for a certain period of time. Capital gains are the difference between the sale price and the adjusted cost basis. Adjusted cost basis is the cost of the property, including most of the closing costs plus any improvements you've made. Keep records of all expenditures you make when you buy and sell property, as well as any improvements you make while you own it. You may need them for tax purposes.

If you own a business or have rental property, your expenses are deducted from your gross revenue to determine net income. There are many deductible expenses. If you have a net loss, it can be subtracted from other income you may have but only up the amount you have at risk. If you own rental property and have a net loss, this loss can offset some other income but only if you actively participate in the rental activity.

If you have a sizable estate when you die, your estate may have to pay substantial estate taxes. Smart estate planning can reduce or, in many cases, eliminate estate taxes entirely. Some ways to minimize estate taxes are discussed in chapter 12 on estate planning.

Deferring Taxes

There are also many ways to defer taxes. Tax deferral can be worth a lot of money. You might be able to defer taxes for forty years or longer. During the time taxes are deferred, you get to use the money you would have paid in taxes for investments. Contributions to traditional IRAs, 401(k)s, and several other retirement savings plans allow you to defer income and, hence, taxes. You might also be allowed to defer a portion of any bonus you might receive. This deferred income and the earnings on it are subject to income taxes but only when you take distributions.

How much is tax deferral worth to you? The answer, of course, depends on how much you defer and how successful you are at investing. Let's take an example. If you defer $10,000 of income and your tax rate on this income was 25%, you would defer $2,500 per year in taxes. The future value of an investment of $2,500 a year (the amount of deferred taxes) is plotted as a function of the number of years it's done and the annual rate of return you achieve, as shown in figure 5-2.

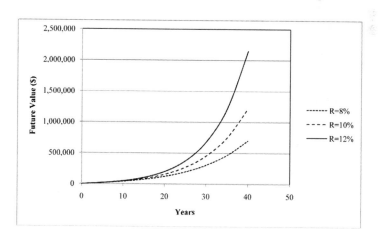

Figure 5-2, Future value of deferred taxes ($2,500 per year)

You can refer to chapter 1 for a discussion of future value. If you do it for thirty years and earn an annualized return of 8%, the investment will grow to a little more than $300,000. Now when you or your beneficiaries take distributions, taxes will likely have to be paid. How much depends on the person's tax bracket at the time distributions are taken. Assuming when you take the distribution you are still in the same 25% tax bracket, a total of about $75,000 in taxes would have to be paid. After taxes are paid, you would have netted about $225,000 from investing the deferred taxes. That's a lot of money. But that's just what the deferred taxes are worth. If you earn 8% on the entire amount of income you've deferred, it is four times as much, or about $1.2 million before taxes are paid and about $900,000 after taxes are paid. It's a big number, but that's because a large amount was invested into a deferred tax account. If you invest for forty years and/or earn a higher annualized return, the amounts are much larger. Another way to look at the benefits of deferral is to compute the present value of the deferred taxes. Present value was discussed in chapter 1. The present value of $75,000 in taxes you pay thirty years in the future is only $7,453 using the 8% earnings rate as the discount rate. However you choose to look at it, the benefits of income and tax deferral are very significant.

Chapter 6

Retirement Planning

Most people dream of the day they will be able to retire, but they do little planning and make little effort to make it happen. They engage in wishful thinking rather than taking action. It's easy to procrastinate about something that may be many years in the future and about which there is such uncertainty. An enjoyable retirement, however, requires advanced planning, and it should begin early in your working life.

Planning requires some thought about what you want to do in retirement: when you want to retire, how long you can expect to live after retirement, how much money you will need, and where this money will come from. Answers to these questions are interrelated not independent. For example, the amount of money you need depends on what you plan to do and how long you might live. In contrast, the amount of money you have may define when you can retire, if at all, and what you will be able to do in retirement.

Americans have been conditioned to expect that they will be able to retire at age sixty-five or younger. A comfortable retirement, however, takes substantial financial resources, and the younger one is the more one needs. Unfortunately, many will not have the required resources. Accumulation of the needed assets takes many years for most people, and the earlier you start the better.

Planning will give you a better chance of controlling your retirement and making it enjoyable. Since things change, retirement planning is not a onetime event, but a process that continues throughout your working life and even into retirement. Start early, develop a plan, and begin to implement it. As life events change, modify the plan accordingly. The plan doesn't have to be written, although if you write it down and look at it periodically, you will have a much better chance of actually taking steps to implement it.

What Will You Do in Retirement?

It's a good idea to think about what you would like to do in retirement well in advance. How will you transition to retirement? How will you spend your additional time? Do you want a second career? Do you want or need to work at all? Where will you live? When do you want to retire? If your spouse works, when does he or she want to retire? What does your spouse want to do? These are some of the questions you need to address. Since the answers will have financial impact, it's smart to think about them while you still have time to accumulate the needed funds.

Will you retire abruptly, or will you transition to retirement? If you're a typical American and have worked full time for many years, you may now find yourself with too much time on your hands when you suddenly no longer go to work each day. Some people may want to gradually cut back on their responsibilities and working hours. If you have a job that lets you semiretire, that's great. Some people enjoy their careers so much they never want to retire; they don't even think of their jobs as work. They are very fortunate. Others want out as quickly as possible, either because of the stress of their jobs or because they have something else they want to do. Whatever your situation, some conscious thought would be beneficial.

What will you do with the extra time? There are many interesting things to do in retirement and many ways for you and your spouse to enjoy retirement. Some people want to travel extensively, and there are many fantastic places to see, both in this country and throughout the world. If you can afford it, it's wonderful. Extensive travel, however, can be expensive; international travel can be particularly expensive if the dollar is weak. Domestic travel is much less expensive, and there are many absolutely marvelous places to see in this country. Some other people want to play golf, and some want to fish or sail. Some may want to sit by the ocean or in the mountains and relax and read. Others may just want to visit with family or friends. Some may want to get more involved in community affairs or help out with charities. Some may want to pursue a second career, and they might go back to school full time or take some courses at the community college to better prepare for what they want to do. Most of these things will cost money, but some can put you in a position to earn money. Whatever you want, if you plan for it, you'll have a much better chance of actually making it happen

Where you live can be important. Some people want to move to a warmer climate, and others may want to move closer to their children or other family members. If you plan to move, check out the new location to make sure you like it. Where you live can have a significant effect on your finances. If you live away from children or move away from children, travel expenses can be large, particularly if you plan to visit frequently. State taxes can also be an important consideration. If you move to a state with no state income tax or a lower income tax, the savings can be quite substantial and can provide funding for some of the activities you want to do. If you move from a low-tax state to a higher one, the opposite is true.

When you retire may also affect what you can do in retirement. Some of the things you want to do may require a certain level of physical fitness. If you wait too long, you may not be able to do them. As you age your physical fitness declines, even if you exercise regularly. When you plan to retire can also affect whether you get to retire at all. I knew a number of people who were eligible to retire but continued working and died, perhaps due to stress. They never got to enjoy the retirement they earned. On the other hand, the earlier you retire the more financial resources you need. Thinking through your wants and alternatives may not be easy, but it will be helpful.

Life Expectancy

How long will you live after you retire? No one can answer that question with certainty. However, the probabilities of your living for various lengths of time, given your current age, can be determined from existing statistical data. Published life expectancy data usually shows the average number of years of life remaining for people in a given group. There are many factors that influence life expectancy: gender, whether you smoke or not, race, and various health factors, to name some. The data in table 6-1 shows the life expectancy for males and females based on their current exact age. This data is taken from the latest Period Life Table published by the Social Security Administration on its website. It is based on mortality rates for 2005. Since mortality rates change very slowly, the data continues to be reasonably accurate.

LIFE EXPECTANCY

Exact Age	Male Life Expectancy	Female Life Expectancy
55	24.37	27.82
56	23.57	26.94
57	22.77	26.08
58	21.97	25.22
59	21.19	24.37
60	20.42	23.53
61	19.66	22.70
62	18.91	21.88
63	18.17	21.08
64	17.44	20.28
65	16.73	19.49
66	16.02	18.70
67	15.32	17.93
68	14.63	17.17
69	13.96	16.42
70	13.30	15.69

Table 6-1, Life expectancy versus age

Since the subject of this chapter is retirement, I've shown only the data for ages fifty-five through seventy, which are the retirement ages for most people. Other than gender, this table makes no distinction for other life determining factors. Keep in mind that these are average life expectancies, and an individual might live much longer. While not shown but of some interest is the life expectancy at birth. It is 74.81 years for males and 79.95 for females. As you grow older, your life expectancy decreases, but at any given age, within reason, there is some probability of your surviving for an additional period of time. For example, if you reach the age of 100 years and you're a female, your life expectancy is still 2.29 years.

How Much Spendable Income Do You Need?

The general rule is that you need 70% to 80% of your income in retirement. Some will need more, some less. Before retirement, most of your income comes from wages. After you retire, however, your income will come mostly from pensions and investment earnings. You don't pay Social Security and Medicare taxes on this type of income, so you save the payroll tax of 7.65% on the first approximately $100K of wages. You generally won't be adding new money to savings and investments either. Assuming that you were saving 10% of your income, that's another 10% reduction. Now how about spending? The largest element of spending for most people is their mortgage payment. If you've managed your finances properly, your mortgage should either be paid off or nearly so. If your mortgage payment including property taxes, and insurance was 20% of your income, your spending might decline by another 15% or so (you still need to pay property taxes and insurance). With these reductions, you're below 70% of income.

Next let's look at other spending items. Clothing expenditures should certainly decline, and since you no longer need to commute back and forth to work, so should gasoline expenditures. Expenditures on many other items could also be reduced, such as gifts and entertainment, for example. The cost of health care, however, will increase. Medical insurance premiums generally go up after you retire. Once you reach sixty-five, you'll be eligible for Medicare, but you have to pay for Medicare part B, and it's wise to purchase a supplemental insurance policy. Considering all these changes, 70% of your income prior to retirement is a reasonably good estimate.

If you or you and your spouse were earning $100,000 per year, you'll need about $70,000 per year in retirement to basically maintain your current lifestyle. If you want to travel extensively or spend lavishly, you might need a lot more. Clearly, the amount you need is a personal matter.

Let's, however, take a bottom-up look at the amount you might actually require to live a reasonably comfortable retirement. Table 6-2 shows possible expenses for a retirement couple living in a modest two-bedroom home, assuming that their mortgage is paid off and that they retire at age sixty-five. The amounts shown are by no means the minimum they could get by on. Allowances for each element are realistic and reasonable. Total spending is somewhat less than $40,000 per year including taxes.

Living expenses—spending for food, clothing, utilities, gas for cars, home and auto maintenance, etc.—are $15,000, and car payments total $4,000. Spending on health care, including health insurance, is substantial and assumes that both husband and wife are on Medicare, both Part A and Part B. Part A covers hospital expenses, and if you are collecting Social Security you're automatically enrolled at sixty-five. You don't pay for this part directly; it's paid out of Medicare tax receipts and the general revenues of the government. Part B covers doctor's costs, but you pay extra for it. In 2011, it costs about $100 per month for most individuals (about $2,400 per year for a couple). I've also assumed that they purchase Medicare supplemental policies with drug coverage, costing $400 per month for the two of them. I have also assumed that they have long-term care policies, purchased when they were younger, costing another $50 per month each. Total spending on health care insurance is $8,400. Additionally, I've assumed that they spend another $1,000 per year for deductibles and dental expenses, giving total health care spending of $9,400 per year. Insurance costs, other than health care, are $3,000 and include automobile, life, liability, and home owner policies. The amount for entertainment is $5,000 and that for gifts is another $1,000, amounts neither minimal nor excessive.

The federal income tax of zero assumes that half of their income of $40,000 comes from Social Security. The federal government currently taxes up to 85% of your Social Security but only if your modified AGI plus half your Social Security is over $44,000 (married filing jointly). Modified AGI excludes your Social Security income. If your modified AGI plus half your Social Security is less than $32,000, none of your Social Security income is taxable. With $20,000 per year in Social Security, their AGI plus half their Social Security is only $30,000 and none of the Social Security income would be taxable. Because of this, their total income for federal tax purposes is only $20,000. Since the sum of their exemptions and standard deduction exceeds $20,000, their federal taxable income is zero. Many states don't tax Social Security, and in many their income tax would be $100 or less.

Item	Amount ($)
Living Expenses	15,000
Car Payments	4,000
Health Costs	9,400
Other Insurance Costs	3,000
Entertainment	5,000
Gifts	1,000
Property Taxes	2,000
Income Taxes	100
TOTAL	39,500

Table 6-2, Hypothetical retirement expenses

Your spending requirements will likely increase each year by about the same percentage as the inflation rate. While no one knows what future inflation rates will be, it is likely that they will be similar to what they were in the past. Over the past 150 years, the CPI (consumer price index) has increased about 2% per year, compounded annually, in the United States; over the past twenty years it's been about 3%, and over the last ten years about 2.5%. Based on the past, it's reasonable to assume an inflation rate of between 2% and 3% per year going forward. Keep in mind, however, that there could be periods in which inflation is much higher. With 2% annual inflation, your spending requirements will double in about thirty-six years, and at 3% they will double in about twenty-four years.

Where Will the Money Come from?

There are various possible sources of income in retirement: Social Security; defined benefit pension plans; savings and investments, including specific retirement savings; business income; part-time employment; and reverse mortgages, to name the most common. You want as many sources of income as possible. Many private and public sector retirement plans were set up to complement income from Social Security with a defined benefit pension and/or a defined contribution retirement savings plan, such as a 401(k) or equivalent. Unfortunately for many in the private sector, defined benefit plans are being phased out, forcing future retirees to rely increasingly on savings, investments, and other income sources.

Social Security provides a guaranteed level of benefits for you and your spouse for as long as you live, and these benefits are currently indexed to inflation through COLAs (cost of living adjustments). Defined benefit pension plans also provide a guaranteed level of benefits for as long as you (and your spouse, if you elect the survivorship option) live. Benefits are not generally indexed to inflation for private sector plans but are for most public sector plans. Savings and investment capital are an important source of retirement income for most people, but it must be well managed to avoid running out. If your Social Security, defined benefit plans, and savings and investments do not meet your income requirements, you can delay retirement, supplement the income you do have by working part time, downsize your home to raise capital and reduce expenses, or, if you have a home that is nearly paid for, you can withdraw equity capital through a reverse mortgage.

It should be the goal of everyone planning for retirement to have an income that at least meets their minimum living needs and is guaranteed for life. Some families' income requirements will be completely satisfied by some combination of Social Security and defined benefit programs (either corporate or government). These people are very fortunate. Most people will have Social Security to provide a base of income for their retirement, but to meet their total income needs they may need a substantial amount of investment capital. If you rely on investment capital for retirement income, you have the risk of outliving this capital, unless you either have a very large amount or earn more than you withdraw each year. An alternative is to use some capital to buy a lifetime income annuity from an insurance company.

Social Security, defined benefit pensions, capital needs, part-time employment, and reverse mortgages are discussed in sections that follow. Various ways to save are discussed in the next chapter.

Social Security Benefits

Social Security currently pays retirement benefits, spousal benefits, survivor benefits, and disability benefits. These are discussed below. The future of Social Security, a hotly debated topic, is also discussed.

Retirement Benefits

The amount of monthly retirement benefits a wage earner is currently entitled to is a function of his or her earnings record and the age he or she elects to begin receiving benefits. Under current law a person can receive reduced benefits at age sixty-two, but the age for full Social Security retirement benefits depends on your birth date. If you were born in 1937 or before, the full retirement age was sixty-five. If you were born between 1938 and 1943, the full retirement age increased two months each year until it reached age sixty-six. For those born between 1943 and 1954, the full retirement age remains at sixty-six. For those born in 1955 or later, the full retirement age again increases two months for each year up to 1960, when it reaches sixty-seven.

The maximum monthly benefit for an individual retiring at full retirement age in 2011 (age sixty-six) is $2,366, a little more than $28,000 a year. If the person begins taking benefits at age sixty-two, the amount is reduced. Monthly benefits are currently indexed to inflation through annual cost of living adjustments. To qualify for the maximum benefit, you must have earned the maximum income subject to the Social Security tax for every year after the age of twenty-one.

The Social Security administration sends a statement to each worker each year showing their earnings record and an estimate of his or her expected benefits at both sixty-two and their full retirement age. To qualify for Social Security retirement benefits, you must have earned forty credits during your working life.

Spousal Benefits

Any current spouse is eligible for benefits, without having to earn benefits on their own. Spousal benefits are half the worker's benefits, if they begin receiving benefits at full retirement age. The percentage is less if the spouse elects to receive benefits early. Divorced or former spouses are also eligible, if the marriage lasted ten years or longer.

Survivors' Benefits

A surviving spouse and a worker's children are also eligible for benefits. Children receive benefits up to the age of eighteen. The earliest age for a surviving spouse who is not disabled to receive benefits is sixty.

Disability Benefits

A worker that has become disabled is eligible for disability benefits, regardless of age. The disabled worker must meet the work requirements in terms of credits and a certain amount of work in the ten years immediately preceding the disability. The benefit amount depends on the worker's age and earnings record.

Future of Social Security

The financing of Social Security is a serious concern for the future. Benefits are paid from the payroll taxes imposed on current workers and their employers. While Social Security is projected to run a surplus for a while longer, the surplus is declining and is projected to continue to decline because the number of retirees continues to increase compared to the number of wage earners paying into the system. According to the 2009 Annual Reports Summary of the Social Security and Medicare Trustees, Social Security's annual surplus of tax income over expenditures will permanently disappear around 2016 (it actually ran a deficit in 2009 due to the recession and could remain in deficit depending on economic conditions). To maintain current benefits, the government will have to begin repaying the funds borrowed from the trust fund. The funds to do this have to come from the government's general revenues. Sometime around 2035, the Social Security Trust Fund will have been repaid all funds borrowed by the government. By then the annual Social Security deficit will be very large, and Social Security will be able to pay only a portion (estimated to be about 75%) of promised benefits. Clearly something will be done long before that. No one wants his or her promised benefits reduced. At some point, however, the young people paying the taxes may decide that they will no longer accept the burden.

What will happen? It is almost beyond imagination that the Social Security program would be allowed to die. Much more likely is that Social

Security taxes will be increased and benefits will be reduced to bring the system into balance. Since the early 1980s that's exactly what's happened. Democrats likely will oppose benefit reductions for all except the wealthy, and Republicans likely will oppose tax increases. A compromise will probably be reached in which the Democrats agree to reduce benefits, and the Republicans agree to raise payroll taxes.

No one knows exactly what changes will be made. Most likely the wage limit subject to Social Security taxes will be increased, and the amount of Social Security benefits potentially subject to income taxes will be increased to 100%. Also, the method used to calculate benefits may change, limiting in some way the amounts paid to high-wage earners. Other changes that might happen are elimination of inflation indexing of benefits, but probably only for higher income people. Another possibility is increasing the retirement age above sixty-seven for full benefits and/or the age for reduced benefits above sixty-two. I believe this is the fairest change. Remember, when the program stated in 1935 the average person was unlikely to live to the retirement age of sixty-five. Today life expectancies are in the mid—to upper seventies, and full Social Security benefits start at sixty-six. Unless the number of people paying into the system compared to the number of retirees is increased, the system will likely continue to have long-term funding problems. One way of doing this is to increase the retirement age and index it to life expectancy. The Social Security program will surely change to keep it viable, and it almost certainly will not be eliminated. Further, I believe, low—to moderate-income individuals will continue to receive full benefits, and these benefits will almost certainly be indexed to inflation.

Defined Benefit Pension Plans

Defined benefit pension plans provide a monthly pension at retirement, independent of the performance of the economy and the financial markets. Many employees in both the private and public sectors have defined benefit plans. Pension amounts are dependent on the employee's salary history and years of service. Contributions required by the employee for these plans have historically been relatively low, while benefits have been quite generous. Normal retirement is sixty-five years of age in the private sector, but most plans allow early retirement, typically at fifty-eight if the employee has thirty or more years of service. Public plans generally allow full retirement at a younger age. Employees in the Federal Employee Retirement System (FERS) can currently retire at unreduced benefits at age fifty-six if they have thirty or more years of service. The retirement age for unreduced benefits will eventually increase to fifty-seven. Certain groups, air traffic controllers and law enforcement officers, for example, can retire with unreduced benefits even younger.

While benefits differ from plan to plan, an employee with thirty years of service might get 30% to 40% of his salary from a defined benefit program. Some state and local plans are much more generous and even allow overtime pay to be used to increase the salary that benefits are based on. If you're employer still provides a defined benefit pension plan, you are very fortunate, and you should be enrolled. Many companies, however, no longer allow new enrollment in their plans. Private pension plan benefits are not generally indexed to inflation, while public plan benefits are. If your pension is not linked to inflation, your spending power can be seriously eroded over time, and this needs to be factored into your planning.

Defined benefit pension plans are slowly being phased out in the private sector because of the financial liabilities associated with them. Efforts to curtail defined benefit plans for public employees are just beginning, but as funding problems become more difficult to handle and more apparent to taxpayers, efforts in this regard can be expected to increase. Employers contribute the majority of funds to defined benefit plans. Funds are generally put into a trust that manages the money by investing mostly in stocks and bonds. The employer has certain legal requirements to provide funding, and plans also have the requirement to pay pensions to eligible employees regardless of the plan's investment performance. Since the value of the plan's assets can decline for various reasons, private sector employers, in particular, have significant risk associated with providing pensions. Employees in private sector plans also have risk, because if the company goes bankrupt and the plan has insufficient funds to pay its obligations, some of their pension might be in jeopardy. If the pension plan is a "qualified plan," the Pension Benefit Guarantee Corporation (PBGC) provides some protection. The protection is limited, particularly for employees that have earned large pensions. The amount of protection also varies with retirement age: for those who choose to retire early the protection is significantly less than for those retiring at sixty-five. Employees in public plans generally don't have these risks. Even if a state or local government went bankrupt, benefits might still have to be paid.

Corporations are required to prepare a detailed accounting of their plans annually and make them available to employees on request; a summary report is sent to each employee yearly. Pension accounting is complicated. Funding status is determined by comparing the present value of the plan's assets to the present value of its obligations. If the obligations exceed the assets, the plan is underfunded. If the underfunding exceeds a certain level, additional contributions are required. Pension contributions are business expenses, and they negatively affect earnings. Since the vast majority of pension obligations are payable in the future, they get discounted to determine their present value. If the discount rate is low, the present value of these obligations is relatively more than if the discount rate is high. Discount rates are affected by interest rates. If interest rates are low for any length of time, a company's pension liability may increase substantially, and the plan can be significantly underfunded, requiring increased contributions. Clearly, companies don't like this. On the other hand, if the plan is overfunded, no contributions are necessary, and, in fact, the company gets to count some of the earnings from the plan as income on its earnings statement.

Public pension plans, other than the federal plan, don't have the same level of regulation or scrutiny as private plans. As a result, taxpayers are largely unaware of the benefits promised to public employees and the financial obligations associated with these benefits. Retiree health cost liabilities, for example, until recently were not required to be disclosed at all. State and local governments and unions opposed disclosure, primarily because they feared negative reactions from taxpayers. Tax revenues fund government contributions and pension obligations, and many public plans are underfunded. As costs for these plans keep rising, squeezing funding for other government services, taxes or employee contributions will likely have to be increased or benefits curtailed in some way in the future.

Savings and Investment

If a significant portion of your retirement income will come from savings and investments, you'll need a substantial amount of capital. You'll also have to manage this capital to both provide the income you need and to preserve the capital for a long time. How long does it have to last? If you retire at sixty-five, you can expect to live about seventeen years in retirement if you're a male and about nineteen years if you're a female. You can refer back to figure 6-1 for your life expectancy, if you plan to retire at some other age. These are average life expectancies, and you might live a lot longer. Further, a couple needs to consider the life expectancy for the last to die (the expected time until both die), and this will be still longer. Thus, whatever savings and investments are used to produce income must last many years. For planning purposes, thirty years would not be unreasonable if you and your spouse plan on retiring at age sixty-five. If you plan on retiring earlier, you should plan on a longer time period.

To keep the risk of running out of income-producing assets low, the amount you can withdraw on a regular basis is a relatively small percentage of starting capital. The exact amount depends on how long you want your capital to last and the returns you earn each year. Various studies have examined sustainable withdrawal rates from retirement portfolios that earn market returns. A relatively recent and comprehensive study, *Guidelines for Withdrawal Rates and Portfolio Safety during Retirement* (John J. Spitzer 2007), determined the probability of running out of money over a thirty-year period for a wide range of real withdrawal rates and different stock and bond portfolios. The study used real (inflation-adjusted) US stock and bond returns from 1926 through 2005. The results are presented in a way that allows an investor to easily see the consequences of selecting a specific withdrawal rate and using a particular mix of stocks and bonds in their portfolio. Both retirees and those planning for retirement should read this paper. Results show, for example, that with 30% to 40% in stocks and the remainder in bonds, a retiree can withdraw about 4% (in real terms) of *initial capital* annually, with a probability of running out of money before the thirty-year period ends of about 5%. One might think that since real (inflation adjusted) average market returns in the past have been higher than 4%, they could safely withdraw more. Unfortunately, returns fluctuate from year to year, and the sequence of returns can make a big difference when you withdraw a fixed or increasing amount annually. If you are unlucky and have an extended period of poor performance at the beginning of your retirement, it will adversely affect your capital balance. When it comes to spending investment capital, retirees need to reevaluate their situation periodically and remain flexible and prepared to reduce spending, if necessary. On the other hand, if you get lucky and have an extended period of good performance at the beginning, you will likely end up with a bigger balance or be able to increase your withdrawal rate.

Higher withdrawal rates are increasingly risky. With a 5% withdrawal rate and a 50%/50% mix of stocks and bonds, for example, the chance of running out before the end of the thirty-year period is about 20%. To reduce the probability of running out of money to 1%, you can only withdraw a little more than 3%. The lower the withdrawal rate, the higher the probability of ending up with a sizable balance that can be left to heirs.

If your spending requirements are $40K in the initial year of retirement and you and your spouse receive $20K from Social Security and don't have any other pensions, the remaining $20K would have to come from savings and investments. If the $20K annual withdrawal were 4% to 5% of initial capital, $400,000 to $500,000 in investment capital would be needed.

If you received the maximum Social Security benefit and your wife received half of your benefit, together you would receive a little more than $40K (actually about $42K) in 2011. If you had a spending requirement in retirement of $70K, you would need another approximately $30K of income. With a defined benefit pension from your employer, you would likely get more, but if it wasn't indexed to inflation, you would need some amount of investment capital to sustain your lifestyle. If you didn't have a defined benefit plan and had to rely on investment income, you would need $600K to $750K, depending on whether you withdraw 4% or 5% of your initial investment capital each year.

For those needing more than $70K annually in retirement, Social Security will provide a decreasing percentage of their spending needs, and they will need increasing amounts of investment capital or defined benefit plans or both.

If you want more certainty of not running out of money, you could purchase a lifetime annuity from an insurance company. A lifetime annuity provides a certain amount of monthly income for as long as you live. The cost depends on the annuitant's age and expectations for future interest rates, but it should be significantly less than the capital amounts discussed above for the same level of income. It should be significantly less because the cost of an annuity is based on one's life expectancy not one's possible lifetime. Annuitants that die before reaching their life expectancy are, in effect, paying for those that live longer than their life expectancy. Buying inflation protection should be seriously considered but will increase the cost of the annuity. The downside of buying a lifetime annuity is that when you die you lose your investment, unless you buy insurance protection.

Insurance, however, also increases the cost. A lifetime annuity is a bet on how long you'll live. The longer you live, the better the deal. If you die early, it's a bad deal (Merrill 2007). Chapter 9 discusses how to calculate the cost of annuities, and there are many websites where you can get cost estimates.

Part-Time Employment

While many might not want to consider the possibility of working in their retirement years, it should be part of most people's retirement planning. Many current retirees supplement their income with part-time employment, and increasing numbers will need to do so in the future.

There are many reasons for considering part-time employment in planning for retirement, including these. First, you may not accumulate the necessary resources to fully retire and may need to work; second, expenses may exceed the amount planned, due perhaps to a major illness in the family or because family members may need financial assistance; third, inflation may exceed that planned for, significantly reducing the spending power of your income, a large part of which may be fixed; forth, an income source you counted on may be reduced or disappear entirely; or fifth, an individual might want to return to the workforce, not because they have to but because they find full retirement boring or unrewarding.

There is much uncertainty in life, and having an income that exceeds expenses, or the ability and energy to increase income, if necessary, provides considerable flexibility to handle unanticipated financial problems. If you plan and prepare in advance for some type of part-time employment, you should be able to retain at least some of this flexibility in your retirement years. You will be much better off if you prepare in advance and retain the option of reentering the workforce with a good-paying, enjoyable job if necessary. Some careers lead naturally to the option of working late into life on a part-time basis; others do not, and some additional education and/or training may be necessary. The knowledge and experience the elderly possess will likely remain valuable in many work areas in the future, and demand for their services may actually increase because of shortages of trained and experienced workers. It's always a good idea to have something to fall back on, and advanced preparation for possible part-time employment should be part of retirement planning.

Reverse Mortgage

A reverse mortgage is a loan against the equity you have in your home. However, unlike a conventional home equity loan that requires you to make monthly payments, with a reverse mortgage you don't make payments; you receive them. You can take the loan funds in different ways: as a lump sum amount, a series of regular monthly payments, or as a line of credit that you can draw on, to name the most common. To qualify, the only requirements are that all home owners must be older than a certain age, typically sixty-two, and must own the home essentially debt free. You may have seen celebrities advertising reverse mortgages on television; they make them seem good. But before you decide to take a reverse mortgage, you should fully understand exactly what they are and how they work, and you should consider alternatives.

Reverse mortgages are designed to appeal to the elderly that wish to continue living in their current homes but who may no longer have the funds to do so. While the loan may permit this, it comes at a significant cost. The loan is secured by the property, and the surviving home owners can continue to live in it even though the loan balance may actually exceed the value of the property at some point. The surviving home owners, of course, must continue to pay property taxes and home insurance and maintain the property to certain standards set by a government agency. When the last of the home owners dies or moves out for some reason, the loan balance must either be paid off or the lending institution will take possession of the property. If the property can be sold for more than the loan balance, either the home owner or their estate will get the balance.

The loan amount the home owner(s) can qualify for depends on their age, the appraised value of the property, and prevailing interest rates, but it will only be a fraction of their equity in the property. It's only a fraction because there must be a large margin between the loan amount and the market value of the home to allow for the substantial amount of interest that can accumulate on the loan. The interest rate on the loan will generally be adjustable, not fixed, and will vary according to some inflation index. There will also be substantial closing costs on the loan. The lender will most likely allow these costs to be added to the loan balance, but this will decrease the funds you can actually take away. Closing costs typically include fees for an appraisal, a title search, a credit check, an inspection, a survey, and recording. You likely will also be required to pay for mortgage insurance to protect the lender against the possibility that the loan balance (loan amount plus accumulated interest) may at some point exceed the value of the property, and title insurance to protect the lender from claims against the property's title. Additionally, the loan will likely have an origination fee and a monthly service charge.

Since no loan payments are being made, the loan balance will grow as the interest on the loan accumulates on a compound basis. With a reverse mortgage, the miracle of compounding works for the benefit of the lending institution and against the borrower. The loan balance can grow very quickly, especially if you take the full amount as a lump sum up front. For example, at an interest rate of 7% per year, the loan balance will double in about ten years. Remember, however, that reverse mortgages are variable rate loans, and if the rates go up, the loan balance will grow more quickly. Since there is usually a cap on the rate and a restriction on how quickly it can increase, the borrower generally has some protection against rising rates. If you take the funds as monthly payments rather than a lump sum, the loan balance will grow more slowly, but still relatively quickly.

If you get a reverse mortgage, you shouldn't count on any equity remaining in your home when you die. There is a fair chance that one of the owners will live long enough that the loan balance exceeds the value of the property. This is, of course, the reason the lending institution makes the borrower pay for mortgage insurance. Also keep in mind that once you finalize the loan, it's difficult to end. If you terminate the loan, the balance must be paid off in full, and people who take these loans are not generally in a financial position to do so.

Before you decide to take a reverse mortgage, you should seriously consider other alternatives. The best alternative financially is to sell the property and either buy a smaller home or rent. This way you get the full amount of equity out of the property. If invested conservatively, and that's the only way these funds should be invested, you may earn enough to pay rent on a nice condo or apartment.

If you feel you must continue to live in your current home, talk to your heirs and see if they will provide the funds you need in exchange for their gradually taking ownership of the property. If they will be getting the property when you die, they might be willing to help financially now, rather than potentially ending up with nothing if you take a reverse mortgage. If you have no heirs or don't care if you leave them anything, and if you just can't bear to move out of your home, then maybe a reverse mortgage is right for you. In my opinion, however, it should be a last resort.

Chapter 7

Disciplined Savings

Savings are essential to accumulation of wealth. Savings together with investments provide the opportunity for the average person to accumulate a significant amount of money. If you spend everything you make, you'll never give yourself this opportunity, and it doesn't matter how much you earn. The first step to accumulating wealth is disciplined savings.

"It takes money to make money" is a common saying. It's true, and the more money you have, the more you can make. You get more money by saving more and by making smart investments. But the initial money comes from savings unless you get lucky and win the lottery, are given a gift, or receive an inheritance. Even then you must save and invest at least a portion. If you constantly add to your investments through a disciplined saving program, you can shorten the time it takes to accumulate wealth.

Americans don't save very much. In fact, by some standards the national savings rate actually went negative in 2006. While this is misleading and has a lot to do with accounting and the definition of savings and investment used in compiling these statistics, it is nevertheless true that Americans don't save very much. The recession of 2008/9, however, caused Americans to revise their savings habits, and according to the National Income Accounts compiled by the Bureau of Economic Analysis, personal savings in 2009 increased to about 5.5% of disposable personal income.[9] For 2010 the personal savings percentage was about the same. It remains

---

[9] Disposable personal income is the amount left after taxes are deducted from personal income. It's the source of funds for consumption expenditures and personal savings.

to be seen how long this refound thrift will last. It is a good idea to make saving a habit, and the earlier you start the better off you will be.

There are many things to save for, including contingencies, a new car, home ownership, education for children or grandchildren, health care spending, retirement, starting a business, and just plain wealth building. For many of these, there are formal savings plans that allow you to defer income and taxes. Many are for retirement savings, but there are also education savings accounts and health savings accounts.

Savings should be made on a regular basis as part of your budget. The best way to save is to put the money away before you spend it, and the best way to do that is to have the money withheld from your paycheck or automatically transferred from your checking account. You can also write checks to yourself, but you need to be very disciplined to do it. Most people could save at least 10% of their income, but every effort should be made to save 20% or more. Many of the ways to save are discussed below.

Contingencies

Everyone should have easily accessible money for contingencies and emergencies. How much is a personal choice, but an amount equal to several months worth of spending would be wise. These funds should be in an interest-bearing account, such as a savings account or a brokerage spending account.

Home Ownership

Home ownership is a form of savings and investment and often is a good way to build wealth. A portion of your mortgage payment is repayment of the loan principal. In the early years of a mortgage, most of the payment is interest, but a portion is payment of principal. This principal payment reduces the loan balance and hence future interest payments. As time goes on more and more of the payment is principal and less is interest. As debt is paid down, your equity in the property increases, even if the market value of the property remains unchanged. If the market value increases, your equity can increase substantially. Since payments are made on a regular schedule, savings increase accordingly.

If you plan on buying a home, you'll need funds for the down payment. These funds can be saved in either a tax-deferred account, like an IRA, or a regular savings/investment account. First-time home buyers can withdraw funds from IRAs and certain other tax-deferred accounts without penalty.

Education

A college education is expensive and getting more so. Scholarships and financial aid are available to those who qualify, and student loans are available to most other students. There are, however, two tax-advantaged programs the government has established to assist in saving for education expenses: Coverdell Education Savings Accounts and Qualified Tuition Programs. Parents can also set up regular savings accounts in their children's names and save on taxes.

Coverdell Education Savings Accounts, (ESAs), are similar in many ways to Roth IRAs. Contributions to these accounts are not tax deductible, but the funds grow tax-free, and qualified distributions are exempt from income taxes. They are usually opened for the benefit of someone other than the contributor. Beneficiaries can be anyone, but they must be under the age of eighteen at the time the contribution is made. The maximum contribution allowed per beneficiary is currently $2,000. The amount was scheduled to drop to $500 at the end of 2010, but the extension of the Bush era tax cuts extended this provision as well. The number of beneficiaries is unlimited, but total contributions are limited by the income of the contributor.

Funds from these accounts can be used to pay qualified expenses at all levels of education from kindergarten to the postgraduate level at eligible institutions. Most institutions qualify, including vocational and religious schools. Qualified expenses include tuition, books, fees, supplies, and room and board, if the person is at least a half-time student. The designated beneficiary of an account can be changed or unused assets rolled over to another ESA. The new beneficiary must, however, be a member of the old beneficiary's family, but the definition of family is very broad.

Qualified Tuition Programs (QTPs), commonly called 529 plans, allow one to either prepay expenses or contribute to an account that is later used to pay qualified education expenses. Contributions are not tax deductible on the federal return but are deductible on some state returns.

As with ESAs, the accounts grow tax free, and the distributions used for qualified education expenses at eligible institutions are exempt from taxes. Eligibility is limited to accredited postsecondary institutions and includes both vocational schools and postgraduate schools. Qualified expenses include tuition, books, fees, supplies, and room and board, provided the individual is enrolled at least as a half-time student. Contributions can be substantial and are not currently limited by income. As with Coverdell Education Savings Accounts, unused funds can be rolled to another QTP for any member of the original beneficiary's family.

For more details on tax-advantaged ways to save for education expenses, the reader should see the latest version of IRS *Publication 970, Tax Benefits for Education.*

Health Care

Health savings accounts are tax-advantaged accounts used to pay current and future medical expenses. Contributions to these accounts are tax deductible, and they grow tax free like contributions to traditional IRAs. Qualified distributions are also exempt from taxes, giving those who qualify for these accounts the best of both worlds. Employers sometimes allow employees to make contributions through paycheck withholdings and may also contribute. Employer contributions are tax free as well. To qualify for one of these accounts, the individual must be enrolled in a health plan that has a high deductible, and they cannot be covered by any other health insurance, including Medicare.

Retirement

There are numerous retirement savings plans both for employees and the self-employed, some sponsored by the employer and some self-directed. Plans include different types of IRAs and defined contribution plans. Rules and contribution limits for these plans can change, and individuals should consult their financial advisors or refer to the latest version of the applicable IRS publication prior to taking action.

Individual Retirement Arrangements (IRAs)

IRAs are tax-advantaged, personal retirement savings plans. There are three types: traditional, Roth, and SIMPLE. With a traditional IRA, contributions up to certain limits reduce taxable income, and the funds grow tax free until distributions are taken. With a Roth IRA, you contribute after-tax money, but your money grows tax free and you never have to pay taxes as long as distributions are taken according to the tax rules. SIMPLE plans, or Savings Incentive Match Plans for Employees, are IRAs set up by small employers for their employees. IRAs are trust or custodial accounts, and the trustee or custodian must be an organization approved by the IRS. Most large financial organizations qualify. Rules for IRAs can be complicated, and contribution limits can change from year to year. You should consult with a qualified financial advisor or refer to the latest version of IRS *Publication 590, Individual Retirement Arrangements (IRAs),* for details. The basics of each type are discussed below.

Traditional IRA

The traditional IRA is the original IRA, and it is sometimes referred to as a regular IRA. A traditional IRA can be set up and contributions made by anyone that received taxable compensation during the year, as long as that person will not be 70½ years old prior to the end of the year. Taxable compensation in this case is generally what's earned from working and does not include all taxable income. It excludes, for example, taxable income such as interest, dividends, and pensions. The maximum deductible contribution per individual is either their taxable compensation or the IRS specified limit. The IRS limit for 2011 is $5,000 ($6,000 if fifty years old or older), the same as for 2010. The amount of the deduction is phased out based on modified adjusted gross income (AGI) and filing status.

The IRS generally allows you to invest your IRA funds in most asset classes, i.e., stocks, bonds, real estate, etc., but you cannot generally invest in collectibles. Investment in certain gold, silver, and platinum coins and bullion, however, is permitted. IRA funds can also be used to invest in annuities, an insurance company product, but cannot be used to buy a life insurance policy. Many custodians or trustees do not allow the full breadth of investments allowed by the IRS.

You can move assets from one IRA to another or from other retirement plans to an IRA. The best way to move assets from one IRA to another is with a trustee-to-trustee transfer; no distribution of assets is involved, and the transfer is completely tax free. The other way to transfer assets is with a rollover. A rollover generally involves a tax-free distribution from one retirement plan and a rollover contribution to another. The rollover contribution must generally be made within sixty days of the distribution. If not, the amount not rolled over is considered a taxable distribution and may be subject to an early withdrawal penalty of 10%.

A good way to transfer assets from a qualified retirement plan to an IRA is with a direct rollover. A direct rollover is similar to a trustee-to-trustee transfer and does not involve a distribution to the owner. There is generally a one-year waiting period between rollovers that can be made; trustee-to-trustee transfers have no such limitation.

You can begin taking distributions from your traditional IRA once you reach the age of 59½. Distributions are subject to ordinary income taxes in the year in which they are taken. If you take distributions prior to age 59½, they are generally subject to the 10% early withdrawal penalty. There are, however, a number of exceptions to the early withdrawal penalty. You can, for example, take a distribution to help buy, build, or rebuild a first home, without incurring the penalty. You can refer to IRS *Publication 590* for specific exceptions.

A minimum distribution must be taken for each year beginning in the year in which you reach age 70½, although you have until April 1 of the following year to take the first distribution (the second distribution must be taken in that year as well). If distributions are not sufficient, you could be subject to a 50% excise tax on the amount of required distribution not taken. The required minimum distribution must be taken each year, and it is determined by dividing the account balance as of December 31 in the year before the distribution by your life expectancy. The IRS provides life expectancy tables in *Publication 590.*

Roth IRA

A Roth IRA is subject to many of the same rules as a traditional IRA. The major difference is that contributions are not tax deductible, but distributions taken according to the rules are completely exempt from taxes.

Contribution limits for Roth IRAs are the same as for traditional IRAs. Participation in an employer maintained retirement plan has no bearing on Roth contributions, and you can contribute even after reaching 70½. Qualified distributions from a Roth IRA are not taxable and include distributions taken after you reach age 59½, distributions made to a beneficiary after your death, and distributions taken for a first-time home purchase. Additionally, there is no requirement to take distributions after you reach 70½.

Traditional IRAs can be converted to Roth IRAs. To qualify for conversion, your modified AGI cannot exceed a certain maximum in the year the withdrawal from the traditional IRA is made, and if married, you cannot file a separate return. Modified AGI for conversion purposes does not include the amount of the conversion itself. Funds you convert that have not been previously taxed are subject to taxes, and they must be included in your gross income for that year.

SIMPLE IRA

SIMPLE IRAs are tax-advantaged retirement savings plans for employees of small businesses (including the self-employed). Employees make salary reduction contributions, and employers either make matching contributions or nonelective contributions. All contributions go into an account in the employee's name. Tax advantages of SIMPLE plans are similar to those of traditional IRAs, except that the contribution limits are higher. Withdrawal and distribution rules are generally the same as for traditional IRAs. Normal distributions are taxed as ordinary income.

Defined Contribution Plans

Defined contribution retirement plans are employer-sponsored, government-approved, tax-advantaged retirement savings plans. With these plans, employers make a defined amount of contributions, but they are not responsible for providing any pension benefits at retirement. There are various defined contribution plans: some intended for large private companies, others for eligible tax-exempt organizations, some for governments, and some for small businesses. The names of these plans generally come from the section of the IRS code authorizing them. Several of these are described below. Contribution limits for these plans, as with

IRAs, can change from year to year but are significantly higher than for IRAs.

401(k) Plans

A 401(k) plan is a company-sponsored, tax-qualified, deferred compensation plan. Plans are set up by employers and must be in writing. A 401(k) plan allows the employee to contribute a significant amount of his or her yearly income tax deferred for retirement savings. Employee contributions are called elective deferrals and are made under a salary reduction agreement. The maximum contribution that can be made depends on the participation at the particular company and IRS regulations. The IRS limit for 2011 is $16,500 if you're age forty-nine or less and $22,000 if age fifty and over, the same as for 2010. Employers can also make contributions, called nonelective contributions. These contributions can be matching contributions, discretionary contributions, or mandatory contributions, depending on the specific plan. Large companies usually contribute a matching amount of some type. The usual match is 50% of the first 6% of wages contributed by the employee, although some companies provide more and some less. Employers' contributions usually vest after a defined number of years. Under the salary reduction agreement, wages of the employee subject to income tax are reduced by the amount of the employee's contribution. Wages subject to Social Security and Medicare taxes, however, are not reduced. Contributions go into an account owned by the employee.

Various investment choices are available to employees, usually a variety of stock and bond mutual funds and money market funds. Funds grow tax free, but distributions are taxed at ordinary income tax rates. Distributions cannot normally be taken until you reach 59½ years of age without paying a 10% penalty, and a minimum distribution must be taken each year beginning in the year you reach the age of 70½. The first distribution must be taken by April 1 of the year following the year in which you turn 70½. There are, however, exceptions that allow you to withdraw funds prior to age 59½ without penalty. If, for example, you're at least 55 when you retire, you can begin taking distributions immediately without penalty. This exception does not apply to an IRA.

403(b) Plans

A 403(b) plan is a retirement plan for employees of public education institutions and certain other tax-exempt organizations. These plans are also referred to as Tax Sheltered Annuity Plans. The plans are offered through employers, and contributions reduce wages subject to income taxes just like with the 401(k) plans. Employees can make both pretax and after-tax contributions. Employers can also make contributions. Investments grow tax free. Individual accounts can be annuity plans through an insurance company or custodial accounts, with funds invested in various stock and bond mutual funds. Contribution limits and the rules for withdrawals and distributions are similar to those for 401(k) plans. Details on these plans can be obtained from IRS *Publication 571.*

Federal Employee Thrift Savings Plan

The Thrift Savings Plan (TSP) is one element of the Federal Employee Retirement System (FERS). TSP is a tax-deferred savings and investment plan similar to 401(k) plans. Employees can currently make contributions up to 10% of their base pay up to the IRS limit for that year. The government also makes contributions. Employees can invest in three different funds: a short-term Government Securities Fund, a Common Stock Index Fund, and a Bond Index Fund. Funds grow tax free until distributions are taken. When an employee retires, he or she has three withdrawal options: a life annuity purchased by the TSP, a lump sum distribution, or monthly payments from the account. Funds can be moved to an IRA as well.

457(b) Plans

A 457(b) plan is an employer-sponsored, deferred-compensation plan for employees of state and local governments and certain tax-exempt organizations. Participating employees make elective contributions through salary reductions. Contributions are tax deferred and grow tax free. Normal distributions are taxed as ordinary income. Contribution limits and distribution rules are similar to those for 401(k) plans.

Small Business Plans

There are several defined contribution type plans for small businesses and the self-employed. These include SEP (Simplified Employee Pensions), profit sharing, money purchase, and 401(k) plans. All these plans allow significant portions of earnings to be deferred. Funds grow on a tax-deferred basis in all these plans. Details can be obtained from IRS *Publication 560, Retirement Plans for Small Business.*

Employers set up SEP plans. Employees can contribute substantial portions of their annual earnings. Employers can also contribute and can vary their contributions from year to year.

Profit sharing plans provide flexibility for employers. Contributions are usually based on profits and can vary from year to year. Contributions can be based on an employee's compensation, or they can be a fixed amount given to all eligible employees. Contribution limits are similar to those for SEP plans.

Money purchase plans limit the flexibility of employers. The contribution percentage must be the same for all employees, and contributions must be made regardless of profitability. Contribution limits are similar to those for SEP plans.

General Wealth Building

While all savings increase your net worth or wealth, those discussed previously have a specific future spending purpose in mind. In addition to saving for specific purposes, it's also important to save for unseen expenses and simply to build your wealth. There are many ways to save and build wealth. Some follow.

Employee Stock Ownership Plans

Many companies have employee stock ownership plans. Most of these programs allow the employees to purchase the company stock at a discount, typically 10%, from the market price. The programs are intended to encourage employee ownership of stock in the company for which they work. If you elect to participate, the company will automatically withhold the amount you decide on from your paycheck and use it to purchase stock on certain predetermined dates. Since you get to buy at a discount, these programs are generally good ways to accumulate stock in your company. First, however, you need to decide whether your company's stock is a good long-term investment. Since you work there, you already have a big investment, and you don't want too many of your resources invested in the same place.

Stock Options

Many companies award stock options to their employees for performance. These options give the owner the option of purchasing the stock at the grant price (the price of the stock on the day the option is granted) at some future time, regardless of how much the stock has appreciated in value. Typically, the owner of the option is given up to ten years to exercise the option. Options are usually exercised after the stock has appreciated substantially, and the stock is sold immediately, providing the owner a risk-free gain. The capital gain is taxable income. Stock options, if you are fortunate enough to receive them, are a great way to increase wealth.

Deferred Bonuses

Many employers that pay bonuses allow employees to defer at least a portion to the future. When income is deferred, the taxes on this income are deferred as well. The employer will frequently allow the employee to convert the bonus money to stock in the company. If the stock appreciates, the employee is entitled to the gain. If the stock price declines, the employee can usually elect to receive the original deferred amount of money plus accumulated interest instead of the stock. Deferred income, in effect, is a loan to the company, and the employee becomes a creditor. As a result, the employee assumes some risk. If, for example, the company goes bankrupt, the employee may lose all his or her deferred income.

Life Insurance

Certain types of life insurance policies, whole life and universal life, for example, are a combination of life insurance and savings/investment. Although premiums are higher for these policies than for term insurance, they pay dividends and have cash values that increase over time. Dividends can be left to accumulate and earn interest, which can be much higher than interest for other low-risk investments. Since you make regular premium payments, part of which become savings, these types of policies provide a means to save and accumulate money. To be cost effective, however, they must be held for a long time period. If you terminate the policy after only a few years, you will generally lose money.

Annuities

Another way to save/invest is with annuities, another insurance company product. There are various types of annuities, as discussed in chapter 9 on investing. You can make a lump sum investment or make regular monthly deposits. Funds invested in annuities grow tax free until you make withdrawals, similar to funds in IRAs. Unlike IRAs, there are no limits on how much you can deposit. Deposited funds, however, are not tax deferred; only the earnings are tax deferred. Like IRAs, you can begin withdrawing funds at 59½ without penalty. A penalty is imposed on early withdrawal of accumulated interest and earnings but not on withdrawal of the amounts originally deposited.

Savings/Investment Accounts

Not all your savings should be in tax-deferred accounts. While tax-deferred accounts are generally advantageous, there are early withdrawal penalties unless the funds are used for certain allowed purposes. Most funds you may need short-term should be in regular savings or investment accounts.

If you plan on buying a second home or other real estate, or starting a business, you'll need funds. While funds from certain tax-deferred accounts can be used for buying a first home without penalty, they cannot be used for second homes or other real estate. Also, while most people buy their automobiles with borrowed money, unless you can consistently earn a greater return on an after-tax basis than the interest rate on the borrowed money, it's often better to pay cash if you can. You should save in advance for this purpose.

You may also want to set aside money for investments outside your retirement accounts. Capital gains and dividends in retirement accounts (except for Roth IRAs) will eventually be taxed at ordinary income tax rates when the funds are withdrawn. Taxes on dividends and long-term capital gains on investments outside retirement accounts may be taxed at lower rates than ordinary income.

Funds can be deposited in savings/investment accounts on a regular basis by using automatic deposits from your paycheck or checking account.

Chapter 8

Investing

To grow your wealth, savings need to be invested. Your money must be put to work, or it will lose value because of inflation. For your money to grow in real terms, your return must be greater than inflation. The higher your earnings growth, the faster you can accumulate wealth, but you need to control your risk and avoid major losses. You want investments that provide consistently good returns, not large returns in one year and big losses in the next. While yearly returns are important, the most important return is the one you achieve over time. Figure 2-1 showed what consistent savings and investment returns and time can do for wealth creation.

There are different kinds of investors. Some do their own research and make all investment decisions themselves; others rely on financial advisors to varying degrees but make final decisions themselves; still others turn all or a portion of their investment funds over to a professional that manages these funds, based on the investor's objectives. There are many things to know about investing, and the more you want to do yourself, the more information and knowledge you need.

If you are going to invest, you should understand something about markets and about supply and demand, since they determine what it costs to buy something and what you receive if you sell. Fear and greed can sometimes rule markets, and investors should be on the alert for these.

Interest rates play a key role in economic activity, and they are a major factor in determining asset values. It is important to understand why.

There are many different asset classes to invest in and various ways to invest in each class. You can, for example, buy stocks by buying individual securities, index funds, mutual funds, or exchange-traded funds. Most important is to understand and value what you're planning to invest in. If you don't understand it, don't invest in it. You want to invest in markets and good assets when they're undervalued. Understanding and valuing possible investments involves research and analysis. Asset valuation is discussed in the next chapter.

All investments have some amount of risk. Investors should know these and the steps that can be taken to reduce them. Diversification is a common way to reduce risk, but buying at the right price can also reduce your risk.

Investors pay in one way or another for financial advice and for buying, selling, and in some cases owning various investments. Sales commissions and any operating expenses and management fees are passed on to the investor, and investors should understand the charges and how they are imposed.

Investing in most asset classes is a non-zero-sum game. Non-zero-sum games are those in which the sum of the gains and losses of all participants can sometimes be more and sometimes less than the amounts they started with. Stock investing is a non-zero-sum game. The total value of US stocks generally increases over time, since the economy grows, and the sum of all gains and losses of participants is greater than zero. Real estate investing is also a non-zero-sum game.

Measurement of Return

It is important to measure your investment return to see how you're doing. It's also important to understand the various ways return can be measured so you can judge data that might be provided to you by various investment companies or advisors. Your cumulative return over a number of years is, of course, what's most important. Your return in any given period is determined by dividing the end amount by the starting amount, subtracting one from the ratio obtained, and converting the result into a percentage. If, for example, you started with $1,000, and after several years of investing it had grown to $5,000, then your cumulative return would be 5,000 divided by 1,000 or a ratio of five minus one, or four times. Converting this to a percentage gives a cumulative return of 400%. Some might ask why the cumulative return is not 500%, and it's because you only earned $4,000 not $5,000. Remember, you started with $1,000.

Another important measure is the return you need each year to earn a certain cumulative return over a given period. Remember, if you remain invested, your returns are compounded. Thus you want the single year (annual) return that, when compounded over the investing period, gives the cumulative amount. This return is called the compound annual growth rate (CAGR); it is also sometimes called the annualized return.[10] Now it is important to realize that this is the return you need each year to obtain the final result. It is *not* the average rate of return. The average return can be misleading. For example, if you have a return of 100% in the first year and a loss of 50% in the second year, you have no cumulative gain at all but are back to square one, although the average return for these two years is 25%. Clearly, as a practical matter, no one will earn the same return each year. Returns will vary, but the best investments are those that provide consistently good returns.

Markets

Markets are the coming together of buyers and sellers of goods and services. There are many different markets: consumer goods markets, financial markets, real estate markets, and used goods markets, to name some. In some markets buyers and sellers meet face to face; in others representatives of the buyers and sellers meet; and in others no one actually meets but transactions take place electronically. Electronic markets, like the NASDAQ stock exchange and eBay's online auction, are becoming more and more common. While we talk of markets such as the stock market as if there was one market, there are actually many different markets. There's literally a market for each individual stock, as well as for various groups of stocks. Similar things could be said about other markets.

---

[10] The total cumulative return is given by: $T = A(1+G)^N$, where A is the starting amount, G the compound annual growth rate, and N, the number of years of investing. This equation must then be solved for G. If the cumulative return in the above example was obtained over a ten-year period, G is 0.175 or 17.5%. In this case the compound annual growth rate was about 17.5%, a nifty return. If the same result had taken twenty years, the CAGR would have been about 8.4%.

Prices in most US markets are determined by supply and demand. Price provides information to potential participants that increases or decreases their interest. Generally, when demand exceeds supply, prices will increase. A higher price will cause supply to increase to meet demand. When supply exceeds demand, prices will fall until demand increases to meet supply. These supply/demand adjustments tend to happen quickly in stock markets. With real estate, it can take a long time to change supply, and increased demand may not be satisfied very quickly, in which case prices may rise significantly. If demand drops suddenly, it can take a long time to reduce supply, and prices will fall.

If you can convert an asset to cash quickly, the market for that asset is said to be highly liquid. Stocks are generally highly liquid; you can, for example, buy or sell most stocks in US markets in fractions of a second. Bonds, except for Treasury securities, are generally less liquid than stocks and tend to have larger bid/ask spreads. Most real estate markets are not highly liquid; it might take many months or even years to buy or sell a property.

Because of human nature, markets can sometimes become irrational. The two emotions of fear and greed can take control of a market. When times are good and prices start to rise, more and more buyers may want to get in, because they think they can make easy money. Continued buying causes prices to rise further and can entice still more buyers, and prices rise until there are no more buyers, at which time prices might begin to fall. Falling prices can increase the number of sellers, and, as more and more sellers appear, the market can collapse as fearful sellers want out at any price.

There have been many asset bubbles throughout history. Perhaps the most irrational was the tulip craze in the Netherlands in 1634–37, in which tulip bulb prices rose to truly unbelievable levels. People actually exchanged real estate and other assets for tulip bulbs. In recent times, we've had the stock market bubble of the late 1990s and the real estate bubble in the mid-2000s. When you see market prices increasing rapidly for any length of time, be careful. As they say, trees may grow tall, but they don't grow to the heavens. The same is true for asset prices. People don't get out because they're either greedy or fearful of missing out when others are making easy money. Many get in late or continue buying until the market collapses. People in powerful positions are fearful of piercing bubbles that they may recognize because they don't want to be blamed for stopping the rise or for causing a collapse.

Influence of Interest Rates

Interest rates play a major role in our economy. They stimulate or restrain economic activity, and they are a key factor in determining the present value of various types of assets and liabilities.

As discussed in chapter 1, the Federal Reserve (US Central Bank) has considerable influence over the money supply and interest rates through its control of bank reserves, and it utilizes this power to alter economic activity. If the economy is entering a recession, the Federal Reserve will take steps to increase the money supply. When money is plentiful, interest rates will be low, and it's generally easy to borrow money to purchase a home or to start a business. It's also easier for corporations to justify investments in new plants and products, since the present value of future returns from these additions is higher. New plants and products require additional workers and generally increase employment. Thus, low interest rates tend to stimulate economic activity. If, on the other hand, the economy is experiencing inflation, the Federal Reserve will reduce the money supply, causing interest rates and borrowing costs to rise and economic activity to slow.

Interest rates affect the value of the dollar in foreign exchange markets (markets where currencies are traded). If yields on dollar assets are relatively lower than those on foreign currency assets, the dollar will be relatively weaker, and if yields are relatively higher, the dollar will be relatively stronger. A weaker dollar makes US goods and services less expensive in foreign markets and foreign goods and services more expensive in the United States, and it generally increases exports relative to imports. An increase in exports relative to imports increases the Gross Domestic Product of the country and increases employment. A weaker dollar, however, can make US assets less expensive for foreigners to acquire. A stronger dollar does just the opposite.

Interest rates affect the value of income-producing assets because they are a major determinant of the discount rate utilized in determining the present value of future financial returns. Because of discounting, future amounts are worth less than the same amount today, and the further in the future these amounts are, the less they are worth today. If interest rates increase, the discount rate increases, and future amounts are worth less today, and the asset is worth less. If interest rates decline, the discount rate decreases, and the value of future earnings and the asset are worth relatively more.

Interest rates change the lump sum value of any future stream of income, such as a pension, you might be entitled to. When rates are low, the lump sum value is relatively higher; when rates are high, the lump sum value is relatively lower.

Interest rates drive the value of previously issued bonds. Except for special types of bonds, such as floating rate and inflation-indexed bonds, the interest or coupon that a bond pays is determined when it is issued, and it remains fixed. If interest rates subsequently increase, the market value of the bond in the secondary market will decline. Conversely, if interest rates decrease, the market value of the bond will increase.

Interest rates have a major impact on stock prices and on the stock market in general. Since borrowing cost is an item of expense to businesses and corporations, low interest rates will reduce interest expense and increase corporate profits, other things being equal. Increased profits generally increase stock prices. Higher interest rates will have the opposite effect. Interest rates, because of their influence on the discount rate as discussed above, are also a major determinant in the price-to-earnings multiple (P/E) that investors are willing to pay. Generally the lower the interest rate, the higher the multiple investors are willing to pay.

For those that doubt the impact that interest rates have on stock prices and price-to-earnings ratios, consider the following historical data.[11] For the seventeen-year period from the beginning of 1965 to the end of 1981, the S&P 500 stock index went from 84 to 123, a roughly 50% increase. Now during that period the GDP of the country went up by nearly a factor of 4. Despite the substantial growth in the economy, stock prices didn't increase much, primarily because of rising interest rates. Rates rose from about 4% to about 14%, and the P/E ratio of the S&P index dropped from about 18 in March of 1965 to about 8 at the end of 1981. Then in

---

[11]   The argument used here is similar to that used by Warren Buffett in an article entitled "Mr. Buffett on the Stock Market," except he used the Dow Jones Industrial average and didn't include the P/E ratios. The article is worth reading. It is available on the Internet.

the next seventeen years things reversed. The S&P 500 index increased from 123 to 1,228, an approximate tenfold increase, while the economy grew by a factor of less than 2. Interest rates, however, dropped from about 14% to about 5%, and the P/E ratio of the S&P 500 index increased from 8 to about 33 over the same period. While other factors, including market psychology, were involved in the increase in market prices and P/E ratios, the decline in interest rates was a major factor.

Interest rates can also affect real estate values, particularly the value of income-producing real estate, both commercial and residential.

Interest rates also drive the present value of liabilities. Lower interest rates, for example, will increase corporate and government pension liabilities, including government Social Security obligations. This happens because lower interest rates result in lower discount rates, and lower discount rates increase the present value of future payments and financial obligations. Again, higher interest rates do just the opposite.

Asset Classes

Investment assets are things you own that have financial value and earnings potential that can be sold or traded. To make them easier to discuss, it is best to divide these assets into classes, placing those with similar characteristics into a given class. There is no hard and fast grouping, and different people use different ones. For example, precious metals are also commodities, but I have placed them into a separate class because they have characteristics that are unique within the commodity category. The two most widely held asset classes, stocks and bonds, are ways to own the equity of corporations and the debt of both corporations and governments. Since corporations are involved in essentially every aspect of both the domestic and foreign economies, stocks and bonds actually provide a vehicle to invest in virtually all other asset classes and sectors of the world economy.

Cash and Cash Equivalents

Cash is currency and coins. Cash equivalents are assets that can be converted relatively quickly to cash—generally assets with maturities of less than one year. Checking account balances, short-term bank deposits, CDs (certificates of deposit), money market accounts, and Treasury bills are considered to be cash equivalents. Currency, of course, earns no interest. Short-term CDs and Treasury bills can be held with different maturities. These earn interest, as do money market accounts. Prior to maturity their value may change depending on interest rates. The FDIC (Federal Deposit Insurance Corporation) up to a limit guarantees bank accounts and CDs, while the US government backs Treasury bills. Money market accounts, typically, are not guaranteed.

Bonds

Bonds are the debt of corporations and government entities. When you buy a bond, you are lending money to a company or a government entity. There are corporate bonds, municipal bonds, federal government bonds, and foreign bonds. Bonds can have different maturities, and most pay a fixed amount of interest, called the coupon value, until maturity. At maturity, the entity that borrowed your money is required to pay back your principal. Bonds can be bought and sold after issue in what is called the secondary market. In this market, prices of fixed coupon bonds fluctuate based on interest rates and risk.

Bonds are rated for risk by several credit rating agencies. In general there are top quality bonds, investment grade bonds, and so-called junk bonds. Junk bonds pay the highest interest rates but also have the highest chance of default. Considering how bad a job the agencies did in rating many bonds prior to the recent recession, it's a good idea to make your own assessment of the ability of an issuer to make the necessary interest payments and to return the principal in the future.

Treasury Securities

The Treasury of the US government issues debt of different maturities, and this debt has different names: Treasury bills are short-term debt and have maturities of one year or less; Treasury notes are medium-term debt and have maturities of ten years or less; and Treasury bonds are long-term debt and have maturities of ten to thirty years. The US government backs all of these, and the owners are guaranteed that they will get their principal back at maturity. Because of this, these are called risk-free investments. Prior to maturity, the prices of these securities fluctuate with changes in interest rates. If interest rates go up, the price of the bond decreases, and if interest rates go down, the price of the bond increases. The amount of the increase or decrease depends on the change in the interest rate and on the maturity date of the bond; the longer the time to maturity, the greater the change. The Treasury also issues Treasury Inflation-Protected Securities called TIPS. Unlike other Treasury issues, the interest payments on these bonds vary with inflation, and the principal returned at maturity increases with inflation. Unlike other bonds, the principal returned can be greater than the face value; it cannot be less. TIPS have different maturities, and are also bought and sold in the secondary market after issue.

GSE Securities

Government-sponsored enterprises (GSEs) also issue securities. Examples are the Federal Home Loan Mortgage Corporation (Freddie Mac), and the Federal National Mortgage Association (Fannie Mae). GSE securities carry an implicit guarantee of the US government, not an explicit one like Treasury securities, and as a result they generally pay slightly higher interest rates.

Municipal Bonds

Municipal bonds are the debt of state and local municipalities. Interest paid on these bonds is exempt from federal income taxes and also from the income taxes of the state and local government that issued them. This tax-exempt feature makes them attractive for investors in the higher income brackets. Unlike Treasury securities, they are not immune to default. Municipal bonds are either general obligation or revenue bonds. The general taxing authority of the municipality provides backing for general obligation bonds. Only the specific revenue generated by a particular capital project, such as a bridge or a highway, funds revenue bonds. General obligation bonds are considered safer than revenue bonds.

Corporate Bonds

Corporate bonds are the debt of corporations. Interest paid on these bonds is a function of general interest rates and risk. Although corporate bondholders have first claim on the company's assets in the event of bankruptcy, there is still risk of default. In this case, the bondholder may only get a small fraction or none of his principal back. Some bonds are callable, i.e., the issuer can redeem them prior to maturity, and some are convertible into the common stock of the corporation. Specific assets of a company secure certain corporate bonds; others, known as debentures, are unsecured. In the event of default, holders of secured bonds have a better chance of getting their principal back.

Stocks

Stocks represent ownership of corporations. There are two basic kinds of stock: common stock and preferred stock. Holders of common stock are the owners of corporations and generally have voting rights. Holders of preferred shares have no voting rights and, in many respects, are similar to bond owners. They are entitled to dividend payments before any dividends are paid to holders of common shares, and they are next, behind bondholders, in claiming assets in the event of bankruptcy. Their dividends are similar in magnitude to the interest that bondholders receive. Unlike a bond, however, preferred stock can appreciate in value independent of interest rates. As a practical matter, however, preferred stock holders, like common stock holders, often get virtually nothing in the event of a bankruptcy, and the value of preferred stock tends not to appreciate very much.

Common share holders are entitled to all the remaining earnings of a company after the preferred stock dividends are paid. Common share holders frequently receive a portion of these residual earnings as dividends, but generally most of the remaining earnings are reinvested in the company, used to buy back shares, or used to further reduce debt. Common share holders benefit from the dividends and any appreciation of the stock price.

There are many kinds of corporations and hence stocks: growth stocks and value stocks; large capitalization stocks and small capitalization stocks; technology stocks, consumer-oriented stocks, and natural resource stocks; utilities and transportation stocks; and homebuilders, to name just a few categories. Common stock prices are generally determined by the prospects for future earnings and by interest rates.

Real Estate

Real estate includes land and associated structures and is usually subdivided into five major categories. Residential real estate includes houses and apartment buildings; commercial includes office buildings and hotels and motels; industrial includes factories and warehouses; agricultural includes farmland, timberland, and pastureland; and special-purpose includes things such as schools, hospitals, airports, and golf courses.

Each of these categories also includes vacant land zoned for that particular use. Land is valuable, particularly since it has a limited supply. No new land is being created, except for the limited amounts created by active volcanoes (as in Hawaii) or being reclaimed from the sea (as in the Netherlands). Zoning plays a large role in determining the value of land. Agricultural land, for example, is generally inexpensive, but it sometimes gets rezoned for residential or other use, and the value can increase dramatically.

Real estate can be purchased in various ways. It can be bought directly or indirectly, through purchase and ownership of shares of a business or corporation that owns real estate. A relatively safe way to invest in real estate is to buy the stock of companies that own real estate. When you buy this way, you're not directly responsible for any loans, and your potential losses are limited to your investment. Many types of companies own real estate; however, a class of companies called real estate investment trusts (REITS) specializes in real estate. There are apartment REITS, shopping center REITS, timberland REITS, office property REITS, and many other types. REITS generally pay good dividends.

Commodities

Commodities are items essentially identical to other items of the same kind that trade primarily on the basis of price. There are many different commodities. Examples include metals such as iron, zinc, and copper; precious metals such as silver and gold; agricultural products such as timber, cotton, wheat, corn, and livestock; and energy resources such as crude oil, natural gas, and coal.

Prices of commodities are determined primarily by supply and demand and can be cyclical. When prices are low, producers don't develop new supply and may actually reduce supply. If demand increases and supply is limited, prices will increase, sometimes substantially. If producers believe demand will continue or increase in the future, they will restore idled supply and also may invest in development of new supply. However, because it can take a long time to develop new supply, the price may remain high for a long period. If there are no sources of new supply, the price of a given commodity may remain high until an alternative or substitute is developed and made producible.

Prices of commodities are also affected by inflation and deflation. Since many commodities are priced in US dollars on world markets, they generally increase in price when the value of the dollar falls in value and decrease when the value of the dollar gets stronger. Prices of commodities often react opposite to that of the stock market, and for that reason commodities are potentially a good asset class for diversification.

There are various ways to invest in commodities, but you don't want to own the commodity directly, unless you're in the business. Much investment in commodities takes place in the futures markets. Here, contracts for the future delivery of particular commodities at specific prices are bought and sold. Many users and producers of commodities use this market to control risk. Institutional investors and speculators also participate. Futures markets, however, are not for the average investor. Average investors can, however, invest in commodities by buying stock in companies that produce or grow the commodity, or by buying a fund that invests in commodities.

Precious Metals

Precious metals are commodities that have high economic value. These include gold, silver, platinum, and palladium. The supply of these metals is very limited, and when the demand is relatively high, they have very high prices. According to the website Ask.com, the total amount of gold, for example, in the world is less than 150,000 metric tons (a metric ton is about 10% heavier than a ton). All these metals are priced in dollars per troy ounce (a troy ounce is about 10% heavier than a US ounce). The price of gold at this writing is substantially more than $1,000 per troy ounce and rising. Platinum is even more expensive.

The demand for precious metals results from both their desirability and industrial use. Because they are physically attractive, don't deteriorate with time, and are scarce, many people want to own them. Precious metals are widely used in jewelry and works of art and are minted as coins. They have been used at various times in the past as currency and the backing for paper money. They also have many industrial uses. Many are, for example, used in a variety of electrical applications, because of their good conductivity.

Owning precious metals is a hedge against inflation and various crises. Because the metals are priced in US dollars on the world market, their price in dollars generally increases as the value of the dollar declines. Additionally, in times of crisis or when people are concerned about the potential failure of paper money, demand can increase significantly and drive the price of these metals much higher. Precious metals, however, earn no interest and incur storage costs, and their attractiveness as investments depends in part on prevailing interest rates.

There are various ways to own or invest in precious metals. The physical metals themselves can be owned in the form of jewelry, artwork, coins, or bullion. Alternately, you can buy stocks of exploration and mining companies, either individually or by buying a mutual fund that holds these types of stock. If you own the metals directly, storage can be a problem. Recently, ETFs (exchange traded funds) have been created that allow the purchase of an interest in some of the metals without having to take possession.

Annuities

Annuities are a class of investments sold by insurance companies. There are various types, including fixed, variable, and equity-indexed annuities. The investment gets its name from the fact that the investor has the option of annuitizing the investment and receiving periodic payments for either a fixed length of time or for life. Most annuities also have a life insurance option. Annuities provide the investor the ability to defer taxes, as with 401(k)s and IRAs. With an annuity, however, there are no dollar limits on the amount you can invest in a given year (see chapter 7).

Fixed annuities are fixed income investments, and they provide the investor a specified return for a given period of time. Variable annuities provide the investor the opportunity to obtain higher returns and are like investing in the stock market in that the investor can also lose principal. Equity-indexed annuities provide the investor the opportunity to share in the gains of various markets without the risk of having their principal decline. In exchange for this protection, however, the investor agrees to accept major limits on the amount of return they can receive. Annuities have contract periods, and if an investor wants to get out early, stiff penalties are generally incurred.

Guarantees provided by insurance companies are only as good as the companies themselves. In the event of bankruptcy, the investor may not get the return they expected, and can lose much of their principal as well. As with other insurance policies, you should only invest with the safest and most financially sound companies.

Private Equity

Private equity is an asset class consisting of private companies engaged in investment activities such as leveraged buyouts and capital investments in promising start-ups, or companies in the early stages of operations. Historically, capital for private equity firms has come from large institutional investors and wealthy individuals. Recently, however, some private equity firms, such as the Blackstone Group, have converted part of their ownership interest to public stock, providing a means for the small investor to gain access.

Private Business Investment

There are many ways to invest in private businesses. You could buy a business or a business franchise, lend capital to someone starting a business, or actually start your own business. Private business investment offers the potential for very high returns, much higher than you can usually earn on stock and bond investments. Many of these investments, however, are risky. If you lend capital to someone, make sure that the potential return is commensurate with the risk. If you're thinking of starting or buying your own business, make sure you carefully evaluate the opportunity. Consider the investment both in time and money required and make sure your assessment of the potential payoff is realistic.

Collectibles

Collectibles are items some people believe worth collecting because the items have some present value or some expected future value. The value may be monetary, or it may simply be the enjoyment the items provide the collector. There are many different collectibles. Some of the most common are stamps, baseball cards, comic books, coins, paintings and other works of art, and various types of antiques.

The monetary value of collectibles depends on how scarce they are. Some rare collectibles are extremely valuable. However, most are not. There likely will be fewer rare collectibles in the future, since more people now save items they think may be valuable.

Ways to Invest

There are various ways to invest. You can buy assets, real estate or businesses, for example, directly or indirectly by buying stocks or bonds of various companies. Few investors have the resources to buy into many of the asset classes directly. Stocks and bonds, however, provide a means for many investors to gain exposure to virtually all asset classes and sectors of the world economy. There are several different ways to buy stocks and bonds: you can buy the stocks or bonds of individual companies, or you can buy mutual funds, index funds, or exchange-traded funds that invest in individual stocks and bonds. You can also hire professionals to manage your investment funds.

Investing in individual stocks and bonds provides the greatest opportunity for gain. Stock and bond picking, however, is not easy, and requires considerable time, effort, and expertise. There are many ways to find investment candidates. Most investment houses have software that allows you to search for candidate companies that have the characteristics you want. Another way is the use of investment newsletters. The best way to find a newsletter you like is to try some. Most will allow you to cancel and will refund your money if you aren't satisfied with their letter. You can also find candidate companies by paying attention to businesses you come across in your daily life. Peter Lynch, manager of the extremely successful Fidelity Magellan Fund for many years, says in his book *One Up On Wall Street* that "the average person comes across a likely prospect two or three times a year—sometimes more." An additional way to find candidates is to follow the highly successful investors and see what they're buying.

However you find candidates, you need to do research and analyses to understand and value them before you decide to invest. This effort is often referred to as fundamental analysis. Some of the questions and things that should be considered in analyzing a company include: products or services the company provides or is expected to provide; whether the company has any competitive advantages and, if so, whether they can be sustained; whether profit margins can endure or if the company has litigation or pension plan funding problems that will reduce future profitability; whether the company has high free cash flow or if all the cash from operations is eaten up by needed capital expenditures; and whether it has too much debt. Another area for investigation is management. Does top management have clear objectives and plans to achieve these objectives, and does it have a good track record? Also of importance is whether the company is being managed to benefit the shareholders or just for the benefit of current management. Other areas to investigate include what might happen to profitability in an economic downturn, and what might happen during inflationary times. Most people spend less time investigating their potential investments than they do buying clothes. Picking winners is relatively easy in the midst of a bull market, but it is considerably more difficult at other times.

If it's a particular stock you're considering, a key element of the analysis should be an estimate of intrinsic value (see chapter 9). If it's a specific bond you're thinking of buying, you should know the bond rating, but you should also make your own assessment of the ability of the company to make interest payments and return the principal at maturity.

An easy way to invest in stocks and bonds is through mutual funds, and there are many mutual funds to choose from. There are many fund families, and most have large cap, small cap, value funds, growth funds, sector funds, and many other stock categories in their families. There are also many bond funds to choose from. A fund might specialize in a particular type of bond, i.e., government, municipal, or corporate; or it might invest only in bonds with terms within a certain range, i.e., short term, intermediate term, or long term.

Most mutual funds are actively managed and buy and sell frequently to try to outperform some benchmark or index. There are both open-end and closed-end funds. Open-end funds issue or eliminate shares as investors buy and sell. When you buy an open-end fund, you pay a price equal to the net asset value per share, determined after the markets close each day. Closed-end funds have a fixed number of shares, and these shares trade like stocks. Because they trade like stocks, they can sometimes be bought for less than their net asset value.

The original advantage of mutual funds was that they provided an easy way to get diversification. Now there are other types of funds that provide diversification but with less cost. Most mutual funds have high fees, and many don't have great track records. William Bernstein, in his book *The Intelligent Asset Allocator*, says that 75% of all professionally managed stock funds underperform the S&P 500 index. While most outperform for periods of time, the results don't persist. If you're a mutual fund investor, the trick is to either find one that outperforms over your investment life or to know when to change funds.

Bond funds provide diversification by holding bonds of many different entities. Don't be misled, however, into believing you can't lose money investing in a bond fund. Bond funds have interest rate risk similar to individual bonds and can decline if interest rates increase. A specific problem with investing in bond funds is that, unlike investing in individual bonds, there is no maturity date on which you get back the face value of the bonds. Bond funds perform very well in a declining interest rate environment and moderately well if interest rates are stable. If interest rates are rising, however, bond funds, particularly those bonds with long-term maturities, can be hazardous to your wealth.

Index funds try to mimic the performance of a particular stock or bond index. The Fidelity Spartan 500, for example, tries to match the performance of the S&P 500 index, an index made up of five hundred of the largest companies. Other funds try to match the performance of other stock indexes, like the Dow Jones Industrial Average, the Willshire 5000 Total Market Index, the Russell 2000 Small Cap Index, or a foreign stock index. Index funds have expense and management fees like mutual funds, although fees are considerably lower. Since these funds are passively managed, portfolio decisions are mostly automatic, and expenses tend to be less. Index funds can be a good way to invest if you're satisfied with the long-run return of the markets, but even with index funds, you shouldn't buy blindly and ignore your investment. Although what the markets have done in the past is well known, no one knows with certainty what the markets will do in the future. If you buy an index fund at or near the top of the market, and the market falls significantly, it can take many, many years just to get back to even. If you buy at or near a market bottom, and the market increases over your investment life, you can make out very well. Investing a fixed amount at periodic intervals can make you less sensitive to the ups and downs of the market, but if the market declines over your investment life, you won't make any money either.

Exchange-traded funds (ETFs) trade very much like stocks and closed-end mutual funds. ETFs have been around since the 1990s, but until 2008 they were restricted to index type funds. In 2008, the government authorized actively managed versions, and since then the number of different ETFs has increased dramatically. There are now many different types, allowing investment in many different asset classes through stock type trading. In addition to index ETFs, there are sector ETFs, foreign country and regional ETFs, bond ETFs, commodity ETFs, currency ETFs, hedge fund ETFs, and leveraged ETFs. There are also inverse ETFs that allow you to essentially bet that the market or a segment of the market is going to decline. ETFs generally have fees less than mutual funds but higher than index funds. Particular care should be exercised when investing in inverse and/or leveraged ETFs. The performance of these can vary significantly from the benchmark they purport to track.

Another way to invest is to have professionals manage some or all of your investment funds. Many firms, including brokerage and financial advisory firms, offer this option. With this type of account, professionals make all investment decisions in accordance with the objectives and risk profile of the client. Managed accounts most often require a certain minimum investment amount. If you decide on this approach, you should be very careful. Investors should never forget the losses suffered by the people that turned their money over to Bernard Madoff, the convicted Ponzi scheme operator, to manage. Keep in mind that his firm was large enough to be regulated by the SEC.

International Investing

Investing a portion of your investment funds in foreign entities adds diversity to your portfolio and allows you take advantage of the higher expected economic growth rates of many foreign countries and regions of the world.

There are several different ways to add foreign exposure to your portfolio. Investors can buy stocks and bonds of foreign companies, either directly or indirectly, or they can invest in American companies that have significant foreign operations and profits. They can also buy bonds issued by foreign governments.

Investors can buy mutual funds or exchange-traded funds that specialize in foreign stocks or bonds. Some are index funds and others are actively managed. Funds provide diversification, a particularly important factor in foreign investing, since valuation of individual foreign securities is more difficult than it is for US securities, and there likely is more risk.

American investors that want to invest in individual foreign securities might be able to buy them directly in the foreign market through the international desk of various brokerage firms. Many foreign-government-issued bonds are bought and sold this way. Many foreign stocks, however, trade on US exchanges as American Depository Receipts (ADRs), and it is more convenient to buy and sell using this vehicle. ADRs are receipts from US banks for shares of foreign stocks, and they trade like securities. Owning an ADR is like owning the foreign stock itself, except that they are bought and sold in US dollars rather than in the currency of the country in which the company is based. ADRs give the owner all the benefits of stock ownership, including dividends, price appreciation, and voting rights.

Investing in foreign securities exposes you to currency risk. Foreign securities trade in the currency of their home market. When you buy a foreign stock, for example, the US dollars you pay are converted to the foreign currency, and that currency is used to buy the stock. When you sell, the foreign currency received is converted back into US dollars. If during the period you own the security, the value of the foreign currency changes compared to the value of the US dollar, the change will affect your return. If the currency loses value compared to the dollar, the change will negatively affect your return. If the currency strengthens relative to the dollar, it will positively affect your return. (International Investing 2010).

Active Versus Passive Management

There has been much debate about whether active management of a portfolio can provide greater returns than the market as a whole or whether passive investment using index funds is better. The debate has been going on at least since index funds were first introduced.

The efficient market theorists say that the market rapidly incorporates all available public information and that stock picking either by small investors or professional money managers cannot beat the market performance in the long run. Further, they say the success of those who do is the result of chance, not due to any superior ability to analyze and pick stocks.

On the other side are those that say that the market is highly inefficient, even irrational at times, and that this inefficiency can be exploited by capable investors. Warren Buffett, for example, has said that he is "convinced there is much inefficiency in the market" and also that "market prices are frequently nonsensical" (Buffett 1984).

Historical data on the S&P 500 index seems to support the argument that the market is often inefficient. Data from 1950 through 2007 shows that market price varies considerably in any given year (Historical S&P Annual Return & Trading Range 1950-2007 and Volatility Ahead n.d.). The average annual variation in prices for the S&P 500 is about 25%, and in nearly 10% of the years the trading range was 40% or more. Given that the S&P 500 index changed by that much in a single year, imagine how much individual stocks must have varied. Now it would be hard to convince me, and many others, I'm sure, that the real value of American corporations taken as a whole varies 25% or more in a typical year and that in many years it varies more than 40%.

Further, there is clear evidence that at least some active money managers have succeeded in beating the market by a substantial margin over a long period of time and that their success was hardly the result of pure chance. Warren Buffett provided convincing evidence in the article entitled "The Super Investors of Graham-and-Doddsville," included as an appendix to a revised edition of Benjamin Graham's book *The Intelligent Investor*. The data presented (nine separate records) clearly shows that each and every one outperformed the market by a substantial margin over a long period of time. Anyone reading the article would have to conclude that the probability that these people all achieved the results they have due to chance is extremely small.

Also, to conclude that even people of superior ability cannot achieve superior results in stock picking, as they have in most other human endeavors, makes little sense. There is no substitute for knowledge and understanding, and those in possession of these, assuming they do the necessary investigation and analysis, will almost certainly outperform in the long run. If you ignore what's happening and refuse to use your intelligence, you do so at your own peril. If, however, you trade a lot (and pay high commissions) and pay a lot of taxes on your gains, as you would in a taxable account, or if you use actively managed mutual funds that have high overall fees, you're laboring under a handicap, and it will be more difficult to beat the market's performance. Unless an investor can acquire the necessary skills or find a proven superior professional money manager, they likely would be better off buying index funds.

Buy and Hold

Many say you should use a buy and hold strategy. Perhaps, but buy and hold shouldn't mean buy and forget or buy at any price. Long-term investing can reduce risk, but it doesn't eliminate it. Nor does it mean that you're guaranteed a greater return. The return investors earn depends on the price at which they buy and the performance of their investments over the time period they actually remain invested. While the long-term trend of the market has been up in the past, and can be expected to be up in the future, there have been periods when it was very much overvalued and long periods in which the market went nowhere or declined, particularly if returns are adjusted for inflation. A little history on the performance of the S&P 500 can be instructive. Data on the S&P 500 used here and in future sections is from the Moneychimp website (Shiller n.d.).

Assume that you bought a fund at the beginning of 1965 that mimicked the S&P 500 index and held it for the next seventeen years. You would have bought when it had a value of 84 and sold at the end of 1981 with the index at 123. Your CAGR over the period, including dividends, would have been about 6.3%. Considering inflation, you would actually have lost money; your annualized return would have been a negative 0.4% (inflation was high in this period). Now if, instead of selling, you held until the end of 2008, a total investment period of forty-four years, your annualized return would have been about 9.0% before inflation and 4.3% after. Your return, however, would have been much better if you didn't invest until the end of 1981, a very good time to buy, and sold at the end of 1998. The annualized return over this seventeen-year period was 18.5%, ignoring inflation, and 14.7% adjusted for inflation. Now to illustrate what can happen if you buy at the wrong time and sell at the wrong time, assume you bought at the beginning of 1999 and sold ten years later at the end of 2008, not quite the market bottom in March of 2009. Your annualized return for that time period would have been about—1.5% before adjusting for inflation and –3.9% after adjusting for inflation. You would have sustained a cumulative loss over the ten years of about 14% before inflation adjustment and a loss of about 33% after inflation. If you had sold in March of 2009, your loss would have been much greater.

Finally, consider what would have happened if you had invested in an index that tracked the NASDAQ Composite in say early November 1999, when the NASDAQ was just above 3,000. Your investment would have been down about 33% in February 2001, and if you had continued to hold, it would have been down more than 50% by the spring of 2003. If you didn't invest until March of 2000, when the NASDAQ crossed 5,000, your investment would have been down more than 60% by the spring of 2003. While the NASDAQ recovered some in the mid-2000s, it got hit hard again in 2008/9. At this writing (mid 2010), the NASDAQ is around 2,300, still down more than 50% from the peak, even before considering inflation.

The above performance should come as no real surprise, since buy and hold investing works if the market goes up over the interval you hold an investment that tracks the market, but it doesn't work if the market goes down, and it is possible for the market to perform poorly over long time periods. You might be much better off if you applied some thought to buying and selling. It's a good idea to buy individual stocks only when you believe their price to be significantly less than your estimate of their fundamental value. This is particularly important if you're considering investing a significant portion of your capital. It's also likely a good idea to sell if stocks are significantly overvalued. Similar comments can be made about mutual fund and exchange-traded fund investments.

Buy and hold doesn't mean that you simply buy something and forget it. Things change, and investments should be reevaluated from time to time. Even Warren Buffett, who says his investment horizon is forever, occasionally sells. He actually sold all the holdings of his first investment partnership in 1969 and returned the money to his partners because he believed the market was significantly overpriced, and there was nothing undervalued to buy.

Investment Risk and Its Reduction

There are many different kinds of investment risk. There is, for example, the risk that an investment may decline or that your entire portfolio may lose money. Usually, however, when financial professionals speak of investment risk, they're referring to the possibility that an investment underperforms expectations. Since asset prices and returns of asset classes fluctuate over time, risk is typically measured in terms of the possible variation from the expected return. Statistical analysis of past performance provides both the expected return and the measure of variability.[12]

There are really no risk-free investments, although some with government guarantees, like US government issued Treasury bills, notes, and bonds, are said to be risk free because owners are assured of getting back their principal if they hold to maturity. All fixed-income investments, however, except those indexed to inflation, have the risk that the return they provide will not keep pace with inflation.

Risk-free investments, typically, don't provide a very high return. If you want higher returns, you generally need to take on more risk. Risk and return, according to financial theory, are related; the higher the potential return, the more risk the investment has. Sometimes, however, contrary to the theory, potential rewards can be high and risk relatively low.

There are risks associated with individual stocks, bonds, and real estate properties, and there are risks that can affect an entire asset class or your entire investment portfolio. The fortunes of individual companies, and hence their stock and bond prices, can change for many reasons. A company's products, for example, may fall out of favor or be replaced by products developed by another company. Many once well-known companies have gone bankrupt and their stocks and bonds made worthless or nearly so. It can happen relatively quickly, as with some high-tech companies, or over a long period of time, as with the US steel and automobile companies.

The value of individual real estate properties or of an entire community or area can decline for many reasons as well. An individual house may be found to have massive termite infestation, or the ground on which it's built may become unstable. The values in a community might drop because a company essential to the area's economic prosperity may have large layoffs, or the company may fail or relocate. Widespread bank foreclosures and vacancies in a community or area can, as we have seen recently, also cause large declines in market values.

---

[12] Risk is usually measured by the standard deviation of the distribution of past returns.

It is well known that rising interest rates cause bond values to decline, but stock prices can also be negatively affected by rising interest rates. The risk that interest rates may increase in the future is thus a significant threat to many investments and even entire portfolios, and deserves serious consideration in investment decisions.

Risks can be reduced in a variety of ways. Some of the more common ways are discussed in the sections that follow.

Hedging

Hedging is a technique to reduce risk or the possibility of loss in a bet or investment. There are many hedging strategies employed by investors. A simple hedging strategy is to buy or sell full positions a portion at a time, rather than all at once. If, for example, you initially buy only a portion of the position you plan to eventually hold, you reduce the amount of loss if you're wrong. Other hedging strategies involve buying counterbalancing positions. You hedge because you're not certain of the outcome of your investment. Hedging, while it generally reduces risk, also generally reduces your potential gain. Diversification and the use of options to limit possible losses are forms of hedging.

Diversification

Most people know or at least have heard that when you invest you shouldn't put all your eggs in one basket. Diversifying, or investing in multiple things, reduces risk, as long as the things you're investing in have returns that are at least partially uncorrelated. If returns are highly correlated (i.e., they go up and down approximately in the same way), diversification doesn't do much good. You can't diversify away risks that affect all assets in the same way. You diversify because you're not sure what will happen in the future; no one is. If you knew with certainty what would happen, you would simply buy the asset that was going to appreciate the most. Even if you think you know, it's prudent to diversify or to hedge your bets. Diversification, or asset allocation, as it's commonly called, reduces variability of your returns and thus risk, but it doesn't eliminate it. William Bernstein, author of the book *The Intelligent Asset Allocator*, says that asset allocation is the single most important factor in the performance of your portfolio. The book explains how to effectively allocate assets and is very informative.

There are three main ways to diversify: diversification within asset classes, investment in multiple asset classes, and diversification over time. To be fully diversified, all three should be used. Since some assets may increase in price and others decline, your asset allocation can change over time. It needs to be reviewed periodically, and some assets may need to be bought and others sold to rebalance the allocation.

Investing in many different stocks can eliminate the risk that a single company's decline can ruin the return of your entire stock portfolio. Also, since the prices of stocks in other countries may not move in exactly the same way as US stocks, a mix of US and international stocks is beneficial, as is a mix of large cap, small cap and other categories as well. Likewise, if you invest in bonds, it's a good idea to hold the bonds of several different entities, including international entities, rather than just one. The same can be said of real estate. Since real estate price changes tend to be locally determined most of the time, it's a good idea to hold real estate in different localities, though this can be very difficult, if not impossible, for most investors that buy real estate directly.

Investing in different asset classes whose prices don't move in lockstep is also highly beneficial. Prices of bonds don't generally change either as quickly or as much as stock prices, and while there are times when they decline or rise together, there are other times when they move in opposite directions. It's thus a good idea to have both stocks and bonds in your portfolio. However, since conventional bonds are negatively affected by inflation and rising interest rates, it's likely a good idea to hold a portion in inflation-protected bonds. Commodity prices also tend to move in opposite directions to stock prices and can be a good asset class to help diversify your investment portfolio. The same is true of real estate, prices of which generally rise with inflation. I have long believed that portfolios should be analyzed for sensitivity to interest rate changes, and the allocation adjusted to lessen the impact.

Use of a bond ladder, a form of diversification over time, can reduce the variation in the return from a bond portfolio. If you, for example, buy ten bonds with maturities one year apart and replace each one as it comes due with a new ten-year bond, your portfolio return will have less variation than if you replaced them all at the same time. With stocks it's also a good idea to invest over time. If you invest equal amounts of money at periodic intervals, you end up buying more shares when the price is low than when it's high, with the result that your average price per share is less. This approach is known as dollar cost averaging, and studies have shown it to be a successful investment approach.

Long-Term Investing

Long-term investing in most asset classes can reduce the risk of loss. Take stocks, for example. Over the last fifty years (from the beginning of 1960 to the end of 2009), the average annual total return (including dividends) of the S&P 500 Index has been about 11% before inflation adjustment. Thus, if the future is like the past, and you invest in an index that mimics the S&P 500, you can expect a return of about 11% in any given year going forward. The actual return could be higher, or it could be much lower or even negative. The annual return has actually been negative about 25% of the time. Your chances of losing money, however, decrease considerably if you remain invested for a number of years. Over the past fifty years, there were only two ten-year periods (the last two) that had a cumulative loss.[13] There have been more, if you consider inflation-adjusted returns.

What about the risk of underperforming expectations? If you're a long-term investor, what counts is the CAGR over the period you remain invested. The CAGR of the S&P 500 (including dividends) for long periods in the past has been about 10% (the CAGR is generally less than the average return over the same period). Over the past fifty years it was about 9.5%, and over the past forty years it was about 10%. This understandably might lead one to believe that they should expect a CAGR of about 10% going forward, but be careful. Over shorter periods, the CAGR has varied considerably. If you look at ten-year intervals within the past fifty years, the CAGR rate, before inflation is taken into account, has varied from about minus 1.5% to about 19%. Over twenty-year periods, it has varied from about 7% to about 18%. These variations are the result of varying economic conditions and varying expectations for corporate earnings and interest rates. Over the past fifty years, earnings of companies in the S&P 500 grew considerably. Additionally, since about the end of

---

13   The periods are rolling ten-year periods, and there are forty-one of them.

1982 interest rates have been in a downtrend and have fallen considerably. Both these factors pushed stock prices higher.

Many economists believe that future economic growth in the United States and other developed economies will be subpar (at least in the near future). Further, at this writing interest rates on ten-year US Treasuries are very low (about 3%). Although they could remain at this level or even decline further if the economy weakens, they are likely to increase in the not too distant future, considering the annual deficits the country is running and is expected to run in the future. If we enter a period of *sustained* interest-rate increases, the market will face a strong headwind, and it will take strong earnings to overcome this headwind. Even though a large percentage of the earnings of the S&P 500 currently are from foreign sources, and this percentage is likely to increase in the future, it is unlikely that earnings growth will be strong enough to offset high interest rates. There is thus significant risk in expecting a CAGR anything close to 10% going forward. The last time interest rates went up over an extended period, from 1965 to 1982, the CAGR of the S&P 500 was 6.3%, and after inflation adjustment the return was actually negative. Also remember, corporate earnings grew considerably over that period.

Value Investing

It should be obvious that your chance of loss decreases if you pay less for an asset than if you pay more and that your potential return is also higher. Value investing, however, doesn't just mean buying low-priced stocks or those with the lowest price-to-earnings or price-to-book ratio, as some have assumed. It means buying stocks, funds, and other assets when they are undervalued. Value investing, if done well, can bring greater rewards with less risk, contrary to the prevailing view that higher risk must accompany higher returns. As Warren Buffett has said, "The greater the potential for reward in the value portfolio, the less risk there is" (Buffett 1984).

Also, solid evidence exists that there is a significant premium for value type investing. According to information in the book *The Intelligent Asset Allocator* (Bernstein 2001, 120-123), a comparison of value portfolio returns and growth stock portfolios of companies of similar size shows an advantage of several percentage points of annualized return over a long period of time for the value portfolios and shows that this increase in returns is accompanied by less risk. There is other convincing evidence as well. The "Super Investors of Graham-and-Doddsville" that Warren Buffett reported on in the article by that title referenced previously, were all value investors. All the investors in this group, according to Mr. Buffett, had "a common intellectual patriarch by the name of Benjamin Graham," the famed value oriented security analyst, and buy only when there is a significant margin of safety between what they estimate to be the value of the underlying business and the price they pay. The article is an excellent testimonial to the fact that value investing works.

Limit Your Losses

No one wants to lose money, but it's better to lose a little than a lot. Not all investments make money and perform the way you expect. If an investment is going up, you want to take advantage of the uptrend to maximize your gain. If it goes up a lot, you might want to protect at least some of your gain, and if the price is falling, you want to limit the amount of your loss. Many advisors and successful investors recommend use of a trailing stop loss strategy for stocks (Steve Sjuggerud 2004). With this strategy you continue to hold if the stock price is going up, but if the price drops a predetermined amount from its high, you sell. Different investors use different percentage drops, measured from the high, before they sell. Some might use 10%, others 20%, 25%, or more. There is no magic number, but since values fluctuate, you don't want to use too small a percentage change. You don't want normal variations to cause you to sell. If, however, the stock drops significantly, it's wise to sell, particularly since you likely don't know what's causing the drop. It's better to take a relatively small loss and retain most of what you've invested than to potentially get wiped out.

Portfolio Insurance

An option is a type of financial instrument whose value is derived from another financial instrument. A put option is one of the two basic types; the other is the call option. Only the put option is discussed here. Buying and selling put options on stocks is like buying and selling insurance. *Buying* a put option can provide downside risk protection for a stock you own. If you own a put option on an individual stock, you have the option of selling that stock at a certain locked-in price, on or before a given date, no matter how far below this price the stock declines. You can think of a put option like an insurance policy with a deductible. The greater the loss you're willing to accept, the less the cost of the insurance. You can buy put options on certain index ETFs as well as on individual stocks. You could, for example buy a put option on the S&P 500 index and possibly protect most of your stock portfolio. Premiums for put options vary depending on the perceived risk, and, like insurance, they expire and must be renewed to maintain protection. Unfortunately, put options can be expensive, particularly if many people think there is a good chance of a significant market decline over the life of the option, or in periods of high market volatility. Selling put options on stocks is very risky and is generally a bad idea for most investors. There are other, more complicated, option strategies that can reduce the cost of insurance, but they are beyond the scope of this book.

Information and Advice

If you plan to invest, you'll need information, a certain amount of expertise, and very likely some professional advice or help. Before investing large amounts of money, you should first decide on your asset allocation, i.e., what fraction of your investment funds to put into various asset categories, such as stocks, bonds, or cash. You can get information on how to allocate assets from books such as *The Intelligent Asset Allocator*, referred to previously, by consulting with an advisor at the brokerage firm you do business with, or from an independent investment advisor or financial planner.

Advisors and financial planners can help you put together an investment plan.[14] They will even make recommendations for specific investments. Remember, though, like anything else in life, you shouldn't just blindly

---

[14] Investment advisors and their representatives register with and are regulated by the SEC or the state. They have a "fiduciary duty" to their clients and must always act in their best interest. Financial planners are also often registered investment advisors. Brokers/agents are currently regulated by the financial industry itself, and unless they are also registered financial advisors, they do not have a "fiduciary duty." They are currently only required to make recommendations "suitable" for their clients. These rules are currently under review and might change.

accept what others recommend. You want to have enough knowledge to be able to evaluate any recommendations and decide if they make sense for you. This is particularly true when it comes to money.

Once you have your asset allocation plan, you need to decide on specific investments in each asset category. A previous section described the various ways to invest. The simplest approach, and the one requiring the least knowledge, expertise, and use of your personal time, is to invest in index funds. Index funds are passively managed funds, either mutual funds or exchange-traded funds (ETFs). These funds are designed to track some type of index, such as the S&P 500 stock index, and your investment returns will reflect this.

If you seek higher returns, you'll want some type of active management. You can be the active manager, in whole or in part, or you can have someone else do most of the active management. Most people will decide to use actively managed mutual funds or exchange-traded funds for most of their investments. If you are this type of investor or an index fund investor, you still need to select the specific funds to use. A good source of information on funds is the independent research company Morningstar Inc. You can subscribe to Morningstar research, but can often get access to their data free through your local library. You can also get information on funds from brokerage fund websites and investment advisors. Fidelity Investments has a particularly good website. It provides research on many funds, both their own and those of other firms, and it provides Morningstar reports and ratings for these funds. The site also provides considerable research data for individual stocks and bonds. Much of their information is even available to those without Fidelity accounts.

Some will decide they want to invest in individual stocks and bonds. This approach requires the most knowledge and expertise. If you decide to invest this way, you'll need to do research and some analysis to understand and value the securities you're considering. There are many sources of information, including brokerage firm websites, investment newsletters, company reports, company websites, and research-company reports. How to find candidates and some of the factors to consider were discussed in a previous section. Valuation is discussed in the next chapter. If you decide on this approach, it's important to understand how to read financial statements and at least the basics of financial statement analysis.

Regardless of how you invest, you shouldn't just buy and forget. Investment performance should be monitored and changes made if investments are significantly underperforming expectations. This doesn't mean that you should become a frequent trader, but you shouldn't be completely passive either. Monitoring performance is easy. You can get monthly statements from your broker, or you can monitor performance as frequently as you like online. Deciding if and when to make changes to your portfolio, however, is not so easy.

Commissions and Fees

Most investment assets are bought and sold through brokers and sales agents that are paid commissions for their services. Additionally, operating and management expenses of businesses, asset managers, investment advisors, and financial planners are passed on to investors through various commissions and fees.

Investors most often use brokerage firms, such as Fidelity Investments, Merrill Lynch, and Scottrade, to buy and sell individual stocks, bonds, and funds. These firms provide the connection to the securities markets and to the entities that issue securities. Brokerage firms provide many services. Services vary widely and range from simple online transaction execution to complete professional management of accounts. There are full-service brokers and discount brokers, although the line between these two categories has become blurred. Generally, however, full-service brokers have research staffs and analysts that produce buy and sell recommendations on securities. They provide more personal attention to clients through personal advisors, but they charge significantly higher commissions and fees. Discount brokers generally make more research and investment information available on their websites, although some, like Fidelity Investments, also make advisors available upon request. Commissions and fees vary widely and differ for stocks, bonds, and funds. A good source of information on fees charged and services provided by various brokers is the Brokerage Review website.

Transaction fees often depend on how many trades are made and whether it's an online trade or a broker-assisted trade. Discount brokers might charge $10 or less for an online stock transaction, while a full-service broker might charge $10 or more. If the order is placed through a personal advisor at a full-service broker, the charge can be up to 2% of the transaction amount. Some firms offer accounts where the investor pays an annual fee (usually a percentage of the account value) and gets essentially an unlimited number of trades. Transaction fees can be avoided if you can buy securities directly from the issuer. When an employee buys stock through an employee stock purchase plan, for example, they don't pay a commission and, in fact, usually buy at a discount. You can also avoid transaction fees on US Treasury securities by buying through Treasury Direct or by signing up for US Treasury auctions at some brokerage firms.

Mutual funds are sold to investors primarily through brokers and sales agents, and many are sold without a broker sales transaction charge. Instead, the fund manager pays commissions to the brokers or agents from fees or expenses the fund charges investors. Sales fees come in different forms. Some funds have a sales charge, called a "front-end" load. Others have a deferred sales charge, known as a "back-end" load, which is paid when shares are sold. Loads can be substantial and might be 5% or more for some funds. There are also so called no-load funds. These funds have no sales loads. No-load funds, however, can have purchase fees and redemption fees. They also have operating expenses and likely have a distribution fee (called a 12b-1 fee), part of which may be used to compensate those that sell fund shares. Funds also have recurring operating and management costs. These include transaction costs associated with buying and selling their portfolio investments and marketing and distribution expenses. These expenses and costs are also paid by investors, but indirectly out of fund assets, and they reduce the fund's net asset value. When buying a fund, the investor should read the fund's prospectus. The prospectus defines the various charges and fees. A good source of information about mutual funds and their fees is a brochure prepared by the US Securities and Exchange Commission and available on its website, entitled *Invest Wisely: An Introduction to Mutual Funds.*

Exchange-traded funds (ETFs) trade like stocks, and they have similar transaction costs. Some firms, however, waive the transaction fees for certain ETFs. ETFs have no sales loads but, like mutual funds, have recurring expenses. As with mutual funds, these expenses are paid indirectly by investors out of the fund's assets, and they reduce the fund's net asset value.

Independent investment advisors provide financial planning, investment advice, and asset management services. They may be compensated by a fixed charge, an hourly rate, a fee charged as a percentage of assets, or from commissions on products they sell.

Various firms offer professional management of accounts. In these accounts, professionals, in accordance with the objectives and risk profile of the client, make all investment decisions. Fees for this type of service are typically 0.5% to 2% of the account value on an annual basis. The larger the account, the lower the percentage fee.

Annuities are sold by insurance companies, sales agents, and also by some mutual fund companies and brokerage firms. Annuities, in general, don't have specific sales charges. Instead, the insurance company pays the sales agent's commission. Commissions for variable annuities and equity-indexed annuities can be substantial and might be 10% or more for an equity-indexed annuity. Commissions are paid indirectly by the buyer of the annuity through costs built into the annuity structure and various fees associated with the annuity. In addition to significantly limiting your upside potential as discussed earlier, annuity contracts also have long durations, and, if the owner wants to get out of the contract, there are high surrender charges. Some have charges as high as 7% of the annuity value if the policy is terminated in the first year. Annuities also usually have a life insurance option paid for by an annual fee (again a percentage of the annuity value) that can be more than it would cost to buy an equivalent insurance policy. There are also other fees, such as investment management fees, subtracted from the value of the annuity that further reduce the investor's return.

When you sell real estate, whether it's an investment property or a residence, you typically sign a listing agreement with a broker and agree to pay a commission for their assistance in selling the property. This commission is typically a percentage of the selling price, and it is paid from funds received by the seller at closing. If there is a different broker representing the buyer, the commission is shared between the two brokers. Sales agents work for the brokers and are paid by them, usually a portion of the commission. Historically, commissions were 7% of the sales price, but they are negotiable. There are also discount brokers that further lower commissions. Additionally, when you own real estate there are property taxes, and there may also be community association and/or condominium fees that must be paid.

Other investments you might buy or sell also generally have fees. If, for example, you want to sell a business you own, you very likely will hire a company to value your business, find buyers, and negotiate the sale. Fees for these services can be quite high.

Chapter 9

Asset Valuation

The intent of this chapter is to acquaint the reader with the subject of valuation and to show how certain assets of interest are valued. There are many reasons to have a general understanding of asset valuation. A person might, for example, want to estimate their net worth as discussed in chapter 2, or they might want to know how much their home is worth or how much a rental property they're considering buying or selling is worth. As part of their retirement planning, they might want to know how much it might cost to buy an immediate monthly annuity from an insurance company. Investors in individual stocks and bonds might want to know what a reasonable value is in order to determine if the market is overpricing or underpricing these assets, and all investors should have some way to judge if the market itself is overvalued or undervalued. The executor of an estate might need to determine the value of different types of assets, and a small-business owner might want to determine or estimate the value of their business.

Asset valuation is a very broad subject. There are many kinds of assets, and assets can have more than one type of value. There is, of course, market value, the value most people mean when they refer to value. Market value can be defined as the most likely selling price in the market at a given time. Other common types of value are assessed value and insurable value for real estate, and book value, going-concern value, and liquidation value for businesses. Businesses and rental real estate also have investment value. Additionally, many believe that certain assets, businesses and their stocks, for example, have an intrinsic value. Intrinsic value is an estimate of value, based on fundamentals, and can differ considerably from the current market price.

Buyers and sellers often have formal valuations done for certain assets by those in the valuation business. For real estate, collectibles, and jewelry, these are called appraisals; for businesses, they are called business valuations. Brokerage houses and independent research firms often do formal valuations of stocks and other securities, and they make them available to clients. For many assets, individuals do their own valuations. Regardless of whether an appraisal or valuation is formal or not, however, the output is only an estimate of value. Valuation, although often done with mathematical models, is not an exact science.

Valuation Approaches

Three basic methods are used to value assets: (1) market approach, (2) cost approach, and (3) income capitalization approach. Not all are applicable to every asset. Where possible, more than one is often used to provide more confidence in the estimate.

Market Approach

Markets determine prices for most assets. The market approach to asset valuation uses sales prices of similar assets to estimate the value of another asset. Some markets have many sales of identical items, and prices are competitively determined and well known. Markets for most publicly traded stocks, bonds, and commodities are like this. Markets for certain other assets may have few, if any, sales of even nearly identical items, and prices are not well known. Comparing the asset being valued to sales of different though similar assets and adjusting prices to account for differences is often how values are estimated in these markets. Sale of comparable properties is the primary method used to estimate value for non-income-producing real estate. The comparable sales approach is also used in business valuations, but the chance of finding recent sales of similar businesses is low. If comparable sales data are insufficient, market prices will not be well known, and the value estimate using this approach is unlikely to be very good.

Market prices are based on perceptions of value not necessarily fundamental values. These perceptions reflect both the knowledge and human emotions of the participants. Demand for an asset can drive the price higher and higher and create a market bubble. Lack of demand can drive the price lower and lower. Under these conditions, prices, although determined by the market, may be irrational and may not be a good representation of value. Nevertheless, they still represent the level at which you must buy or sell if you're in the market.

Cost Approach

For some assets, cost, or adjusted cost, is used as an indication of market value. In certain appraisals or valuations, the cost to build or buy comparable assets is determined and used as an indication of value. In other cases an adjusted cost is used. One way to value a home property, for example, is to estimate the cost to a build a similar structure and add it to an estimate of land value.

Businesses and companies have values recorded in their accounting books, commonly referred to as book values. Assets are usually recorded in the books at their original acquisition cost minus accumulated depreciation. Often companies are valued by updating these book values to reflect current market values. For a going-concern, values are often greater than the book values. Sometimes the value of certain assets, land or minerals (such as gold, oil, or natural gas), for example, may be worth many times the amounts in the accounting books. For a company going out of business and liquidating its assets, values can be less than existing book values.

The cost approach is particularly important if sales of comparable assets are lacking and if the asset is not income producing.

Income Capitalization Approach

Many assets generate income on an ongoing basis. Pensions and annuities provide regular income streams. Businesses and companies generally produce regular earnings and cash flow, and some pay dividends. Bonds provide regular interest payments, and most rental properties produce income for their owners. Assets that produce income of some type are most often valued by capitalizing their income streams

Two general techniques are used for capitalizing income: discounted cash flow analysis (also known as yield capitalization in real estate appraisal) and direct capitalization. In discounted cash flow analysis, estimates of future incomes and possibly the future sale price of the asset are converted to present values by discounting them using appropriate discount rates. The resulting present values are summed to determine the capitalized value. With direct capitalization, an estimate of a single year's income is directly capitalized by dividing by an overall capitalization rate or by multiplying by a suitable factor. The mathematical and conceptual basis for these two approaches was established many years ago by two great economists: Alfred Marshall, who identified interest rate as the connection between income and value; and Irving Fisher, who analyzed the proposition that *value is the present worth of future benefits* (Shea-Joyce 1992). This simple statement has great significance, and it is the basis for present value analysis using discounted cash flow.

Income capitalization is a powerful technique used to value many types of assets. It is, for example, utilized to determine the lump sum value of annuities, the rational market price of bonds, the investment and intrinsic values of businesses and corporations and their stock, and the investment and market value of income-producing real estate. Although not ordinarily used to value non-income-producing real estate, it could be, if there are similar properties used as rentals in the area. If it is used rationally, the technique can prevent you from unknowingly overpaying for an asset you are buying or unknowingly underpricing an asset you are selling. You may still overpay because you want something so much, but at least then it will be a conscious decision or choice.

Annuities and Pensions

An annuity is the payment of an amount of money at regular intervals. If the payments go on forever, it's called a perpetual annuity. The periodic rent on a parcel of land, for example, is a perpetual annuity. Annuities can also be for a fixed amount of time or for life. If you win the lottery, for example, you generally win an annuity. A million dollar win is normally $50K a year for twenty years, a total payment over that time period of $1 million. The Social Security check you might get each month is an example of a lifetime annuity.

An annuity has a present value and can be converted to a lump sum amount. The present lump sum value of a perpetual annuity that pays a fixed amount of income, A, at periodic intervals is given by the following simple relationship:

$$V = A/ D.$$

In this relationship, D is the discount rate (in decimal terms) used to discount future payments. The income payment might be rent on a parcel of land, interest on a savings account where the interest is withdrawn each time it's paid (no compounding), or some other payment. This relationship is the closed form solution to an infinite series of constant periodic payments discounted at the interest rate (or rental rate) being earned (see appendix I for the derivation). The terms A and D must be consistent: if A is an annual payment, then D must be the yearly rate, and if A is a monthly payment, D is the monthly rate. The equation shows how interest rate forms the connection between the value of an income-producing asset and the income it provides. Most people are familiar with this relationship but in a slightly different form, where the amount of interest received (the payment) equals the principal (the asset value) times the interest rate (equal to the discount rate) being earned. Few people, however, understand the full significance of this simple relationship and the insight it can provide into how income-producing assets are valued.

Another relationship of particular interest is that for the lump sum value of a perpetual series of periodic payments that grow (or decline) at a constant rate, G. As shown in Appendix I, the present lump sum value in this case is given by:

$$V = A/(D-G).$$

For this expression to be valid, the value of the discount rate, D, must be greater than the value of G. As will be seen in subsequent sections, this relationship has wide application in the valuation of assets. It is often referred to as the perpetuity equation, and that is how it will be referenced in future sections.

Defined-benefit pension plans typically provide a fixed monthly payment at retirement for life, with the amount determined by years of service and earnings record. Some companies will allow you to take your pension either as an annuity or as a lump sum payment. The lump sum payment will be a function of the number of payments the firm expects to make and the discount rate, and it can be calculated using an annuity equation. Equations for the present lump sum value of both fixed and growing pensions or annuities with a fixed number of payments are provided in Appendix I. The discount rate for pensions is determined by prevailing interest rates and can be obtained from the Pension Benefit Guarantee Corporation (PBGC) hotline (202-326-4041). The rate they provide is the yearly rate, and it is updated monthly. For lump sum pension calculations, the number of payments is based on life expectancy.

You can use the PV and NPV formula functions in Excel on a PC or in Numbers on a Mac to determine the present value of different types of annuities. PV is used for constant income streams, while the NPV function allows you to specify different amounts for each element in the stream. Income elements must be periodic with both functions.

An alternate method of calculating lump sum pensions is to multiply each regular future payment by the probability that the person will live to that date, discount each of these products appropriately to bring them back to the present, and sum each of the elements. With this method, one needs to go out far enough in time that the probability of living to that date is extremely low.

If the annuity will not begin until sometime in the future, the lump sum value of the annuity can be calculated at that future time using one of the above methods and then discounted to bring it back to the present time. As discussed in chapter 1, a future lump sum value can be brought back to the present by multiplying by the discount factor, $1/(1+D)^N$, where N is now the number of periods between the present time and the future start of the annuity.

You can buy various kinds of annuities from insurance companies. Period-certain annuities provide a fixed number of payments, and lifetime annuities make payments until the annuitant dies. These can be bought either as an immediate annuity for a lump sum payment or by investing with an insurance company over a period of time and annuitizing the investment at some future time. The cost of the annuity depends on the amount and number of future payments and expected future interest rates. You can also buy inflation protection for the annuity. The insurance company might charge a premium for the annuity, and the cost could be higher than what you calculate.

Bonds

After issue, bonds are bought and sold in the secondary market, and prices for these bonds are determined by supply and demand, like prices for many other assets. What, however, is the intrinsic value, or, as some would say, the rational market price of a bond in the secondary market? There are both fixed coupon bonds and variable coupon bonds. Most bonds, however, have fixed coupons. Fixed coupon bond values are determined by interest rates, bond maturity, and the riskiness of the specific bond. Prior to maturity, the value of the bond will fluctuate as interest rates or the risk of the bond changes. Variable coupon bond values tend to be independent of interest rate changes. The discussion that follows pertains primarily to bonds with fixed coupon values.

The future benefits one gets as the owner of a bond are periodic interest payments, called the coupon values, and, at maturity, the face value (or principal value) of the bond. The intrinsic value of the bond is the present value of these future benefits. To determine the present value, each of these future benefits must be discounted to bring them back to the present. The present value of the bond is the sum of the discounted values of all the interest payments plus the discounted face value of the bond. The periodic interest payments can be considered an annuity, and the discounted value of these payments can be calculated using the annuity equation for a fixed number of payments, as discussed previously. The discounted value of the face amount due at maturity is the face amount multiplied by the discount factor. The discount rate is the expected rate of return on the bond investment, and this return is the risk-free rate plus a premium for the risk of the particular bond under consideration.

The present value of an existing fixed coupon bond varies inversely with prevailing interest rates, i.e., as interest rates increase compared to the coupon rate, the bond value decreases, and as interest rates decrease compared to the coupon rate, the value of the bond increases. Existing bonds must be competitive with new bonds. If new bonds are offering a coupon different than existing bonds, the price of the existing bond will adjust to equalize the yield. Bonds with longer maturities have greater changes in value. Short-term bonds are thus less affected by interest rates than long-term bonds. Of course, if you hold the bond to maturity, you will get back the full face value of the bond (unless the issuer defaults).

Since government bonds are risk free, the discount rate contains no risk premium and is simply the current market rate of interest for the specific bond. If you know the interest rate and maturity date, the value of a US government bond paying a fixed coupon amount is completely determined, and the intrinsic and market values are the same.

The present values of other types of bonds, e.g., corporate and municipal bonds that are not risk free, are a function of both interest rates and riskiness. The present values of these bonds can be estimated using the same technique described above. The discount rate, however, now is higher than the risk-free rate because of the risk premium. How much higher depends on the riskiness of the particular bond, and different investors may have different views of the risk.

Business/Stock Valuation

If you're a private business owner, how much might your business be worth, and how can you estimate its value? If you're an investor, what's the fundamental value of a company you're interested in, and what should its common stock price be? Valuing businesses and their stocks can be complicated; books have been written on the subject, and there are organizations that do valuation as a business. A comprehensive treatment of the subject is beyond the scope of this book, but the basic concepts employed are relatively simple, and business owners and investors should understand them. They should also understand the key factors that drive business value.

A business entity may have both operating and nonoperating assets, and the value of the entity is the sum of both these pieces. These assets are employed in various ways to earn money, and the operating assets may earn a lot of money. Because of this, the market value may be considerably more than the value of the assets themselves. The market value of a business entity is the market value of its equity plus the value of its debt. The market value of the equity of a public company, often called the market capitalization, is equal to the market value of the common stock plus the market value of any preferred stock outstanding.

The owners of the common stock are the owners of the business. The equity they have in the business, like the equity people have in homes they own, is equal to the entity value less the debt and other claims against the entity.[15] If you sell a business outright, you sell all its assets (unless you remove some from the sale). You, however, must pay off the debt and claims against the business (unless the buyer as part of the deal assumes them), and you end up with an amount of money equal to the equity you had in the business. Alternately, when you buy a business outright, you buy all its assets by paying an amount equal to the value of the equity and either paying off or assuming responsibility for all the claims. If the business has nonoperating assets, these could be sold and the cash received used to reduce the outlay in acquiring the business. When a public company is bought or taken over, the acquiring organization often pays more than the current market price for the stock. This usually happens because both management of the company being acquired and the buyer believe the stock to be undervalued or because the buyer believes the company's value can be enhanced by new ownership.

Businesses also have accounting values called book values. Book values refer to the amounts shown in the accounting books for items such as assets, liabilities, and owners' or shareholders' equity. Assets are generally recorded in the books at their original cost and depreciated over time, but most are not updated to reflect current market values. The book value of the business entity's assets minus its liabilities is the book value of shareholders' or owners' equity. Since retained earnings are added to shareholders' equity in the accounting books, the book value of shareholders' equity generally increases over time. The book value of the common stock is the book value of the shareholders' equity less the value of any preferred stock. It is usually expressed on a per share basis.

The market price of a company's common stock fluctuates for many reasons, but most often it's greater than the book value. What's the fundamental or intrinsic value of a stock, and how, if at all, is it related to its book value? The intrinsic value can be related to the corresponding book value under certain conditions by a simple relationship. Such a relationship is discussed later in this chapter.

---

[15]   The equity you have in your home is the market value of your home minus the value of the remaining mortgage and any home equity loans you may have (the claims others have against your home).

Some companies are made up of a number of different businesses. The value of a multibusiness company is often determined by valuing each of its business segments separately and adding the pieces.

Intrinsic Value

To quote Warren Buffet, perhaps the greatest investor of all time, "Intrinsic value is an all-important concept that offers the only logical approach to evaluating the relative attractiveness of investments and businesses. Intrinsic value can be defined simply: it is the discounted value of the cash that can be taken out of a business during its remaining life."[16] Note that these amounts are the "future benefits" to the owners of the business, and his statement is equivalent to that of Irving Fisher given earlier in the chapter. If the business is an ongoing business, the money that can be safely taken out, on an ongoing basis, without negatively affecting the business is what's called the "free cash flow." Free cash flow (FCF) is the cash generated by business operations less capital expenditures and less any dividends payable to preferred shareholders. Free cash flow is that portion of the money generated by the business that belongs to the owners or, in the case of a public company, the owners of the common stock. These funds could be paid out as dividends to the shareholders, used to pay down additional debt or to buy back shares, or invested to further expand the business. Note that the free cash flow is money that could technically all be paid out as dividends but usually is not. The management of the company is the custodian of this shareholder money. If they are good custodians, the money not paid out in dividends will grow tax free as the company grows, and this will be beneficial to shareholders (if it's paid out as dividends, the shareholders will pay income tax on it). Unfortunately, some companies use a large portion of their free cash flow to buy back shares previously issued as stock options to management. Some of these companies are being run for the benefit of management not shareholders. To make the estimate of intrinsic or fundamental value as accurate as possible, the portion of free cash flow used for this purpose should be subtracted.

---

[16] This statement appears in many Berkshire Hathaway annual reports. It appears, for example, on page 73 of the 2007 report and on page 77 of the 2006 report.

As discussed in the book *Valuation* (Tom Copeland 1995, 133-135), you can value the equity portion of a business by directly discounting the expected future free cash flow belonging to the common equity investors or by using what they call the entity DCF model. In the entity model, the expected future free cash generated by the entity (sometimes called free cash flow to the firm) is used. The free cash flow of the entity is similar to the free cash flow belonging to the common equity investors, except it is before interest payments on debt and any dividends on preferred stock are subtracted. The entity free cash flow is the cash flow from which potential payments are made to the various capital providers, i.e., debt holders and owners of both preferred and common equity. For corporations, after-tax cash flows are normally used. For unincorporated businesses or subchapter S corporations, the pretax cash flow is generally used. The discounted value of these expected future free cash flows gives the value of the operating portion of the business entity. Any nonoperating portion is added to this value to obtain the value of the business entity. The common equity value is then obtained by subtracting the outstanding debt and the value of any preferred stock from the business entity value. The two methods give the same result for the common equity value, providing that the two cash flows are appropriately discounted.

What discount rate do you use? If you directly discount the free cash flow belonging to the equity investors, the correct discount rate is the cost of equity. The cost of equity is the annual return that an investor expects to receive on his investment in the particular stock. The annual return a rational investor in common stocks expects is equal to the risk-free return (typically the ten-year treasury rate) plus a premium, based on the riskiness of the investment, called the equity risk premium. If you use the entity model and discount the entity operating free cash flows, the discount rate used is what's called the weighted average cost of capital. Weighted average cost of capital combines the different costs for each type of capital, using weights that reflect the proportion of each type of capital (common equity, preferred equity, and debt) the business uses.

Intrinsic value calculations are based on estimates of future free cash flows, future interest rates, and investment risk, and these calculations are necessarily *estimates* of the present value or worth of a business. Expectations for future inflation will influence these estimates and, therefore, the estimate of intrinsic value. Not everyone will make the same cash flow estimates or use the same discount rate, and thus different analysts can have different estimates of intrinsic value. If the estimates of free cash flow change or if the discount rate changes, the estimate of intrinsic value changes.

Accurately estimating cash flows gets increasingly difficult the further into the future you go, and the calculations can get cumbersome if one makes individual estimates for each year. To be accurate you have to go out many years into the future, until the last term becomes insignificant. Fortunately, approaches have been developed to simplify the task. They basically involve breaking up the time frame into two (or more) periods. The first period is called the explicit forecast period, and the free cash flow is estimated for each year in this period. Each of these values is discounted to the present, and the discounted values are summed to determine the value for the explicit forecast period. The explicit forecast period has also been called the excess growth period. The explicit forecast period can be five years, or it can be fifteen years or longer, depending on the company and how long it can sustain its competitive advantage and high levels of growth. The second period is the time after the explicit forecast period, and this continues indefinitely for an ongoing business. The present value of free cash flows for this period is called the continuing value. If the cash flow grows at a constant rate, G, during this period, and the discount rate, D, is constant going forward, the calculation is very simple. The present value of these future free cash flows is given by the perpetuity equation, discussed previously in connection with annuities, with A equal to the FCF (free cash flow):

$$V=FCF/(D-G).$$

The FCF used here is the value in the first year of the continuing value period. In applying this equation, considerable care must be used to ensure that the values of FCF and G are consistent. Lower growth rates imply less capital spending, and assuming a lower growth rate without adjusting the FCF upward can lead to significant undervaluation. The continuing value thus obtained needs to be brought back to the present. This is done by multiplying by the discount factor $1/(1+D)^N$. The present values for the two periods are then added to obtain the business value.

It's very difficult for the average investor to do a discounted cash flow analysis for a company or its stock. It is not easy to estimate free cash flows into the future, even for the management. You can obtain historical data from annual reports, but that's very time consuming, and it's past data. A good source of data is Value Line. Value Line provides both historical data and estimates of growth rates going forward. Future growth rates can also be obtained from a number of online sources such as First Call and Zacks.

An excellent alternative is the Value Pro Online Valuation Service.[17] They have a website that will do the analysis for most companies on the US stock exchanges. The site basically uses the entity DCF model and the two-step method described above, except that it doesn't directly estimate free cash flows; instead, it calculates them from input data. The software program imports data from other sites that maintain corporate data. The site will calculate the intrinsic stock value if you enter the company stock symbol and will display the input data used. The user has the option of changing many of these inputs and recalculating the intrinsic value based on the changes.

Price-to-Earnings (P/E) Multiples

The price of a given stock is equal to the P/E multiple, or ratio, multiplied by the annual earnings. If the earnings increase and the P/E multiple remains unchanged, the price of the stock increases. The price-to-earnings multiple is a popular metric used to evaluate stocks. Stock prices are available in the newspapers and on many websites, and corporate earnings are reported quarterly and are quickly made public. P/E ratios can be calculated using trailing earnings (earnings for the past twelve months) or forward earnings (earnings estimated for the next twelve months). While the current P/E ratio using trailing earnings is a fact, the P/E ratio, in and of itself, doesn't tell much about value unless you have some idea of what a reasonable P/E is for a given stock. Just because the P/E ratio is low doesn't mean the stock is undervalued. Nor if the P/E ratio is high does it mean the stock is overvalued.

So, what's a reasonable P/E ratio for a given stock? As discussed in the previous section, the intrinsic value of a given stock depends on estimates of the present value of the future free cash flows the business

---

[17]   "The 4-Step DCF Valuation Technique," Value Pro. Available on the Internet: http://valuepro.net.

is expected to generate. While future free cash flows depend very much on future earnings, they also depend on the amount of new capital that the company plans to invest and how effectively this capital is employed (this determines the growth in FCF and earnings). Further, present values depend on the discount rate, and the discount rate depends on estimates of future interest rates and risk.

By making a number of simplifying assumptions, an expression for the P/E ratio that takes these factors into account can be derived. With G, the FCF growth rate (in decimal terms); R, the rate of return on net new capital investment (in decimal terms); and D, the discount rate (in decimal terms), P/E ratio is given by:

$$P/E = (1-(G/R))/(D-G).$$

The relationship is from the book *Valuation* (Tom Copeland 1995, 75). A derivation is provided in Appendix II. While only an approximation, the equation is very useful because it shows what the key determinants are and how they affect the P/E multiple. The numerator can be interpreted as the fraction of earnings not reinvested in the business and thus available for payout to the common shareholder. The following key points can be seen from the equation:

(1) The P/E ratio is inversely related to future interest rates, through the discount rate. Thus, the higher expected future interest rates, the lower the P/E multiple should be, and the lower expected future interest rates, the higher the P/E multiple should be.

(2) Higher growth rates increase the P/E multiple. Low-growth-rate companies have lower P/E multiples, and higher-growth-rate companies have higher P/E multiples.

(3) Companies that employ capital more effectively should have a higher P/E ratio. This results from the fact that the more effectively capital is employed, the less new capital investment is required to achieve a given growth rate, and the more money that's available for payout to the common share holders.

Although not apparent from the equation, a company can have small or even negative current free cash flow and yet command a high price. This happens when the prospect for future free cash flows is high and the present value of these future values is also high, even though they may be several years in the future and, hence, severely discounted.

Price to Book Value

If it is assumed that a company has no debt, the above expression for the P/E ratio can be converted into a simple expression for the price-to-book (P/B) ratio, and this is done in Appendix II. The expression is given below[18]:

$$P/B = (R-G)/(D-G).$$

In this relationship, B is the per share book value of the common equity; R is the rate of return on common equity (in decimal terms); D is the cost of equity (in decimal terms); and G is the growth rate for earnings and free cash flow (in decimal terms).

The relationship shows clearly why a company with a return on equity equal to its cost of equity should have a stock price close to its common equity book value. It also shows why a company with a return on equity greater than its cost of equity should have a stock price greater than its common equity book value, while a company with a return on equity less than its cost of equity should have a stock price lower than its book value.

This relationship should be of interest to investors. It can be used to give some idea of what price-to-book multiple is reasonable for a given stock. As an example, assume that a company has a return on equity of 15% and an expected growth rate for the foreseeable future of 5%, and that the return an investor expects to make on this stock, i.e., the cost of equity, is 10%. Under these assumptions, the ratio of intrinsic value to book value is:

$$P/B = (0.15-0.05)/(0.1-0.05) = 0.10/0.05 = 2.$$

---

[18]   The expression might be recognizable by some. It is the same as the basic Westinghouse VABASTRAM (value based strategic management) equation that Westinghouse used to make successful strategic decisions for a number of years, although the derivation is different.

The stock is thus worth about twice its book value to the investor. Since the relationship is valid only under a limited set of circumstances, it shouldn't be used to value stocks in general, but it can give a reasonably accurate estimate of this ratio for many companies with little or no debt.

Relationship of Business Value to Invested Capital

The next expression, also derived in Appendix II, relates the value of the operating portion of a business to the amount of capital invested. This value is given by:

$$V = IC\ (R-G)/(D-G).$$

Here IC is the amount of capital invested in the business operations; R is the rate of return on invested capital (in decimal terms); D is the weighted cost of capital (in decimal terms); and G is the growth rate for operating earnings and free cash flow (in decimal terms).

Unlike the previous equation, this one is valid even if a company has some debt. What this expression basically says is that the value of a business depends on the amount of invested capital and how well that capital is employed. Return on invested capital measures how effectively capital is employed. The higher the return on invested capital, the less the fraction of free cash flow that needs to be invested back into the business to achieve a given growth rate, and the more of that free cash flow that's available to be paid as dividends or for buying back stock, both of which directly benefit the common share holder. The equation also shows that if the return on invested capital is equal to the weighted cost of capital, the value of the business is equal to the invested capital. If the return is greater than the weighted cost of capital, the value of the business is greater than the amount of invested capital, and if the return is less, the value of the business is less than the invested capital. Companies that have a return on invested capital less than their weighted cost of capital for any length of time are destroying value, not creating it.

Market Valuation

Markets can be overvalued, fairly valued, or undervalued, and every investor, regardless of how they invest, should have some ability to assess the value of markets they invest in. Ideally, you want to buy when things are cheap and sell if they're too expensive. Having an ability to assess value should make you a more successful investor.

When it comes to the stock market, there are a number of different techniques for sizing up the market. You can make an estimate of intrinsic value using the DCF technique and/or you can use various other numerical measures to help decide the value condition of the market. Making an accurate estimate of the intrinsic value of the market using the DCF technique, however, is difficult for most investors. Many research firms make these estimates, but they are not readily available. Many of the other numerical measures, on the other hand, are simple ratios that are easily calculated, and up-to-date values for most are available on the Internet. These metrics provide an *indication of risk and reward* in the market at any given time. Markets, however, can remain undervalued or overvalued for long periods of time. The metrics discussed here only provide an indication of whether the market may be overvalued or undervalued; they are *not market timing signals*, and they do not indicate when it might reverse. None are perfect, and all have been challenged in one way or another. If you use these metrics, it's likely a good idea to track several of them rather than relying on just one.

Price to Earnings

The P/E ratio is a popular metric used to value stocks and was discussed in a previous section in relationship to individual stocks. Often the P/E of the S&P 500, using trailing earnings, is used to value the market as a whole. This ratio has varied from about 5 to more than 40 over most of the past one hundred years. To judge the market's valuation, many compare the current P/E to its long-term average of about 15. If the current P/E is higher, they conclude the market is overvalued, and if it's lower, they conclude it's undervalued. While simple, this approach is not entirely correct. Fair value of the P/E ratio depends on interest rates. If interest rates are low and are expected to stay low or go lower, a reasonable P/E could be higher than 20. If interest rates are high and are expected to stay high or go even higher, a reasonable P/E could be 10 or less. If you use this metric, you should be comparing the current P/E to a P/E value characteristic of the interest rate environment prevailing at that time.

A problem with using a P/E ratio calculated with a single year's earnings, as described above, is that when earnings are low, as in a recession, the ratio can get abnormally high, as it did in March of 2009 when it was greater than 100 for a short period of time. To overcome this problem, economists and analysts use an average of several years of earnings. An increasingly popular measure is one developed by Robert Shiller, the prominent Yale economist. In this approach, P/E ratios are calculated using inflation-adjusted prices and the prior ten-year mean of inflation adjusted earnings (R. J. Shiller 2009).

Price to Book

The price-to-book value for individual stocks was also discussed in a previous section. As with the P/E ratio, this ratio can also be calculated for the S&P 500 index. The ratio indicates how the market is valuing stocks compared to their book value. The P/B for the S&P 500 has been greater than 1 for essentially all of the past one hundred years and has varied from about 1 to 5 over the past thirty years. The average value over the past thirty years is about 2.4. Unlike earnings, book value is relatively insensitive to changes in economic conditions, and the ratio fluctuates less than the P/E ratio. Like the P/E ratio, however, a fair value for the P/B ratio depends on interest rates, and one cannot simply compare the current value to the long-term average and conclude the market is overvalued or undervalued. The ratio increased dramatically from about 1.2 to nearly 5.0, for example, from 1982 to 1999/2000. For much of that time the increase was justified, as interest rates declined from nearly 14% to less than 5%. Toward the end of the period, however, the market became overheated and eventually crashed. Rapid increases occurred prior to both the 1929 and 1999/2000 crashes, and these increases were clearly warning signs.

Dividend Yield

Dividends and dividend yield are an important factor in individual stock selection, and dividends can contribute a large portion of the total return of an investor's portfolio. While some still use the dividend yield to judge the market's value, it has not, in my opinion, been a good indicator of overvaluation or undervaluation for many years. Dividend yield of the

S&P 500 is the annual dividend divided by market value of the index. If the market value increases without a corresponding increase in the annual dividend, the dividend yield will decline. Dividends are clearly related to earnings, and if earnings increase, dividends can be expected to increase as well. If the market is going up in value primarily because of increased earnings, the yield can be expected to remain reasonably constant. If, however, market value is increasing primarily because interest rates are falling, the dividend yield will decline. This latter situation is, in fact, what's happened since the early 1980s. Because of declining interest rates, stock prices increased considerably more than earnings alone would dictate, and dividend yields declined. In the previous two decades, earnings increased substantially but stock prices hardly changed because of rising interest rates, and dividend yields increased. In neither period was the change in yield evidence of overvaluation or undervaluation.

Fed Model

Another relatively simple measure is a model named the Fed's Stock Valuation Model by Dr. Edward Yardeni, a prominent investment strategist, in 1997. He named it the Fed Model because he derived it from some research done at the Federal Reserve. The Federal Reserve has not endorsed the model, and he later named it Stock Valuation Model #1 (SVM-1). The model basically compares the earnings yield of the stock market (most often the S&P 500 index) to the yield on the ten-year Treasury note. The earnings yield of the market is the inverse of the P/E ratio or E/P. In this model the forward-looking earnings yield is used. If the earnings yield is lower than the Treasury yield, the market is considered overvalued compared to bonds. If the earnings yield is higher than the Treasury yield, the market is considered undervalued compared to bonds. The model also uses the inverse of the Treasury yield to estimate a "fair value" for the market P/E. From this and the estimate of future earnings, an estimate of the "fair value" of the S&P index is calculated. The model seems to have worked quite well in identifying if stock prices were excessively overvalued or undervalued but not in predicting absolute values. Dr. Yardeni developed a second model in 1999, called SVM-2, because the market value began to diverge significantly from that predicted by SVM-1. He warned that neither model was likely to work well if interest rates were low and likely to stay low or go lower because of deflationary conditions for the economy and earnings (Yardeni 2003).

Tobin's Q Ratio

James Tobin of Yale University, a Nobel laureate in economics, originated the Q ratio. The ratio indicates whether the stock market is undervalued or overvalued by comparing the actual value of the market to the cost to replace the net assets of all the companies comprising the market. Fair value of Q was determined by Smithers and Wright to be 0.65 rather than 1.0 (Busch 2010). The accuracy of Tobin's Q ratio has been questioned because of the difficulty of accurately determining the cost to replace the net assets of all the companies making up the market. The value of Q going back about one hundred years, however, has been a reliable indicator of large changes in the market. When the Q value is near 0.3, it indicates the market is extremely undervalued, and when it's above 1.0, it indicates significant overvaluation. In 1920, for example, the value of Q was about 0.3. From that point, the market rose appreciably until 1929, and Q rose to about 1.05. Then, as the market crashed, the value of Q fell back to 0.3. In the early 1980s, the value of Q was again down to about 0.3 when the market took off and the value of Q rose to about 1.8 in 2000 as the market rose to record highs. Subsequently, the market fell about 50%, and the value of Q declined toward its long-term average of about 0.7.

Market Cap to GDP Ratio

A metric less commonly used but the one that Warren Buffett said "is probably the best single measure of where valuations stand at any given moment" is the ratio of the market value of all publically traded securities to the gross national product (GNP) of the country. He also said "if the percentage ratio falls to 70 to 80%, buying stocks is likely to work out well. If the ratio approaches 200% as it did in 1999 and early 2000 . . . you are playing with fire" (Warren Buffett 2001). The ratio actually reached about 180% in this time period. Although Warren Buffett said GNP, others use GDP, and for this purpose there is no significant difference. Others say that fair value is a ratio between 75% and 90%, and that anything over about 115% indicates significant overvaluation (Wolinsky 2010). Using the 115% criterion indicates that the market was significantly overvalued for much of the last decade. Jacob Wolinsky updates this metric and most of the others on a monthly basis in an article entitled "Stock Market Valuation (date), "available on the Internet.

Estimating the Value of a Small Business

If you're a small-business owner, you're very likely interested in what the business might be worth, even if you're not interested in selling. You should also be interested in what factors make your business more valuable. Your business may be worth more (or possibly less) to you than to potential buyers. The investment value depends both on cash flows the business is expected to generate in the future, and on the return on invested capital expected by an investor. Potential buyers might expect higher returns and hence place a lower value on your business.

To value your business you need to determine the value of the operating portion and then add any nonoperating pieces. The valuation process utilizing DCF is essentially the same as that discussed in the earlier section on business/stock valuation. If, however, the business is characterized by low to moderate growth (many small businesses are), the perpetuity equation can be used to quickly provide a rough estimate of the present value of the operating portion. Since you're valuing the entire business, not just the equity portion, the FCF that the business operations are expected to generate in the future must be estimated. You want these estimates to be as high as possible, but they need to be credible. Past performance is likely the best indication of future performance, and business records should be used to determine both the present value of FCF and recent growth.

Note that the FCF from the business operations is not the same as the net income that's determined on the business tax return. Adjustments are made for many reasons. The business may have some debt, and any interest charges should be added back to net income. Additionally, noncash charges, such as depreciation, should also be added back. Further, if you're drawing a significant salary that's been deducted as an expense of the business, at least a portion of this could possibly be added back to get a better estimate of the FCF from the business operations. Business owners frequently pay themselves more to manage their business than they would need to pay a manager. Also, since the business is most likely a subchapter

S corporation and the net income flows through to the owner's personal tax return, the FCF that you should be using in valuing the business is the pretax entity FCF.

Next, you need to get some idea of the rate of return a prospective buyer would expect on their investment. Keep in mind that the rate of return expected by an investor in a small business might be fairly high because of the potential risk involved. Future inflation expectations will also affect the expected return. Expected returns of 20% or more would not be unusual, and they could be much higher.

If the expected return is 20% and the FCF is not growing and you don't expect it to grow, and assuming an all cash transaction for simplicity, then the present value of the business using the perpetuity equation is five times the entity FCF. You can increase the estimated value if you can make a case that the FCF generated by the business has been growing and is expected to continue to grow in the future. If you can, for example, justify a 5% growth rate going forward, the present value of the business would be about seven times the current entity FCF, a substantial increase. It should also be clear that if you can find a buyer that doesn't expect quite as high a return on his investment, you might get more money for your business. If you found a buyer that only expected or was willing to accept a 15% return, the multiple of FCF increases from 5 to 7 for no growth, and from 7 to 10 for 5% growth. If the growth rates are higher than the investors' expected return, the perpetuity equation cannot be used directly. If the growth rates are close to the expected return, the equation does not provide a very good estimate, not because the equation is wrong, but because high growth rates cannot be sustained indefinitely. Under both these conditions you would need to use the two-step procedure, described in the previous section. Anyone actually considering selling his or her business should have an expert in valuation assist them in making as accurate an estimate as possible.

Estimating the Value of a Home

There are various ways to estimate the market value of homes. These include: home valuation websites, use of real estate agents, and formal appraisals. Which method or methods you should use depends on your purpose. If you want an estimate of your home's value for a net worth calculation, or simply because you're curious, use of a home valuation website should be adequate. If you're interested in knowing what the market value of your home might be because you would consider selling if the price were right, use of a home valuation website would be a good starting point. If you begin to get serious about selling, discussions with a real estate agent would be appropriate. If you decide that you're putting your home on the market, it might be a good idea to have a formal appraisal done. Formal appraisals are often done on behalf of buyers, because lenders require them, but sellers might want their own independent appraisal done.

Historically, buyers and sellers have not been well informed about real estate markets and home values. Potential buyers and sellers were largely dependent on real estate agents and appraisers for estimates of market value. Agents and appraisers had access to data not directly available to buyers and sellers. In recent years, the development of home valuation websites has made data on real estate markets more accessible by the public. Sites provide potential buyers and sellers, and curious individuals, considerable information on market prices and home values. By accessing a site and simply typing in an address or a neighborhood, an individual can obtain data on recent sales and homes currently listed for sale in an area of interest.

A good site is Zillow.com. In addition to the above data, the site will also provide an estimate of market value for a home with a specific address, called a Zestimate. The estimate is a computer calculated comparative analysis using publicly available data. Public records of home characteristics and even sale prices can often be in error, so the database is far from perfect, limiting the accuracy of Zestimate. Accuracy can be improved using a tool the site provides, called My Estimator, which allows the user to update data on the specific home being valued. The estimates, while very useful, are not appraisals and likely cannot be used for actions requiring an appraisal.

Real estate agents have access to comparable sales and listings of various kinds and most understand local market conditions very well. Using this information, they can make an estimate of market value for a specific property. Many real estate agents will also provide a comparative market analysis (CMA) to prospective clients. These reports can provide data on active listings, pending home sales, and comparative sales, some of the data they and appraisers use in estimating market values. Agents can help a seller establish an asking price and a buyer an offering price.

Real estate appraisers do research and perform various analyses to establish value estimates for clients. Formal appraisals by professionals are required for many reasons. An appraisal is normally required to obtain a mortgage and is often required to legally establish property value for an estate or settlement of some type. Estimates made by appraisers are considered more accurate than those provided by home valuation websites and real estate agents.

Two basic methods are generally used to estimate the market value of homes: the sales comparison approach and the cost approach. The primary method is the sales comparison approach. The cost approach becomes primary only if there are insufficient sales of similar properties to provide a reliable estimate of market value. Although cost and value are closely related in the minds of buyers, desirable homes are often worth much more than the cost to build them.

In the sales comparison approach, an estimate of market value is made by comparing the property of interest to recent sales of comparable properties in the area. Many different factors are compared, including rights conveyed, financing terms, conditions of sale, location, physical characteristics, and market conditions. Adjustments are made to the price of each comparable property for the factors that differ from those of the property of interest.

In the cost approach, the cost to develop a similar property is determined and used as an estimate of market value. The appraiser separately estimates the cost of the land, site improvements, and the cost to build or construct a comparable structure, and sums them to obtain an estimate of property value. For an older home, an estimate of depreciation is made for the structure and site improvements and subtracted from the total. Depreciation doesn't apply to land. Cost can be reproduction cost or replacement cost. Reproduction cost is the current cost to construct a duplicate of the house being valued including the same materials, construction, quality of workmanship, etc. Replacement cost is the current cost to construct a functionally equivalent home using modern materials, construction, etc.

The cost approach is also used to determine insurable value. The insurable value of a property is the cost to reproduce or replace the structure or buildings; it does not include the land value.

Appraisals provide the basis for an initial offer (or asking price) and support for negotiations, but there is no reason why a seller can't ask for more than the appraised value or a buyer can't offer less. Many buyers, however, may not be able to pay more than the appraised value since the lending institution usually limits the borrowing amount based on the appraisal.

Regardless of how the value of a home is estimated, keep in mind that the selling price is ultimately determined by negotiations between buyer and seller or their representatives.

Estimating the Value of Income-Producing Real Estate

Income-producing real estate is generally purchased for its investment value. Investment value is the property value to a particular investor and will likely differ from investor to investor and may differ from the general market value. Differences usually result from the different returns on investment that are expected.

To determine the investment value of a property, both an estimate of the cash flow expected to be generated by the property each year it is owned plus any amount expected to be received if the property were sold are discounted to determine their present worth, and the discounted values are summed. The correct cash flow to use is that generated by the property's operations before taxes. It is called net operating income (NOI) in the book *The Appraisal of Real Estate*. NOI is defined as the income left after subtracting all operating expenses from gross revenues but before mortgage debt service and depreciation are deducted. It is similar to the entity free cash flow used in valuing a business discussed previously, except for taxes. The discount rate used is the cost of capital. If you assume it's an all-cash transaction, then the cost of capital is the cost of equity capital. If debt capital is used in combination with equity capital, then the discount rate is the weighted cost of capital, where the different costs of capital are weighted according to the proportions used. It should be noted that expected future inflation could affect both the NOI and the discount rate that are used.

There are several ways to compute the value estimate for the property. You can use the DCF series directly and forecast the cash flows for each year of the useful life of the property. This might, however, require forecasting for fifty or more years. Another approach is to use the multistep method used in analysis of businesses and stocks. Recall that with a two-step approach, the future is divided into the explicit forecast period (in which the cash flow is forecast for each year) and the remaining time (for which a continuing value is determined). The present values of cash flows for each of these periods are added to obtain the property value. This approach allows use of specific cash flows and discount rates for the explicit forecast period. For the continuing value period, one could use an estimate of the sales price one might expect to get at that future time or alternately calculate a value assuming that the property continues to be rented. If it is assumed that the cash flow grows at a constant rate in perpetuity and that the discount rate is constant, the continuing value is given by the perpetuity equation:

$$V = NOI/(D-G).$$

Here NOI is the net operating income in the first year of the continuing value period; D is the discount rate (in decimal terms); and G is the growth rate for NOI (in decimal terms).

Use of this equation overstates the value somewhat because it assumes the useful life to be unlimited, but if the useful life is fifty years or so, the error is only a few percent. Rather than assume rents in perpetuity, one could assume a limited life and cash flows either fixed or growing (or declining) at a constant rate and use the annuity formulation for a fixed number of payments (see the section on annuities). However it's calculated, the continuing value, calculated at some point in the future, needs to be brought back to the present. This is done, as usual, by multiplying by the discount factor.

A very simple approach is to calculate the continuing value, using the perpetuity equation, from day one and have no explicit forecast period at all.[19] With this simple approach, both the cash flow growth rate and discount rate would remain fixed for the entire life of the property. The cash flow value now is the cash flow estimate in the first year of ownership.

---

[19] Although some might think that this approach doesn't count the amount one could get from selling the property at some point in time, it actually does. Remember that the value of the property at any point in time is the sum of the discounted values of the cash flows that the property produces from that point on. Whether the cash flow is from selling the property or from continuing to rent it, the results will be the same if the cash flows and the selling price are consistent.

This approach, though not as accurate as the other approaches, can provide a rough estimate of the investment value of a property very quickly.

The perpetuity equation can come in handy for anyone considering buying rental property as an investment. A few simple calculations might prevent the investor from overpaying for a property. An example will show its usefulness. Back in 2006, the apartment building where my daughter was renting was being converted to condominiums, and the units were put up for sale. At the time she was renting a one-thousand-square-foot, two-bedroom unit for about $1,000 per month. The builders were asking between $250,000 and $275,000 for units like hers, and I suppose there were appraisals showing comparable sales at these prices. The condo fee was to be $200 per month. I looked at the units as a potential rental investment and concluded that they were substantially overpriced. My reasoning was as follows. I assumed the unit could be rented for $1,200 per month and, after paying the condo fee, the cash flow generated by the unit would be $1,000 per month or $12,000 per year (for simplicity, other expenses such as maintenance, insurance, and property taxes were ignored). I also assumed the cash flow could be increased each year in the future by the inflation rate, which I assumed would be 3% per year going forward. Then I made two simple calculations. In the first, I assumed that I would buy the unit for cash and would expect a return on my investment of 15%. Based on these assumptions, the investment value of the property was:

$$V = NOI/(D-G) = \$12,000/(0.15-0.03) = \$ 100,000$$

(Had I been willing to accept a return of 10%, the investment value would have increased to about $170,000). The return an investor might be willing to accept depends in large measure on their view of the investment risk.

For the second calculation, I assumed I would buy the unit using a large amount of debt financing. Now if I used a significant amount of debt, my cost of capital could be lower. Under these conditions, as an investor I might be willing to pay more for the property. For example, if I financed 80% and had a fixed rate 8% interest loan, my cost of capital would drop to 9.4%. Again assuming a 3% annual increase in cash flow, the investment value of the property increased to $187,500, still significantly lower than the asking price. Also, remember I actually overstated the cash flow number because I ignored many of the operating expenses. Had the rough estimate of property value been close to the asking price, a more accurate analysis might have been warranted. Now clearly the value of real estate depends on location, and this was a good location, but that should already be reflected in the rent figure.

After the short analysis, I decided not to buy. Many people, both investors and tenants, assumed that the property value would continue to appreciate, and that they would get their investment back plus a nice profit when they sold in a few years. While that might have been possible, it wasn't very likely at the time, and it turns out that I was correct, as that was just about the peak of the real estate market in the Phoenix/Scottsdale area (and elsewhere as well). Obviously the people that bought units were unable to flip them for a higher price. In fact, I'm sure that the market price has now decreased substantially and that many of the buyers have either defaulted on their loans or are losing money on their investments.

Chapter 10

Insurance

Insurance provides protection for you and your family against many of the possible financial risks associated with living in a modern society. It allows individuals and families to limit their downside risk by spreading it across a large group of people. You can buy insurance to protect against almost any kind of financial risk. One should, however, only buy insurance for those probable risks that could impose a significant financial burden. For some risks, self-insurance can be a good option.

The specific insurance that people need depends on their individual circumstances. Everyone should have some type of health insurance, and most people of working age should have disability insurance. If you own a home, home insurance is a must, as is automobile insurance if you own a car. If you rent, you should have a renter's policy. Both home owner and renter policies typically provide a certain amount of liability insurance, but the amounts are usually insufficient. In our litigious society, it is generally a good idea to have a liability umbrella policy for added protection. Life insurance should be a top priority for married people, particularly those with children. When you buy property, a home, for example, it's a good idea to buy title insurance. Long-term care insurance should be given careful consideration for those approaching old age, and it should be a high priority for many.

Many people have some insurance that they may be unaware of, since they don't pay for it directly. Social Security, for example, in addition to providing retirement benefits, also provides survivor benefits to children under the age of eighteen and a level of disability protection to qualified participants. Most companies provide a limited amount of life insurance, and some provide short-term disability insurance to employees at no charge. One should understand these benefits before deciding on the amounts of insurance to buy.

There are many other types of insurance. There are, for example, extended warranty contracts for automobiles, appliances, and electronic equipment. These are generally not cost effective, and people that can afford repair or replacement costs should not buy them. If you're an investor, you can even insure your portfolio (see chapter 8).

Whether or not you buy a particular type of insurance is a personal financial decision, but it should be made with a full understanding of the risks and consequences of not having the insurance, the benefits the insurance provides, and the cost. Since insurance needs change, you should review your needs periodically. You should find an insurance agent or broker you trust to deal with, but you should understand as much as you can about insurance beforehand. You want to be an informed buyer. Shopping around is always a good idea, but in most cases you'll get significant discounts and the policies will be coordinated if you buy all the policies from the same company. Insurance should only be purchased from financially strong companies. While state guaranty funds provide some protection, if your insurance company goes bankrupt you may not have the insurance you thought you had.

Health Insurance

Health insurance provides a means of limiting what you pay for possible future medical expenses, and it should be a top priority for everyone. Treatment for a serious illness or injury can be costly and can create large and perhaps unmanageable debt, if you don't have adequate health insurance.

The Health Care Reform Bill, signed into law in the spring of 2010 has a large impact on health insurance, but it maintains the private US health care system. Beginning in 2011, every American will be required to have health insurance or pay a fine.[20] Individuals and families making up to 400% of the federal poverty level will be eligible for government subsidies to help pay for their insurance, but not until 2014.

---

[20]   Several states are challenging the legality of this provision in the courts.

There are various health insurance plans. Some are fee-for-service type plans and others are managed care plans, although some managed care plans are, at least in part, also fee-for-service plans. Some are private plans and others such as Medicaid are administered and funded by the government. Some plans pay for most expenses and have high premiums. Others pay only for major medical expenses and have lower premiums.

Fee-for-service plans allow the insured to select the health providers they want without the need for referrals from a primary care physician or preapproval for services. In fee-for-service plans, the insured pays a monthly premium and, in addition, a charge or co-pay for each service provided. The insured pays the full amount of the charges until a certain amount, called the yearly deductible, is met. Thereafter the patient pays a percentage, typically 20%, of each charge; the other 80% is covered by the insurance until the maximum out-of-pocket amount for the year is reached. Once the maximum yearly amount is reached, the insurance is responsible for the full amount of charges. Historically, plans have had a limit on the total amount of insurance that companies would pay over the life of a patient, called the lifetime cap. The 2010 Health Care Reform Bill eliminated these caps.

Catastrophic or major medical plans are fee-for-service type plans that allow you to pay lower premiums in exchange for very high deductibles—usually the higher the deductible, the lower the premium. Deductibles can be several thousand dollars. With this kind of plan, you're only paying premiums to cover major medical expenses. Since premiums are lower, you can save money if you remain healthy.

Managed care plans were created to help reduce the cost of health care and there are several types. All limit your choice of health care providers to a certain extent in exchange for lower costs. Plans use networks of providers that have agreed to provide discounts for covered services. Health maintenance organizations (HMOs), preferred provider organizations (PPOs), and point of service (POS) plans are all managed care type plans.

HMOs generally provide the least expensive care, but with an HMO you must choose a primary care physician and use the health care providers that are part of the HMO network. Most HMOs charge small co-payments for services.

PPO plans give the participants discounts when providers in the network are used. Unlike an HMO you don't select a primary care physician, but, like a fee-for-service plan, there are deductibles, co-pays, and out-of-pocket maximums. PPO plans are generally less expensive than fee-for-service plans but more expensive than HMOs.

With a POS plan, as with an HMO, you must select a primary care physician from the network of providers. This physician becomes your point of service. If you use a facility or physician in the POS network, the plan functions similar to an HMO. Your physician can make referrals outside the POS network, but then there are deductibles that must be met and higher co-pays.

Health insurance can be obtained from a variety of sources. Most employers and many alumni, fraternal, and professional organizations offer group health insurance to employees and members and their families. If you don't qualify for a group plan, you can buy individual or family health insurance directly from an insurance company. Insurance companies also offer short-term or temporary insurance. Most Americans sixty-five and older qualify for Medicare, and many poor qualify for Medicaid, both of which are government-run health care programs. There is also a government plan for children and pregnant women from relatively poor families called the Children's Health Insurance Program or CHIP. Under the 2010 Health Care Insurance Bill, the uninsured and self-employed will eventually be able to purchase insurance through state-based health insurance exchanges.

Group plans ordinarily have the lowest premiums, since providers have negotiating power with the insurers. Also, many employers subsidize their plans. Additionally, individuals and family members can usually enroll without regard for existing conditions. If you have a group plan provided by an employer, you have a degree of portability mandated by law. If your employer had more than twenty employees, then you're generally eligible under COBRA, Consolidated Omnibus Reconciliation Act of 1985, to continue your coverage for up to eighteen months after you leave your job. Unfortunately, COBRA is expensive; the premiums you pay are the same as what your employer paid plus an administrative fee. Also, under HIPAA, Health Insurance Portability and Accountability Act of 1996, you must be covered under any new employer's health plan if you were covered under your old employer's plan. You can't be denied coverage because of any preexisting conditions.

Individual or family plans purchased directly from an insurance company are more expensive. Choosing higher deductibles and out-of-pocket maximums can reduce premiums. The state-based insurance exchanges are intended to give individuals negotiating power, similar to that of group plans, and should help lower premiums. Individual coverage currently requires medical underwriting and can be denied for preexisting conditions. However, under HIPAA, if you had group coverage or COBRA, insurance companies must provide individual insurance coverage if you apply within sixty-three days after your coverage runs out. This HIPAA coverage, however, is very expensive. Under the 2010 Health Care Reform Bill, insurance companies will no longer be able to deny coverage to those with preexisting conditions. While this provision applies in 2010 for children, it doesn't apply to adults until 2014.

Medicare is a government-run health insurance program for people sixty-five and older and for people under sixty-five with certain disabilities. Medicare has four parts. Part A, hospital insurance, Part B, medical insurance, and Part D, prescription drug coverage, make up the basic Medicare program. These parts don't cover all your medical expenses, and many people elect to buy supplemental policies from private insurance companies. Part C is a separate comprehensive insurance plan, called Medicare Advantage. Medicare Advantage plans are run by private companies, approved by Medicare, and provide more coverage than the basic Medicare program. The 2010 Health Care Reform Bill reduces government funding for Medicare Advantage plans.

There is no charge for Medicare Part A if you or your spouse paid Medicare taxes while working. Part B, if elected, requires payment of a monthly premium that depends on your modified gross income. Part B has a deductible that must be paid before Medicare pays for any doctor's services. Part D also requires payment of monthly premiums and has yearly deductibles and co-payments. Like Part B and Part D, Part C participants pay a monthly premium.

Medicaid is a health insurance program for those in certain designated eligibility groups with limited income and assets. It is a joint federal and state program administered by the states. There are no premiums for Medicaid, but in some states the Medicaid recipient might be expected to pay small co-pays for services. The Health Care Reform Bill increases the number of individuals and families eligible for Medicaid substantially.

The CHIP program, formerly known as SCHIP (State Children's Health Insurance Program), was renewed and expanded in February 2009. It is a joint state and federal program for uninsured children and pregnant women in families with income too high to qualify for Medicaid, but too low to afford private health care. States design and run these programs using federal guidelines.

Disability Insurance

If you become disabled, you might lose your ability to earn the income that supports you and your family. Disability insurance can replace at least a portion of this income if the insured is unable to work for an extended period of time. In contrast to death, individuals and families give little thought to the consequences of disability, even though for many the chances of being disabled may actually be greater than that of dying. Bread-earners should generally have insurance to replace a high percentage of their income unless they have significant assets that they and their families can live off for an extended period of time. Also bear in mind that you need less disability insurance as your financial obligations decline and your financial assets increase.

There are various possible sources of income for the disabled. These include Social Security disability, workmen's compensation, employer disability insurance, and private policies. Disabled veterans are entitled to special government benefits, but these are not discussed here.

Social Security not only provides retirement benefits, it also provides disability payments to eligible individuals and their families. To qualify, the individual must have sufficient work credits, and he or she must satisfy Social Security's definition of disability. Social Security only pays benefits for "total disability"; no benefits are paid for partial or short-term disability. The amount it pays depends on your average lifetime earnings. To get an estimate of how much Social Security will provide, you can go to their website and use their disability calculator.

States provide workers' compensation. Workers' compensation, however, only applies if the person is injured on the job. Benefits include payment of medical expenses, weekly payments to replace wages, and compensation for economic loss. Benefits are also payable to dependents of a worker killed on the job.

Many private companies provide short-term disability insurance, and some offer long-term disability coverage. The short-term coverage is often free, while the long-term coverage usually requires the employee to pay a monthly premium. Short-term disability coverage generally only provides benefits for a year or less. Long-term disability may provide benefits until you reach normal retirement age or, in some cases, for life. These policies typically pay about 60% of the employee's income. Premiums should be less than for a comparable private policy, since employees pay group rates. If your employer offers disability insurance, you should check on the coverage, but it's generally smart to enroll in the plan.

Private disability insurance policies are available from various insurance companies. Even if your employer provides long-term disability insurance, you might want a private plan to supplement what your employer provides. Private plans can be purchased for different amounts and different durations. Premiums for private plans depend on the amount of income you want to replace, the percentage of your salary it represents, your age and health, the type and riskiness of the job you have, and how long you want benefits to last. They also depend on when you want benefits to begin. When buying private disability insurance, you should always check to make sure the policy covers all disabilities, regardless of the cause. Also make sure that the policy can't be cancelled and that it can be renewed at the same premium regardless of changes to your health. As for all insurance, you should shop around and compare premiums.

Home Owner Insurance

A home owner's (HO) policy protects your home (both the dwelling and unattached structures) and personal possessions from financial loss caused by various perils such as fire, lightning, theft, windstorms, hail, and vandalism. Your home and personal possessions likely are your most valuable possessions and should be insured. HO policies also provide coverage for increases in living expenses you incur if your home becomes uninhabitable, but only for a limited time. Additionally, they provide a certain amount of liability protection for bodily injury and/or property damage claims brought against the insured and for medical payments to others for covered accidents. "Insured" usually means the policyholder, other relatives that are residents of the household, and other residents (under the age of twenty-one) in the care of the previously named residents.

There are various kinds of policies, designated HO-1, HO-2, HO-3, etc., and generally referred to as forms. These provide different types of coverage and protect against somewhat different perils. HO-1, HO-2, and HO-3 are early forms of combined coverage policies. The HO-1 form provided basic coverage for both the home and personal property, while the HO-2 policy covered more perils. The HO-3 form provided "all risk" coverage on the dwelling and "named peril" coverage on the contents. Almost all new policies are HO-5 type polices. HO-5 provides "all risk" coverage on both the home and its contents. "All risk" actually doesn't mean that it covers all perils; it generally means that the policy covers all perils except those specifically excluded by the policy. HO-4 is a form for renters or tenants, and it covers personal possessions and provides some liability protection. HO-6 is for condo owners. None of the policies insures for damage due to neglect, floods, earth movement (including earthquakes), war, or nuclear hazards, although you can buy special insurance to cover floods and earthquakes.

Home owner policies provide coverage for the home, but they don't cover the land or the costs that might be required to stabilize or restore the land if an insurable event occurs. Thus you only want enough insurance to cover your home, not both the home and the land. You therefore need to know the value of your property less the value of the land, and you should have an estimate of what it would cost to rebuild the dwelling and extensions if destroyed. There are two basic types of loss settlement provisions that you can choose in home owner policies: replacement cost and cash value. With a replacement cost provision, the insurance company will pay the actual cost to repair or replace the dwelling, even if this cost exceeds (usually up to 20%) the value specified in the policy. There are actually two different replacement cost choices: one in which they will repair or replace the dwelling with construction *similar* to that of the original dwelling, and another in which they will repair or replace the dwelling with what is called *common* construction. Common construction means use of materials and construction techniques commonly used in new construction. If your home was built with custom materials and construction, they likely won't pay for this unless your policy specifies similar construction. With a cash value type policy, the insurance company will only pay the policyholder the amount specified in the policy if the home is totally destroyed. If the market value has increased since the time the policy was issued, you still only get the amount specified in the policy. Additionally, if the home is only partially damaged, and it is insured for less than the cost to rebuild, you will likely only get a percentage of the cost to repair the damage. To receive the full cost of repair, the home must normally be insured for at least 80% of the full replacement cost. You should always insure for the full cost to replace the home. Also, since inflation generally increases the cost, you want some type of inflation protection.

Coverage for personal possessions is usually related to the amount of dwelling coverage. Personal property is often covered, even if it is off the premises, but then special limits apply. Special limits also apply to certain categories of personal property such as securities, checks, traveler's checks, stamps and trading cards, silverware, and firearms. Similar to coverage for the dwelling, you can get a policy that will repair or replace personal possessions either lost or damaged, with certain exceptions. Exceptions typically include antiques, fine arts, paintings, and similar items, for which there are limits to what they will pay. The loss settlement for personal items in many policies is only their depreciated value. Depreciated value is the original cost less the accumulated depreciation over the time period the items have been owned. You want a replacement cost provision for personal items; depreciated values for furniture and other personal possessions can be surprisingly small. You should also have some type of record of all your personal items, together with documentation to verify your claim since you will need to provide an itemized list of damaged, destroyed, or stolen personal items to the insurance company. Photos or a video showing these items together with receipts showing what each cost would be good to have and should be stored off the premises.

HO liability coverage generally provides protection to the insured for claims or lawsuits brought for bodily injury to others and damage to property of others, even if the incident happens off your premises. It covers your legal defense, as well as those damages that the insured is legally liable for up to the limits of the particular policy's coverage. Certain types of damage claims, such as those that result from intentional or willful and malicious acts of the insured, are typically excluded from protection.

As mentioned earlier, home owner policies don't normally cover damage from floods or earthquakes. Coverage for these hazards, however, might be available as options. Flood coverage is mandatory for homes in designated high-risk flood areas if the mortgage is federally insured. In this case, flood insurance can be obtained through the National Flood Insurance Program. Earthquake insurance is usually available as an add-on to your home owner's policy. Its cost depends on where you live. It is extremely expensive in California, for example, and deductibles are large.

Costs for home owner policies depend on the amount and extent of the coverage provided. Having higher deductibles, a home security system, and multiple policies with the same insurance company, for example, can hold down costs. Policies differ but all have limitations and exclusions. Policies should always be read and understood before purchasing.

Auto Insurance

Ownership and/or use of motor vehicles can be hazardous. An accident can result in serious injuries, deaths, and major property damage and can expose you to substantial financial liability. Automobile insurance is an absolute necessity. Insurance can provide liability protection and cover medical expenses, provide economic protection for you and others in your car in a crash caused by an uninsured or underinsured motor vehicle, and coverage for physical damage to your car or a nonowned vehicle in your possession. Insurance companies offer many different types of coverage: some mandated by law, and others that are optional.

When you buy automobile insurance, you protect yourself as well as certain others. Policies cover those people defined in the "insured" section or sections of the policy, and generally include the policy owner, spouse, relatives of the policy owner named in the declarations, and other persons using your vehicle authorized by you or your spouse.

Liability coverage protects the insured for bodily injury to others and damage or destruction to the property of others because of an accident involving use of their car. It covers claims for injuries to all involved in an accident, including those in other cars, pedestrians, and passengers in your car. *Liability coverage* usually extends to the use of a newly acquired car (usually only for fourteen days) and a nonowned or rental car as well. If you borrow someone's car, the owner of that car has primary liability responsibility. Similarly, if you lend your car to someone, you have primary liability responsibility. Liability coverage typically has different dollar limits for bodily injury to a single person and the total allowed for injuries to all people. A third amount applies to the total property damage. The limits allowed by any specific policy are shown on the declarations page under limits of liability. Additionally, the insurance company will defend the insured against lawsuits resulting from an accident and pay legal fees, but they will generally not defend or pay legal fees for amounts above the liability limit.

It is extremely important to have adequate liability coverage. States require that you carry certain minimums, but these are usually insufficient. The financial liability from a serious accident can easily be hundreds of thousands of dollars or more. Generally the more assets you have, the more liability insurance you should carry. It only takes one serious accident to wipe you out financially if you're not adequately protected. See the next section on personal liability umbrella insurance for more information.

The medical payments portion of a policy covers medical expenses of the insured and those of any passengers in the insured's car due to injuries sustained in an accident. This portion of the policy covers medical expenses up to the policy limit, regardless of who was at fault.

Comprehensive and collision portions of a policy cover physical damage to the insured's vehicle from various causes. Comprehensive covers damage or loss from most perils, e.g., fire, theft, earthquakes, wind, hail, water, flood, and vandalism. Collision covers damage or loss resulting from a collision with another vehicle or object. Comprehensive and collision coverage may apply to a newly acquired car and a nonowned or rental car for a limited time period, but you should check with your insurance agent to make sure of the specifics of your policy. The insurance company's liability limit for these types of coverage is the lower of the cost of repair or the actual cash value of the vehicle. Actual cash value is the market value at the time of the loss (usually less than the Kelley Blue Book value).

Comprehensive and collision are optional and may not be cost-effective for all vehicles. Both have deductibles associated with them, and the insurance company will only pay the amount of damage or loss over and above the specified deductible. The decision as to whether to carry these depends on the cost of the coverage and the value of the vehicle. Collision coverage on a car that's not worth much, for example, is most likely not cost-effective. You can reduce premiums by using larger deductibles. Other optional types of coverage include emergency road service and car rental and travel expenses if your car is not drivable for certain reasons.

Uninsured and underinsured motor vehicle coverage provides protection for bodily injury to the insured caused by an accident involving a vehicle without insurance or without adequate insurance. These portions of a policy protect you against hit-and-run drivers, drivers without liability insurance or with insufficient liability insurance, and insured drivers whose insurance companies can't pay the value of the claim because of insolvency. They effectively treat your insurance company as though they provided liability coverage for the uninsured or underinsured vehicle.

Rates depend on where you live and your risk profile. Risk factors include: age, gender, annual mileage driven, type of vehicle, marital status, and driving record. Discounts are often given for various things such as insuring multiple cars with the same company, an accident-free record, good grades if you're are a student, and having safety devices (air bags and antilock brakes, for example) or antitheft devices installed in your vehicle.

You should read and understand the policy you're buying. If you don't understand any part of the policy, have your agent explain it to you.

Personal Liability Umbrella Insurance

Liability insurance protects the insured against many, but not all, possible legal actions or claims that might be brought against them. Both the legal defense costs and any legal liability the insured might be responsible for are covered up to the specific limits of the policy. Both auto insurance and home owner insurance policies typically provide some liability protection, but these policies are limited both in the scope and amount of coverage. Auto policy liability coverage, for example, covers bodily injury and property damage claims resulting from ownership or use of a car, but the amount of protection likely is inadequate. A serious auto accident could result in claims against a person for hundreds of thousands of dollars or more. If the legal liability is higher than the protection, a person could end up losing their home or other assets. In our litigious society, broader and higher levels of coverage are almost a necessity. A liability umbrella policy provides higher levels of protection, additional funds for legal defense, and can protect against things other policies don't cover. Umbrella policies complement your other policies.

Policies usually require that a certain minimum level of liability protection, called the retained limit, be maintained in your other policies. It's thus, generally, a good idea to buy all the policies from the same company to ensure that they're properly coordinated. Costs are usually reasonable, even for multimillion dollar policies, but they depend on the underlying coverage you have on other policies and the number of people in your household. There is no magic number for how much liability coverage you need. Some say you should have enough to cover the value of your assets, but a claim could be for more than that. How much you actually need, unfortunately, can only be determined after the fact. It depends on the seriousness of the harm you or other covered members of your household do to others and your suability factor. Your suability factor, according to the author of the book *Insurance for Dummies*, depends not only on your current assets and income but also on your future income and any future assets you may accumulate or even inherit (Hungelmann 2009, 47). In general when it comes to liability protection, more is better.

Life Insurance

The primary reason to buy life insurance is to provide funds to cover the financial consequences of one's death. These include death expenses, lost income, and possibly estate taxes. Death expenses for most people include funeral costs and possibly probate court and other legal and administrative costs. If you're a bread-earner, the main reason to have life insurance is to replace lost income that would have supported or helped support dependents. Non-bread-earners may also want life insurance to cover added household expenses that could result from their death. Child-care, for example, can be a major financial burden to a working spouse if the nonworking spouse dies. One could also have debts that they don't want their spouse or estate burdened with. For those with large estates, there may also be estate taxes. Not everyone, however, needs life insurance. If you're single and have no dependents, for example, you probably don't need life insurance.

How Much Insurance Do You Need?

Funds required for funeral costs are relatively small, and range from a few thousand dollars to $15,000 or more depending on the type and extravagance of the funeral. Probate costs—the costs for the court to supervise the legal distribution of your probate property—vary from state to state but are typically a small percent of the value of the probate estate. Probate costs, however, can be entirely avoided by good estate planning (see chapter 12). Other legal and administrative costs are relatively small if the needed information is readily available. If it's not, it could be costly to pay someone to determine assets and liabilities and locate necessary documents. Good estate planning can also minimize these costs.

Replacement of lost income requires the largest amount of insurance for most families. The amount of life insurance required to replace lost income is equal to the present or capitalized value of the needed income stream. Some agents and financial advisors may use a simple multiple of income to estimate how much insurance you need, but this approach can be misleading unless it's related to how long you need the income. Chapter 9 discussed how to determine the present value of different types of income streams, and appendix I provides equations that can be used to calculate present values. To utilize these equations you need to know the amount of income you're trying to replace, the time period over which you want to replace it, and the earnings return you can expect to make on the capital going forward. The first step is to decide how much income you want to replace. You may want to replace the entire expected income of the bread-earner going forward or only enough income to meet minimum needs. The amount clearly depends on each family and their situation. It might be $25K, or it could exceed $100K per year. To allow for likely future inflation, the income stream should be increased by a certain percentage annually. Next you need to determine how long the future income stream is needed. This duration clearly depends on the age of the bread-earner and how many earning years they have remaining. The duration also depends on whether you're trying to provide the income stream for the life of your spouse or for some lesser time period like until the children, if any, graduate from high school or college. The final piece of information required to calculate the amount of needed life insurance is the return you can expect to make on the capital going forward. Since investment of this capital should be very conservative, the expected rate shouldn't be very high.

To get a feel for how much insurance one might need under different circumstances, an example might be beneficial. Let's assume initially that the bread-earner's spouse is thirty years old and that they want their full income of $50K per year replaced until the spouse is sixty-two years old, a period of thirty-two years. Let's further assume that they want this income stream to increase 3% per year because of expected inflation. Let's also assume that they can safely expect to earn 5% per year on the capital. The present value of this income stream can be calculated using the annuity equation for a growing income stream that persists for a limited number of years (see appendix I). Using these numbers, the amount of capital and hence the amount of life insurance needed is about $1.15M. If the initial income you want to replace were $100K, then the amount of insurance needed would be about $2.3M. These amounts may surprise many people, and many will find that they are underinsured when it comes to replacing income. If one only wants to replace the income stream until the children complete college, the amount of insurance needed is less. As the bread-earner ages, fewer years of lost income need to be replaced and less life insurance is needed for this purpose unless their financial obligations increase for other reasons. Similar reasoning can be used to determine the amount of insurance a non-bread-earner might need to cover any additional family expenses that might result from death.

Estate taxes depend on the size of one's estate and on the estate tax laws prevailing at the time of death. Most people don't need to worry about federal estate taxes because their estates will not be large enough to result in any tax liability. They might, however, need to consider estate taxes that might be due the state they live in. If your estate is sufficiently large, however, there may be large federal estate taxes that, in the absence of insurance, might require asset sales (possibly at distressed prices) to satisfy (see chapter 12). Although life insurance proceeds are not subject to income taxes, life insurance proceeds are part of the policy owner's estate. It is important that individuals make estimates of the value of their estates periodically and, if their estates are large enough, take the estate planning steps that minimize any estate taxes. Various techniques are available to minimize estate taxes, including titling assets so that each spouse takes advantage of the estate tax exemption to which they're entitled, gifting, and creating an irrevocable life insurance trust, so that life insurance proceeds do not end up as part their estate.

The total amount of life insurance needed is the sum of the amounts needed for the various purposes. Not all this insurance needs to be purchased. You likely have life insurance provided by your employer, and remember that Social Security provides income benefits to survivors of eligible people. Before buying insurance, you should make sure you understand what you have from these other sources.

Types of Policies

There are two basic kinds of life insurance policies: those that provide temporary insurance and those that provide more permanent insurance. Temporary life insurance is called term insurance, and, as the name implies, is purchased for a period of time, or a term: five, ten, or fifteen years, for example. Term insurance is the purest form of life insurance and the least expensive; premiums are for insurance only. Term policies generally don't pay dividends, and there is no accumulation of cash value. The older you are and the longer the term, the higher the premiums. Rates also depend on gender and health and lifestyle. Policies can be bought that have constant annual premiums or premiums that change each year. It's usually a good idea to sign up for the length of time you need initially than to buy for a short term and plan to renew. Rates when you renew will be based on your age and health at that time and will be higher, and possibly much higher. If you think you might renew, it's likely a good idea to buy an option that guarantees your ability to renew regardless of health. You can buy level term, decreasing term, or increasing term. Which you should buy depends on whether you expect your financial obligations to increase or decrease over time. Since premiums vary from company to company, you should comparison shop for life insurance. Rate comparisons among term insurance providers are relatively easy.

Whole life, universal life, and variable life are common forms of permanent life insurance. With these types of policies, there is no need to renew: they remain in effect as long as you continue paying the premiums. Premiums generally remain fixed, but they can increase on some policies after a number of years. These policies are a combination of life insurance and investment/savings, and, as a result, premiums are significantly higher than for term insurance. Because of the investment aspect, the policies have a cash value that increases over time. Cash value is the amount that will be returned to you if you terminate the policy. Be aware, however, that if you only hold the policy for a short period of time and terminate it, you will take a substantial loss. These policies also pay dividends that can be left to accumulate and earn compound interest. Dividends can also be used to reduce premiums. Because policies differ from provider to provider, comparison of policies is very difficult. Most people should have some combination of permanent insurance and term insurance. In general, however, the bulk of most people's insurance needs should be covered with term insurance.

Long-Term Care Insurance

Americans are living longer, and many will need some type of assistance with daily living as they age. Their families might provide assistance, but, increasingly, paid outside help is needed. Help might be some kind of home care service, or it might mean use of an assisted living facility or nursing home. Long-term care (LTC) insurance provides protection for the financial risks resulting from the need for some type of extended health care service.

According to a study done by the US Department of Health and Human Services, a sixty-five-year-old has at least a 40% risk of entering a nursing home sometime in his or her life, and about 10% of these will remain for at least five years *(Guide to Long-Term Care (LTC) Insurance* n.d.). Neither Medicare nor supplemental insurance covers long-term care needs. Medicaid pays for long-term care, but Medicaid is for those in poverty or near poverty. If you have resources and no long-term care insurance, you will have to pay for the care out of your own pocket. Once you exhaust your savings, you may qualify for Medicaid. You can't, however, simply give resources away and claim poverty to get Medicare to pay for LTC. States will consider gifts you made within the last three years in determining whether you qualify. LTC partnership insurance policies, however, are available and allow a person to qualify for Medicaid coverage without having to spend down all their savings.

Long-term care costs depend on where you live but are high. Based on cost estimates made by the AARP Public Policy Institute, average nursing home costs in most states in 2006 exceeded $50K per year and in some few states were in excess of $100K *(What Does Long-Term Care Cost in Your State?* n.d.). Average costs for assisted living were about half those for nursing homes. Costs have surely increased since then and can be expected to increase more in the future. Home care is much less expensive but still costly. Long-term care is a financial risk that many should insure against.

Premiums for long-term care insurance depend on the level of coverage, when benefits begin, and a person's age when they buy the insurance.

Coverage is not cheap, and policies might exclude payments for certain conditions. The higher the daily limit and the longer the benefit period, the more the policy will cost. How long you're willing to wait after care starts and benefits begin (called the elimination or deductible period) also affects cost. Age, however, makes the most difference. If, for example, you wait until age seventy to buy a policy, it will cost about twice what it would have cost at age sixty and about four times what you would have paid at fifty. There is, however, no guarantee that the premiums will not increase. While insurance companies cannot single out individuals for premium increases, they can increase premiums for everyone in the same category. Since costs for long-term care continue to escalate, some type of inflation protection is necessary to fully protect yourself, but inflation protection is costly.

Policies generally pay benefits in one of two ways: a daily, or per diem rate, or for expenses as they are incurred. A per diem rate policy, called an indemnity policy, pays the daily/weekly/monthly benefit amount specified in the policy, once eligibility has been established, and the benefit period begins. With an expense-incurred policy, you're reimbursed for covered expenses actually incurred up to the policy daily/weekly/monthly limit.

Policies can differ in the type of care covered. Some may only pay for approved stays in nursing homes, while others might only pay for home care services. Most new policies, however, pay for a range of services from home care to nursing home stays, although per diem limits will likely be different for different types of care.

As with other kinds of health insurance, there are both group policies, sometimes offered by employers and certain associations, and individual policies that can be purchased directly from insurance companies. Group policies are generally less costly and often have a provision that allows continuation of the policy when you leave your employer. If you qualify for a group policy, it should be given serious consideration.

LTC partnership insurance policies combine private insurance with the Medicaid program. Holders of these policies can qualify for Medicaid coverage without having to spend down all their savings. They can usually protect assets equal to the benefits paid by the policy. Legislation allowing all states to create partnership programs was enacted in 2005, but after a relatively long trial period in a few states.

As with all insurance policies, you should fully understand what it is you're buying before signing up. This is particularly important, however, for long-term care insurance, since it may be many years in the future (hopefully never) before you need any benefits, and by then it will be too late to change policies if the coverage differs from what you thought you had.

Title Insurance

Title insurance protects property buyers and their lenders against the possibility that the title may not be valid. Unfortunately, separate policies are required for the two parties. When you buy a piece of property or a home with borrowed money, the lender almost always requires that the borrower buy title insurance to protect the lender from risk, the amount dependent on how much is borrowed. The borrower pays for this insurance at closing. Title insurance that protects the buyer is optional, but it is generally a smart investment. Buyer's title insurance needs to be purchased only once, while title insurance that protects the lender must be purchased each time you borrow or refinance.

Chapter 11

Identity Theft Protection

Identity theft is defined by the United States Department of Justice as "all types of crime in which someone wrongfully obtains and uses another person's personal data in some way that involves fraud or deception, typically for economic gain" *(Identity Theft and Fraud* n.d.). Identity theft is a serious and growing crime in the United States, affecting several million people each year. Some of these crimes can be resolved quickly, with no significant impact to the victim; others can take a long time, requiring legal and other assistance, and cost a lot of money to resolve.

The best defense against identity theft is to prevent it from happening in the first place. If prevention fails, you want to detect it quickly. If you detect or suspect it, you want to take immediate action to prevent or correct any damage, including financial loss or damage to your credit or reputation. Because of the growing awareness of this crime, the difficulty in preventing it, and the time and cost of recovering from it if you are a victim, identity theft insurance is rapidly becoming a part of the solution.

This chapter covers the personal data you should protect, some ways identity thieves obtain this data, and some of the fraudulent and criminal acts they can commit in your name. It also covers things you can do prevent or minimize the chances of identity theft, how it can be detected, and steps you should take if you or a family member become a victim. Finally, identity theft insurance and the services and protection it provides are briefly covered.

Identity Theft

Personal Data

Identity theft occurs when some or all of your personal information is wrongfully obtained, including by those with legal access, and used to commit a criminal act. Protecting this personal data is difficult. There may be a lot of it, and due in large part to our credit-oriented society and increasing use of the Internet, many people potentially have access. What personal data should you be concerned about protecting? Other than your name, address, and phone number, you should protect all other personal information. This includes: Social Security numbers; tax information and returns; financial account information, including account numbers, user and personal identification numbers, passwords, and account statements; driver's licenses; passports; car registrations; health insurance cards, particularly Medicare cards, since they have your Social Security number on them; birth certificates; city of birth; other family member names, including mother's maiden name; e-mail addresses; and beneficiary designation documents.

Protecting your Social Security number is particularly important, since it links a lot of personal information together. Unlike your name, your Social Security number is a unique identifier; no two people have the same number. Because of its uniqueness, it is used as an identifier for most of your personal data and records. The government issues it, and it is used to identify you as a taxpayer and keep track of your tax information and payments into and out of the Social Security and Medicare systems. Many organizations are required to report financial data to the government and need your Social Security number. Other organizations may need it to check your credit.

Pay special attention to protection of your financial account numbers, user and personal identification numbers, and passwords. Use of an ATM machine to get cash, or use of a computer or phone to do online banking or investing is extremely convenient and efficient for both customers and businesses. Anytime you access an account using these devices, however, you expose yourself to possible theft of your personal data. While financial institutions generally provide guarantees that cover financial losses resulting from unauthorized activity in your accounts, you're required to take certain steps and precautions to protect your personal information for these guarantees to apply. Although these steps and precautions are mostly what a reasonable person would consider safe practices, you should read the specifics of your financial company's guarantee to become aware of your responsibilities.

Protecting your credit report is also very important, since your personal identification data and much of your financial data is aggregated in these files, and many people have legal access. Credit reports are prepared by the major credit bureaus from information provided to them by creditors, lenders, landlords, utilities, etc., that you as a consumer have had some type of relationship with. The report contains all kinds of personal information, including identification data, employer, credit score, credit history, any court records that may exist, and a list of companies that have accessed your credit report or were authorized to see it. The reports are prepared for the primary benefit of the credit agencies' customers. The Fair Credit Reporting Act (FCRA) defines who has access. It basically permits organizations you have initiated some type of business relationship with, to gain legal access. Thus, existing creditors and potential lenders—banks, credit card companies, car dealerships, landlords, insurers, and other businesses—have a legal right to access your credit report. They generally need your personal identification data to do so. Potential employers can also view your report, but you must provide written authorization. Different types of customers get different versions. Additionally, telemarketers and other companies can get your name and address from the credit bureaus to send you preapproved credit cards and other offers.

Ways Thieves Can Get Your Personal Data

The Federal Trade Commission (FTC) has identified many common ways that thieves can gain access to your personal information (*About Identity Theft* n.d.). These are included below together with some additional information.

1. **"Dumpster Diving**. They rummage through trash looking for bills or other paper with your personal information on it."
2. **"Skimming**. They steal credit/debit card numbers by using a special storage device when processing your card."

3. **"Phishing.** They pretend to be financial institutions or companies and send spam or pop-up messages to get you to reveal your personal information."

4. **"Changing Your Address**. They divert your billing statements to another location by completing a change of address form."

5. **"Old-Fashioned Stealing**. They steal wallets and purses; mail, including bank and credit card statements; pre-approved credit offers; and new checks or tax information. They steal personnel records, or bribe employees who have access." If they break into your home, they can steal many other things as well, including Social Security cards, tax returns, birth certificates, passports and medical records (if they're kept there). If they steal your car or break into it, they can get your car registration.

6. **"Pretexting**. They use false pretenses to obtain your personal information from financial institutions, telephone companies, and other sources." They do the same thing to get information from you over the phone or to get your credit report from one of the credit agencies.

7. **Other methods**. Some other ways, perhaps not common, and not specifically listed in the above FTC website, but ones you should be concerned about include: stealing personal data by looking over your shoulder as you enter it into a computer in a public place or overhearing you speak it into a phone; intercepting your data with a receiver designed for that purpose, when you use wireless access to the Internet; and use of spyware installed on your computer without your knowledge to steal personal information that you may store or enter into your computer. The latter two methods, although more sophisticated and perhaps less common, nevertheless should be of concern because of the damage that can be done.

Some Ways Thieves Can Use Your Personal Data

Once someone has your personal information, there are many possible ways it can be used to commit criminal acts. What they might be able to do depends on what information they have. Examples are given below:

1. If they have your credit card or credit card number, they can charge merchandise to your name. Also, if they have your credit card, they could get a cell phone and wireless service in your name. A credit check would likely be required, and, if so, they would need your Social Security number.

2. If they have your bank card and password, they can withdraw funds from your bank accounts at an ATM machine.

3. If they have the ID, password, and account number for your brokerage account, they can make trades in your account and perhaps transfer funds to another account.

4. If they have three types of identification belonging to you, one of which is a picture ID (with their photo replacing yours), they can potentially get a driver's license in your name but with their photo. Once they have an official driver's license, there are many other things they can do. If, for example, they have one of your checks and another form of ID, they could make the check out to cash and potentially cash it at your bank.

5. If they have your Social Security number and other information about you, they can do a lot more. With your Social Security number and knowledge of your background, they might be able to get a job using your identification.

6. If they have your Social Security number and birth date, they might be able to rent an apartment in your name and get utility and phone service in your name. Your Social Security number lets the rental agent check your credit.

7. If they have your Social Security number together with a driver's license in your name but with their photo and your employer's name and address, they might be able to buy a car in your name with a loan taken out in your name.

8. If they have your Social Security number and birth certificate, they might be able to get a passport in your name but with their photo.

Steps to Take to Help Prevent Identity Theft

While it is impossible to totally protect yourself from the possibility of identity theft, you can take steps to minimize its probability. Taking steps to protect your personal information is essential. However, even if you do all you can, you remain at the mercy of organizations (including the government) with possession of or access to your personal information. If you think they will fully protect your information, think again. While they have procedures in place, the procedures may not be sufficient, and they must be followed to be effective. As mentioned previously, Medicare puts Social Security numbers on Medicare cards. Why? Probably because it was easy to do originally, and to change now would be very costly. Years ago the Department of Motor Vehicles in Maryland was selling the personal information of car registrants without their permission. More recently there was an article in *Business Week* magazine about how universities were selling students' personal information to the credit card companies. Many institutions can legally share your information with other institutions unless you take steps to prevent it. Read the privacy policy statements that banks and other institutions send you. These statements tell you how they "safeguard" your personal information. Read them carefully, and you'll see the broad range of organizations they actually share your information with, all legal and for your "benefit," of course. Regardless of your dependence on others, you should still do everything you can to protect your personal information. The fewer people and organizations that have your personal data or access to it, the better off you'll be.

In addition to doing what you can to safeguard your personal information, there are certain other things you can do to help prevent identity theft. You can, for example, opt out of allowing sharing of your personal information by institutions, you can place a fraud alert in your files at the credit monitoring agencies, you can freeze your credit files, you can secure your computer, and you can diversify where you hold your financial accounts. Additionally, to protect yourself further, you can buy identity theft insurance.

Safeguard Your Personal Information

To prevent or minimize the chances of anyone getting your personal information, there are a number of things you should do. The FTC has identified many of these (*ID Theft: What It's All About* n.d.). Most are common-sense actions, but they require extra effort, and people don't do them. You should make the following actions habits:

1. Shred all documents and papers containing personal information after you're finished with them. This means shredding all financial documents, bills, credit card offers, etc., before putting them in the trash. It's best to use a shredder that pulverizes the paper rather than one that merely cuts it into strips.

2. Avoid giving out personal information unnecessarily. Most importantly, protect your Social Security number. Many people who ask for it don't really need it. If you must give out personal information, make sure you know the party that you're dealing with and know that they have a legitimate reason for needing the information. Don't give it out in connection with a promotion or a questionnaire, and don't give it out over the phone. Also don't write or have it printed on checks.

3. If at all possible when paying with a credit card, don't let the sales person or waiter/waitress process your card without watching them to ensure that they're not copying your information. If you charge purchases online, use only one card, and one with a low credit limit.

4. Protect your mail. You need to be concerned about both the mail sent to you and the mail you send. To minimize the possibility of mail sent to you being stolen, pick it up daily from your mailbox, or, better yet, if mail theft is a problem in your area, use a post office box. You can also sign up for online delivery of bank and brokerage statements and notifications, and keep this information out of the mail. If you mail anything with your personal information, mail it so it can be tracked, and you know that the party that you mailed it to actually received it. As a minimum, use certified mail. Certified mail has a tracking number, and you can track it online.

5. Protect your passwords. People have passwords for many different things, and they have difficulty remembering them. Thus, many write them down or use phone numbers, mother's maiden name, or some similar device as passwords. Passwords shouldn't use obvious elements that others can figure out if they made the necessary effort. If you do write them down, they shouldn't be kept in your wallet or purse but in a very safe place that only you know about. The best place is a safe deposit box. Also, if you use your password over the phone, don't use it in a public place where

it can be overheard. In addition, if you key in your password, keep in mind that your phone remembers numbers you key in. Additionally, you should always shield the keypad when you enter PIN numbers. Also it makes sense to use different passwords for different things and to change passwords often to make it more difficult for those attempting to steal them.

6. Store personal information in a safe place. Certain documents and information should be stored in a safe deposit box, including Social Security cards, passports, birth certificates, beneficiary designation statements, and passwords, if you have to write them down. We all have various records—bills, tax returns, and other records containing personal information that we keep at home. These should be stored in a place not easily accessible by visitors, outside help or workers, or roommates, if you have them. They should also be difficult for anyone breaking in to find. A good precaution is to remove your Social Security number from documents stored at home.

7. Close accounts that you are not using and do not plan to use. You may have more than one credit card and more than one checking account, and you may have active accounts at various department stores. Stores frequently give discounts to get you to open a charge account. Some people may have so many accounts that they have trouble keeping track of them. The more accounts you have, the more information you have to protect, and the greater chance that someone may obtain access. Close any unneeded accounts, and, when you do, make sure that you get a letter from the firm or credit card company confirming the action. Retain the letter in a safe place. Also, since they still have the legal right to share your information with other institutions even if your accounts are closed, make sure you tell them you don't want your personal information shared with anyone.

Opt Out of Personal Information Sharing

You have the legal right to opt out of personal information sharing by the institutions you do business with. The privacy policy statements or notices they send you define the types of organizations they share your information with, the choices you have to prevent or minimize this sharing, and how you inform them if you want to opt out. These policy statements are generally sent to you when you open an account and then annually thereafter. To minimize the sharing, you must opt out, and if it's a joint account, each of the joint account holders must opt out individually. If you don't opt out, they can share your information, and they likely will.

Set a Fraud Alert

You can place a fraud alert in your credit files by calling one of the three nationwide credit monitoring and reporting agencies. That credit agency will inform the other two agencies. The purpose of the fraud alert is to inform the credit agencies that someone other than you may try to open a credit account in your name. Once a fraud alert is in place, you should be contacted by the agency if anyone attempts to open a credit account in your name. Your phone number is added to the credit report with a note telling the creditor to call prior to extending any credit. Fraud alerts typically remain in effect for ninety days and thus need to be renewed every ninety days, if you want this protection to continue. If you have filed an identity theft report with a law enforcement agency, you can obtain an extended alert that will remain in effect for seven years.

Freeze Your Credit

A powerful way to hinder identity thieves is to freeze your credit files. A credit freeze, or security freeze, as it's called by the credit agencies, prevents anyone from accessing your credit file without your agreement. Thus, it prevents thieves from getting much of your personal data quite easily. Since lenders, for the most part, won't grant credit without checking the creditworthiness of the applicant with the bureaus, this procedure also essentially prevents thieves from obtaining credit in your name. This service was only recently made available to people in all states. Prior to this action, only victims of identity theft could request freezes in most states. It should be noted that many businesses, including the credit bureaus, opposed this legislation, saying it would hurt consumers because it would prevent them from getting instant credit. It would appear that they weren't much interested in giving consumers the ability to restrict access to their reports. At this writing, the service costs $10 per agency each time you initiate the freeze and $10 if you want to lift the freeze, either permanently or temporarily. The freeze needs to be activated and lifted with each of the credit agencies separately. The freeze does not affect existing credit accounts, only new ones. Thus, if you won't need new credit anytime soon, the service is relatively inexpensive for the protection it provides. You must apply for the freeze in writing, and the application requires personal information, including your Social Security number. It should be sent certified mail, with return receipt requested. Specifics may be different for each of the three credit bureaus and can be obtained from their websites.

Keep Your Computer Secure

Many people have personal computers, and they store lots of data on them. If you store personal or financial information on your personal computer, it's vulnerable to theft, and you need to take steps to protect it. A thief can potentially gain access to your data, by stealing the computer itself or by "hacking" into it. If the computer has open access, guests or workers in your home could steal your data. Laptops are particularly vulnerable and can be lost or stolen, especially if you carry them with you. Use of wireless access, increasingly popular, increases your vulnerability. Additionally, if you use your computer for various online financial services, such as banking or investing, you potentially put your money at risk. Although the banking and brokerage sites you access are very secure, and it's in the best interests of these institutions to keep them that way, the potential for problems exists on your end. To access your accounts online you enter your user identification and a password. Anyone in possession of these can access your accounts and perform whatever functions you can perform. That's why it's so important to protect them. While you may not knowingly give them out, it's possible that someone might obtain them by gaining access to or control of your computer with spyware. Spyware can be installed on your computer without your knowledge in a variety of ways. These include software you download from a website offering free software, or software in an e-mail attachment with a virus that infects your computer when you open it. Spyware can provide a thief with access to your financial accounts. Once they have access, they can electronically transfer or withdraw funds from your account or create other problems for you.

To reduce your risk, there are a number of things you should and shouldn't do. Following are some recommendations. Most are from the FTC website previously referenced and another government-run website, OnGuardOnLine (*Investing Wisely On-Line* n.d.).

1. Make accessing data stored on your computer more difficult by using a computer log-in password that only you know. You can also password protect specific files or folders. Biometric hardware devices are also now available that use fingerprint matching for access.

2. Use a firewall, either a hardware or software implementation or both, to protect against unauthorized access. Hardware firewalls are usually part of a router and protect a network; software firewalls are part of a computer's operating system and protect an individual computer. If you have a software firewall in your computer, check to make sure it's been activated and that the appropriate selections have been made to prevent unwanted guests from getting access.

3. Make sure you use antivirus and antispyware software and that it's from reputable sources. Update them often.

4. Set your computer to check for patches and updates to the operating system and have them automatically downloaded and installed. Also keep your web browser up to date.

5. Don't install unknown software of any kind, either downloads or software that's obtained from another person.

6. Don't open files or e-mail attachments, or click on links in e-mail from strangers. Even if you know the source, you still need to be careful.

7. Don't click on pop-ups. Close them instead.

8. If you access your financial accounts online, make sure the site you're using is secure. Secure sites are indicated by a closed lock on the status bar or a website address that begins with "https." The "s" indicates security. Keep in mind, however, that there is no absolute certainty when it comes to security.

9   Minimize the use of wireless access for financial accounts, and don't use a public computer for this purpose. Better yet, don't use wireless access for this purpose either.

10 Don't store financial data or information on a computer you use for Internet access. Either store it on a removable flash memory or use a separate computer.

11. When you are finished using a site, log out completely by clicking on the "logout" button and closing your browser. Don't allow your browser to remember your username and password. If you have a high-speed Internet connection to your computer, shut your computer down when not in use.

12. When you dispose of your computer, delete all personal data, and use a special utility that overwrites the entire hard drive. Better yet, remove the hard drive and destroy it.

Diversify Your Financial Account Institutions

Many people have several types of financial accounts, e.g., checking, savings, equity lines of credit, investment, etc., and many have all their accounts at the same institution. It is certainly convenient to do all your financial business at one institution, and, additionally, organizations encourage it, and they may make it attractive by offering better interest rates and other benefits. If, however, you are concerned with someone fraudulently obtaining and using your personal information to illegally transfer or withdraw funds from your accounts, you can reduce your risk by utilizing different institutions for different accounts. Most financial institutions make it more difficult to move or transfer funds to an account outside their institution than they do to move funds among accounts within their institution. To transfer funds from one account to another within the same institution usually requires nothing more than a user ID and password. Many institutions actually preclude electronic transfer of funds to an account outside their institution unless a specific channel and receiving site are set up. The bill pay function in online banking, however, allows payments to individuals as well to businesses. Thus, a thief with your user ID and password could transfer money from your savings or equity line of credit to your checking account and then, using the bill pay function, pay money to themselves or other conspirators. These payments would most likely be by check, and the individual receiving the fraudulent check still has to cash it to draw funds from your account. Personally, I think the online bill pay function coupled with the ease of transferring funds between accounts at the same institution is risky. A much safer approach would be to have your savings and investment accounts at one institution and your checking account with online banking at a different one.

Identity Theft Detection

Since it is nearly impossible to totally protect yourself from the possibility of identity theft, it is important to detect any evidence of possible identity theft as soon as possible. This requires that you be observant. You should monitor and carefully check all the data available to you. Be alert to suspicious or irregular activity involving your personal information and particularly your finances. Following are some actions recommended by the FTC.

Check all the financial information that comes to you—bills, bank and credit account statements, and brokerage account statements. Make sure that you receive bills and statements when you expect them. If you don't receive them in a timely manner, it's possible that they may have been delivered to the wrong address (if you have them mailed) or stolen or that an identity thief has changed your address. In any case, your personal information may have fallen into the wrong hands. If this happens don't just ignore it; follow up to determine what actually happened. When you receive your bills and statements, review them promptly and in detail to ensure that all activity was either done or authorized by you. If you access your financial accounts online, check them frequently for any irregularities.

A good way to detect potential problems is to monitor credit activity in your name. The three nationwide credit monitoring agencies—Equifax, Experian, and Transunion—maintain credit records. You should review your credit report periodically. You are entitled by law to receive a free credit report once each year from each of the three agencies. Alternately you can sign up for continuous monitoring and reporting of credit activity. There are a variety of companies providing this service, including the credit monitoring agencies themselves. Some of these services provide continuous access to your credit report, including alerts when changes and inquiries occur. Others only provide periodic updates.

Other suspicious or irregular activities you should be on the lookout for include receipt of or denial of a credit card you did not apply for. Obviously, you should also be concerned if you receive a bill for items you didn't purchase; a bill or statement for an account that you didn't open; or calls, letters, or other correspondence from collection agencies or companies for charges or bills you're not responsible for.

What to Do If You're a Victim

If you are a victim of identity theft or suspect you are a victim, there are a number of actions you should take immediately. These actions will help to minimize or prevent damage to your finances and your reputation as well as begin investigations by the appropriate authorities. Following are brief descriptions of actions recommended by the Department of Justice and the Federal Trade Commission on their websites:

1. Contact the FTC to report the situation and file a complaint. The FTC is the government organization responsible for handling and coordinating complaints from people who suspect they may be victims. The FTC's toll free number is 1-877-ID THEFT. Depending on the nature of the theft, you might also need to contact other organizations: the Postal Inspection Service, if the mail was involved; the Social Security Administration, if your Social Security number was involved; or the Internal Revenue Service, if taxes were involved.

2. Call the fraud units of the three major nationwide credit reporting agencies to report your concerns and to set fraud alerts on your credit reports. Phone numbers are: Equifax, 800-525-6285; Experian, 888-397-3747; and Trans Union, 800-680-7289. Setting fraud alerts lets you get a free copy of your credit report from each of the agencies. You, however, need to request them. Read the reports carefully to determine what's happening. See the section entitled "Set a Fraud Alert" for more information.

3. Contact all creditors and institutions involved and speak with someone that handles fraud. Close all accounts in which your name or identifying data have been used fraudulently or that you suspect might have been tampered with. To be safe, I would also call all other organizations that I had accounts with just to alert them.

4. File an identity theft report with police, either your local police or the police in the community where the theft occurred. Some

states, but apparently not all of them, have laws requiring local police departments to accept the report. If your local police are unreceptive, try the state police, or the state attorney general's office.

You should keep detailed records of all correspondence with organizations you've contacted. Retain copies of all identity theft reports and complaints you've filed, and follow up phone contacts with letters confirming the action. Send all correspondence certified mail, with return receipt requested.

For more detail on actions you should take, consult the US Department of Justice and the Federal Trade Commission identity theft and fraud websites.

Identity Theft Insurance

A number of companies offer identity theft protection services, including identity theft insurance. Identity theft insurance is different than credit monitoring. The credit bureaus and others provide credit monitoring. A credit monitoring service does just that; they monitor your credit and provide you with copies of your credit report, either by mail or online, and in some cases they provide an alert if someone tries to open credit in your name. Identity theft protection services do things to try to prevent identity theft, and they cover the cost of restoring your credit, good name, and lost funds if you're a victim. Different companies provide somewhat different services and protection (*Identity Theft Protection Services* n.d.). Benefits can include:

1. Credit reports—either quarterly or annually.
2. Credit monitoring—monitor credit files at credit bureaus and provide alerts.
3. Prevention—set and renew fraud alerts in your credit files.
4. Fraud monitoring—monitoring of websites for illegal activities involving your personal information and changes of address.
5. Mail list removal—have your name removed from preapproved credit offers and junk mail.

6. Wallet loss assistance—help cancel affected accounts and take steps necessary to replace them. Also help to get lost documents replaced.
7. ID theft insurance—basically identity restoration insurance that manages and pays for efforts required to restore your good name and lost funds in the event you become a victim.

These insurance services generally cost about $10 to $15 per month per adult. Most companies offer discounts if you pay for a year's service in advance. You could actually do some of these services yourself for free. However, some of these functions need to be done over and over again and take discipline and effort on your part. If you buy the insurance, you're paying the company to do the work and to provide the insurance protection. Even if you buy the insurance, however, you still need to take actions necessary to guard your personal data and prevent becoming a victim of identity theft in the first place.

Chapter 12

Estate Planning

The primary purpose of estate planning is to ensure that your intentions are carried out as closely as possible when you die and to maximize transmission of your wealth to the parties you choose. How do you hold title to the property you own? Do you need a trust, or is a will good enough? How do you minimize or avoid estate taxes? The answers to these questions and others like them are the province of estate planning.

Like retirement planning, estate planning requires thinking through what it is that you want to do. To do it right requires specialized knowledge. Even in the early planning stage, most people should get professional help. Use of a qualified estate-planning attorney is very important in implementing your plan. Before seeking professional help, however, you should have a basic understanding of what the process entails and the choices you have. Professional help can be expensive, and the more you know about the subject, the more likely you are to set up a plan that implements your intentions at a reasonable cost. You can often get invited to free seminars on the subject. These can be quite good, and I advise you to take advantage of the opportunity to learn and to evaluate the speakers as professionals that you might want to hire in the future. There are also many good books on the subject. Two that I've used are: *Protect Your Estate* and *Encyclopedia of Estate Planning*.

Your estate plan may require use of a will, or it may involve the use of several trusts. What you need and how involved the plan needs to be depends largely on the size of your estate and your preferences. Your first step should be to determine and define your intentions. Do you want to leave all your assets to your spouse, or do you want to leave them to your children but give your spouse use of them while she is alive? Do you want your children to get the assets outright on your death or your spouse's death, or do you want them held in trust for your children and only allow them to have a certain amount each year? Beneficiary documents, a property title, a will, or a revocable trust can be changed during your lifetime. On your death, however, they become irrevocable, so it is of the utmost importance that they accurately reflect your intentions.

Depending on the size of your taxable estate, it may be subject to estate taxes, and present rates are very high. There are, however, many things you can do to minimize or avoid them. Some are easy to do, and others require expert knowledge.

Finally, there is the matter of information. Your executor should know the assets and liabilities you have and the location of important documents. A good way to do this is in a letter. Writing this information down in one place will ease the process for your heirs and minimize the chance that something is forgotten.

Estate Planning Tools

Estate planning can be relatively simple, or it can be complicated. Generally the more you try to do, the more involved it gets. The more wealth you have and the more control you want to exercise over how it is spent, the more likely the plan will end up being complex. There are various tools available to implement your intentions, and you should understand as much as you can about what they can and cannot do.

How you hold title to property that you have an interest in determines whether you have a legal right to leave it to persons of your choosing. If you hold title jointly there is a right of survivorship that governs, and the surviving partner or partners automatically get full title to the property after your death, no matter what your will or trust may say. There are also possible tax consequences to how you hold title to property.

Beneficiary designations control the passing of certain types of assets to heirs. Even if you have a will or a trust, you still need to make beneficiary designations for insurance policies and pension type assets. Designating beneficiaries is simple and straightforward and costs you nothing.

Many people have wills, but not many understand what a will can or cannot do. A will by itself is insufficient for many people; it can only control the transfer of some of the property they might own. Also, a will must go through the probate process, and probate takes time and costs money.

Much of estate planning can be accomplished with a trust, and there are a variety of different types. To be useful, however, a trust, once created, must be funded. You fund a trust by putting property into it either during your life or after your death. Trusts can allow the maker (the person for whom the trust is made) to exercise considerable control over the trust property even after their death.

When should you get started? Actually, the sooner you get started the better. If you've named beneficiaries for insurance policies and/or retirement plans, you've already begun. How much more you should do depends on the assets you've accumulated and whether you have children. The information in the next few pages should help you get started.

Property Ownership

Private property is of two basic types: real property and personal property. Real property is basically real estate. Personal property is all property other than real property and includes things like motor vehicles, various financial assets, and intellectual property.

Real estate is land and all the structures permanently attached to it. It includes everything that is a natural part of land such as trees, minerals, and water. There is a set, or "bundle of rights," associated with the ownership of real estate. These include the right to use, lease, sell, or give away all or only a portion of a real estate property. If you own property, you could own all or only some of the rights. If you own only some of the rights, you have a partial interest in the property. If you own all the rights, you could, for example, sell or lease the entire property or only the buildings, or you could sell or lease only the mineral rights. (Shea-Joyce 1992, 6).

How do you own property? How do you legally hold title to it? These are important questions that affect the value of your estate, the amount of estate taxes you might be subject to, and your right to transfer property when you die. Private property can be owned individually or together with others. Following are brief descriptions of various ways to own property, with the rights each gives you.

Fee-Simple

If you own property fee-simple, you own it entirely, including all rights associated with absolute ownership. You can use, lease, sell, or give away all or only a portion of the property or the property rights. You can leave the entire property or partial interests in the property to whomever you want on your death. The value of the portion you still own at your death is part of your gross estate.

Tenancy in Common

Tenancy in common is property ownership with other people. If you hold title to property this way, you own your share or percentage absolutely. You can sell your share, give it away, or leave it to whomever you choose at your death. There is *no right* of survivorship, i.e., if one party dies, the other parties do not automatically acquire the dead party's share. The value of the portion you own at your death becomes part of your gross estate.

Joint Tenancy

Joint tenancy is a type of ownership with other people but has the right of survivorship. Survivorship means that as each of the joint owners dies, the remaining owners automatically acquire title to the dead person's interest in the property. While the parties are alive, this form of ownership functions like tenancy in common. That is, each party can give away or sell their interest in the property, but then the new party owns it jointly with the other parties. With joint tenancy you *cannot* pass title of your interest via a will or trust. If the property is owned jointly with your spouse, one half of the value of the property becomes part of your gross estate. If it is owned jointly with others, the value of the entire property might be part of your gross estate. The executor of your estate would need to justify taking any other position.

Tenancy by the Entirety

Tenancy by the entirety is another kind of joint ownership. A husband and wife sometimes use this method for ownership of real estate, and it works very much like joint tenancy. That is, upon the death of one of the parties, the other automatically acquires full title to the property. The difference is that while both are alive and married, there is *no right* to split the property. As with joint tenancy, you cannot pass title of your interest via a will or trust. Since this form of joint ownership is between a husband and wife, one half of the value of the property becomes part of your gross estate when you die.

Community Property

At this writing ten states have community property laws. Arizona is such a state. In a community property state, property acquired during marriage generally belongs to both husband and wife, and each owns 50%. The property each owned before marriage remains their individual property. Gifts or inheritances received by either party during marriage belong to the recipient. Individually owned property, money for example, can become community property if it is commigled with community property. Community property laws vary from state to state. In some states, property can be held as community property with a right of survivorship similar to that of joint tenancy.

Deeds, Title Documents, and Evidence of Ownership

The United States has a well-established private property system, and recorded deeds and title documents are used for many types of private property.

Deeds are ordinarily used to show ownership of real estate and to transfer title. Property deeds need to be recorded by the recorder of deeds in the county in which the property is located.

Title documents are used to designate and transfer ownership of motor vehicles. A transfer form is on the back of the title document. When you transfer ownership, it is important to notify the Department of Motor Vehicles where the vehicle is registered to ensure the vehicle is no longer registered in your name.

Intellectual property ownership in the United States is usually indicated by copyright, patent, trademark, or similar means granted by an entity of government. Intellectual property rights are usually transferred by contract.

Retirement (IRA, 401(k), etc.) plans are set up in the name of the owner, using his or her Social Security number as an additional identifier. Ownership of IRAs, 401(k)s, and other pension holdings are transferred by beneficiary designations at the owner's death.

Ownership of personal property for which there is no title document is often determined by possession. A purchase receipt can often help provide proof of ownership.

Deeds and titles for all private property you own should be retained and stored in a safe place, preferably a safe deposit box.

Beneficiary Designations

Certain types of assets are normally transferred to heirs by beneficiary designations that you make while you are alive. These assets include life insurance policies, IRAs, 401(k)s, and other types of pension and fringe benefits. You should designate both primary and contingent beneficiaries. When you die, these assets become part of your gross estate, but they belong to the named beneficiaries. If you name an adult or a living trust as the beneficiary, the proceeds can avoid probate court. Be aware, however, that for retirement plans governed by the Employee Retirement Income Security Act such as 401(k) plans, spouses have certain rights, and beneficiary designations need to comply with the plan rules.

A few states (Arizona included) allow real estate to be legally transferred by a beneficiary document, called a beneficiary deed. A beneficiary deed functions like other beneficiary documents in that it transfers ownership, effective on the death of the owner, directly to the beneficiary or beneficiaries without probate court involvement. Unlike other beneficiary documents but like other real estate, deeds must be recorded in the office of the recorder of deeds for the county in which the property is located prior to the death of the last remaining owner to be valid. The owner can change or revoke a beneficiary deed at any time prior to his or her death, but the change must be recorded. There may also be tax consequences to use of a beneficiary deed. Before deciding to use a beneficiary deed, the individual should consult with an experienced estate-planning attorney to fully understand both the benefits and possible problems. (*Avoiding Probate with a Beneficiary Deed* n.d.).

The custodian or provider of the asset or benefit should send you a beneficiary designation form. After naming your beneficiaries and signing the form, you should retain a copy and forward the original to the custodian or provider. They should return a signed copy, and you should retain it in a safe place as part of your records. Beneficiary designations should be kept up to date. It is particularly important to do this when you get married or if you get divorced. It is very important that you understand that the beneficiary designations control the transmission of these assets to your heirs. Also, if you do not name a beneficiary the courts will decide who gets these assets.

Wills

A will is a legal statement, usually a document, of an individual's directions for the disposition of his or her property after death. It specifies who is to receive the property and when they are to get it. If you have left a legally valid will, you have died "testate." If you die without a will, you have died "intestate," and the courts will distribute your property according to state laws.

A will can only control the transfer of some of the property you might own. A will *cannot* direct the disposition of property that has a named beneficiary. Insurance policies and retirement plans such as IRAs and 401(k)s have beneficiary designations, and a will cannot countermand the named beneficiaries. *Nor* can a will control the disposition of jointly owned property such as a home, since this form of ownership has a right of survivorship. On your death, property held this way goes to the surviving joint owner or owners. You have no right to bequeath "your portion" of joint property to anyone no matter what your will may say. Many people don't understand this and believe they have the right to leave "their portion" to whomever they choose through their will. Sadly for their intended heirs, they don't.

Also, even with a valid, well-written will, you might not have complete control over what happens to your property. State laws may require that you leave a certain percentage to your surviving spouse or to surviving children, regardless of what the will may say.

A will needs to be filed with the local probate court after the maker dies. Once it goes to probate, it's open to the public. Probate is the process of proving that the will, submitted as a last will and testament, is genuine.

The probate court also supervises the distribution of property to heirs (after making sure that creditors are paid), but only that property that legally passes through the will. Probate costs money and takes time, sometimes a long time. Probate fees vary considerably from state to state and can be substantial in some. Your estate pays these fees.

A qualified attorney should write a will. The maker should review the document, making sure that he or she understands the language and that it complies with their intentions.

A properly written will should name an executor or executors to administer your estate. The executor's job is to file the will with the probate court, locate all your assets, ensure that all tax returns are prepared and filed, pay your debts including funeral costs, and dispose of remaining probate assets in accordance with your stated intentions. The executor must coordinate the dispersal of funds with the probate court. If you don't name an executor, the court will appoint an administrator for your estate.

A will can be amended or completely rewritten and replaced while you are alive. It cannot be changed after your death, thus you should make sure that any current will reflects your intentions as accurately as possible.

Trusts

Trusts are the most comprehensive of the estate planning tools, and there are many different types. They permit people to transfer property either during their lifetime or at their death and, in many cases, to exercise considerable control over their property even after death. As the authors of the book *Protect Your Estate* say, "trusts allow property to be passed to others with 'strings attached'." (Robert A. Esperti 1993, 84). Many books have been written on trusts; only the very basics are discussed here. The person for whom the trust is created is called the maker; the person administering the trust is called the trustee.

There are two basic categories of trusts: living trusts and death trusts. The most common type is the living trust, and only living trusts are discussed here.

Living trusts are created while the maker is still alive, and there are two types: revocable and irrevocable. Revocable living trusts, as the name implies, can be changed or revoked by the maker while he or she is living.

Irrevocable trusts are just that; once they are created, they cannot be changed or revoked, except possibly by the courts. A revocable living trust becomes irrevocable when the maker dies. Trusts, to be useful, must be funded. The maker funds them by transferring property into them either during their lifetime or after their death. This is done either by retitling property in the name of the trust during the maker's lifetime or by making the trust the beneficiary of certain property, using beneficiary designation forms. Pour over wills, usually written in conjunction with trusts, are also used to put property into trusts after the death of their makers. With a revocable living trust you can move property in or out of the trust, if you so desire, anytime during your life. (Robert A. Esperti 1993, 91-93).

Not everyone, however, needs a trust. The most often cited advantage is that they avoid probate. While this is true, property with beneficiary designations, such as life insurance, retirement plans, and even real estate in some states, avoids probate. If the total value of your other property is less than the minimum probate requirement, you can completely avoid probate without a trust. Additionally, just because you have a trust doesn't mean you avoid probate. Only those assets actually in the trust avoid probate; hence it must be properly funded. Also, a husband and wife don't need a trust to each take full advantage of the unified tax credit; they only need to title sufficient assets in each of their names. Use of a trust, however, can provide flexibility in the passing of assets not provided by simply retitling assets. A trust can, for example, allow a surviving spouse use of assets during their lifetime, rather than transferring assets fully to children or others on one's death as would otherwise be necessary to make full use of the unified tax credit. Trusts, however, cost money, anywhere from $500 to many thousands of dollars, and they need to be kept up to date.

Generally the more wealth you have and the more control you want to exercise over how it's spent after your death, the more likely you are to benefit from having a trust. A comprehensive trust written by a qualified estate-planning attorney can accomplish virtually anything you want. Trusts can be complicated and are not easily understood. They are written in legal language, and they are full of decisions that you have technically made but most likely don't fully understand. Even assuming that the implementation is perfect, there is ample opportunity for mistakes. You may not, for example, have fully thought through some of the decisions you made or not fully understand the consequences of these decisions, or the lawyer drawing up the plan may not have fully understood what you wanted to do or adequately explained the consequences. There is no substitute for understanding, and you should make sure you understand to the fullest extent possible what the trust documents say and do. The documents need to be read and reread until you do understand them. If you don't understand them, ask the attorney questions and continue to ask questions until you do. Once you sign them and you die, you are locked in. If you sign them but later discover that they don't do what you intended or your intentions change, they can be modified or redone. Trusts also need to be reviewed periodically, not just created and forgotten.

Tax Considerations

Tax considerations are an important part of estate planning. No estate planning or poor estate planning can result in substantial taxes on the wealth that you transmit to your heirs, while good planning can minimize or potentially eliminate these taxes for most people. Taxes to be concerned about include gift and estate taxes, and income taxes that the beneficiaries of deferred income and pension assets might be subject to. The primary estate tax is the federal estate tax; however, states also have estate taxes in one form or another. Information on federal estate and gift taxes can be obtained from the latest version of IRS *Publication 950, Introduction to Estate and Gift Taxes,* and the instructions for form 706, the tax form used to file an estate tax return.

Gift taxes are imposed on the person making the gift, and estate taxes are imposed on estates above a certain minimum amount. Gifts and inheritances that people receive are not considered income to them, so in general there is no income tax on the value of these. However, there are income tax consequences resulting from inheritance of deferred income type assets, including pensions.

Gifts of money or property made during your life that exceed the annual exclusion amount are subject to the federal gift tax; estate taxes are levied on the value of your taxable estate, and beneficiaries pay the income taxes on deferred income as they withdraw funds from these accounts or as they receive pension checks. Because there is a unified tax credit, however, gift and estate taxes are only due on gifts and estates over certain amounts, and under current law these values are relatively high. Tax laws, however, are subject to change, and you need to be cognizant of any changes and be prepared to modify your plan as appropriate.

The various taxes and some of the strategies that you can employ to minimize these taxes are discussed in the following pages. These sections are intended to give you a general knowledge of the subject, make you aware of some of some of the choices you have, and encourage planning. Before implementing any of these, you should speak to knowledgeable estate-planning and tax specialists.

Gift Taxes

Gift taxes apply to gifts of money or property you make that exceed the annual gift tax exclusion. The annual gift tax exclusion applies separately to each person you make a gift to. Gifts to your spouse, to charity, or paid directly to an institution for college tuition or medical expenses, however, are not subject to the tax. If married, you and your spouse can each separately give up to the annual exclusion amount to the same person without incurring the tax. The individual annual exclusion for 2010 was $ 13,000, and it remains at that level for 2011. Thus if you are married, you and your spouse together could give $26,000 to each person in 2010 and also 2011. The annual exclusion could increase in the future due to inflation.

If you give more than the annual exclusion amount to any one person other than your spouse, you must file a gift tax return for that year. If you or your spouse makes a gift of more than the annual exclusion, it can be considered as coming one half from you and one half from your spouse. This is called gift splitting. If, however, it exceeds your individual gift exclusion, you must file a gift tax return to show that you and your spouse agreed to use gift splitting. To avoid having to file a gift tax return, you should each individually write a check for your portions of the gift.

Unified Tax Credit

Under the old law, the credit for estate taxes increased from $345,800 in 2002 to $1,455,800 in 2009 while that for gifts remained fixed at $345,800. The corresponding exclusion amounts (amounts of taxable estates exempt from federal estate taxes) increased from $1 million to $3.5 million. Also, under the old law, there was no estate tax for tax year 2010, and the estate tax laws were scheduled to revert back to the 2002 level for years 2011 and beyond.

The estate tax laws, however, were modified in December 2010, increasing the individual exclusion amount to $5 million (an estate tax credit of $1,730,800) for tax years 2011 and 2012. There is also a portability provision in the new law for 2011 and 2012 that potentially allows any unused exemption amount to be used by a spouse. The gift tax exclusion also increases to $5 million for tax years 2011 and 2012. Both the estate and gift tax levels are scheduled to revert back to those of 2002 for tax years 2013 and beyond. The new law means that very few people will owe any federal estate taxes for 2010, 2011, and 2012 (How the new tax law may affect you 2010). You can, however, expect that the estate tax laws will be revisited again for tax years 2013 and beyond. The levels will likely be determined by the outcome of the 2012 elections.

You can apply the unified credit to any gift tax that you might owe. The credit used reduces the amount of remaining lifetime credit you have for gifts made in future years and the amount which your estate will have available to offset any estate taxes due when you die. As a practical matter, this means that most people can give away a substantial amount of money or property during their lifetime without actually having to pay any gift taxes.

Federal Estate Taxes

To properly do estate planning, you need to know the approximate value of your final estate and if married that of your spouse. Since neither of you know when you will die, the best you can do is to estimate the current value and continue to do this throughout your lives. If you have been measuring your individual or household net worth periodically, as discussed in chapter 2 on personal net worth, you have a good start on estimating the value of your taxable estates. It is important that individuals make estimates of the value of their death estates periodically just as they should make estimates of their net worth. Married individuals should make estimates two ways: first, assuming that they die first, and, second, assuming that their spouse dies first. If this is done, they should have a good idea of whether their individual estates may be subject to estate taxes and if they need insurance to cover these taxes. They will also know if they need to take steps to reduce their estates to avoid or minimize these taxes.

Keep in mind that insurance policy benefits become part of the policy owner's estate when they die.

An individual's taxable estate is their gross estate minus certain allowable deductions. For estate tax purposes, you want your taxable estate to be as small as legally possible, even though your ego may want you to make it high.

Your gross estate includes the value of all property that you had an ownership interest in at the time of your death. Thus, to estimate your gross estate you need to know how you hold title to property. In general the value used in your taxable estate is equal to the proportion that you own at your death. For property held jointly with your spouse, the courts have ruled that half the value is considered yours for tax purposes. As stated in IRS *Publication 950 (Rev. December 2009)*, the following are also included in your gross estate:

1. Life insurance proceeds payable to your estate or, if you owned the policy, to your heirs;
2. The value of certain annuities payable to your estate or your heirs;
3. The value of certain property you transferred within 3 years before your death.

Life insurance proceeds can be kept out of your gross estate by creating an irrevocable life insurance trust that owns the policies.

In determining your taxable estate, you are allowed certain deductions from your gross estate. According to IRS *Publication 950*, these include:

1. Funeral expenses paid out of your estate,
2. Debts that you owed at the time of your death,
3. The marital deduction (generally, the value of the property that passes from your estate to your surviving spouse),
4. The charitable deduction (generally, the value of the property that passes from your estate to the United States, any state, a political subdivision of a state, the District of Columbia, or to a qualifying charity for exclusively charitable purposes), and
5. The state death tax deduction (generally any estate, inheritance, legacy, or succession taxes paid as the result of the decedent's death to any state or the District of Columbia.)

The full marital deduction is allowed only if the spouse is a US citizen. You are also allowed to deduct certain administrative expenses paid out of your estate (see the instructions for tax form 706).

You and your spouse are also each individually allowed a tax credit to reduce your estate taxes. The credit applicable to estate taxes is the amount of the unified tax credit discussed in the previous section less any amount used for gift taxes. It is important to understand that while the credit is available to both a husband and wife individually, assets must be titled properly for both to be able to claim the credit, except for tax years 2011 and 2012, in which the credit is portable and any unused amount can potentially be used by a spouse, as mentioned previously.

State "Death Taxes"

While federal estate taxes have declined in recent years, the same cannot be said about estate taxes imposed by the states. States have various ways to obtain "death taxes." Some have estate taxes, and some have inheritance taxes. All states, however, have probate systems of some type that charge fees to probate an estate.

Before 2005, federal estate tax laws provided a credit for estate taxes paid to the states, and many states imposed just this amount of tax. The federal credit was eliminated in 2005 and replaced with a deduction for actual taxes paid to the states or to the District of Columbia. Also, the exclusion amount for federal estate taxes has increased substantially since 2002, resulting in fewer people actually being subject to federal estate taxes. Because of these federal tax law changes, states have generally made changes in their laws to make up for the declining revenues.

So-called "inheritance tax" states tax the amounts that pass to beneficiaries rather than the estate itself. Typically, these states have tax rates that depend on the relationship of the beneficiary to the deceased. The closer the relationship, the lower the tax rate and the amount of inheritance tax.

Probate fees in many states are small, and the process is relatively quick. In some states, California and Florida, for example, probate can be time consuming and expensive.

It's a good idea to understand both the probate and estate tax system for the state applicable to your estate. The article "State Estate Taxes," included in the reference list, provides a convenient way to find out about the estate and inheritance taxes applicable to the fifty states, the District of Columbia, and Puerto Rico, and is a good place to start. While it's always important to get help on estate planning from a qualified estate-planning attorney, it's particularly important if you live in one of the states with high "death taxes."

Inherited IRAs

An IRA beneficiary can be any person or entity the owner wants to receive the benefits when the owner dies. The money in a traditional IRA, unless it has a basis, is considered deferred income, since no income taxes have yet been paid on it. Even though the decedent's estate may have paid estate taxes on the value of the IRA, the government still wants the income taxes. Beneficiaries of traditional IRAs must include IRA withdrawals or distributions in their gross income for the year in which they receive the distributions, and they must pay any income taxes that are due.

It is highly beneficial from an investment point of view for the recipient of an IRA to defer income taxes as long as possible. With deferral you get to use the tax money for investment. Chapter 5 discussed the advantages of deferring taxes. You cannot, however, keep funds in a traditional IRA forever. The owner of a traditional IRA must generally take a certain minimum distribution each year starting with the year they turn 70½. The amount that must be taken each year is called the required minimum distribution (RMD). The owner, however, has until April 1 of the year following the year they turn 70½ to take the initial minimum distribution, but they must also take the next distribution by December 31 of that year. Individuals that are *beneficiaries* of traditional IRAs must begin taking distributions under the rules for beneficiaries. The rules are complicated and won't be discussed in detail here. Generally, however, beneficiaries must begin taking distributions in the year following the death of the owner. Rules are contained in IRS *Publication 590* on IRAs. If distributions are not taken when or in the amount required, severe penalties might be imposed.

Beneficiaries of traditional IRAs have choices to make. These are also defined in IRS *Publication 590*. Anyone with an IRA should understand these choices and make sure that their heirs understand them. Basically your beneficiary can withdraw all the funds within five years and pay the income taxes, or they can "stretch" the IRA. If they cash it out, the added income may put them in a tax bracket where they pay over 40% of the total value of the IRA in taxes (including federal, state, and local). If they stretch the IRA, they reduce the amount of each required distribution and likely the tax rate, and they can continue investing the remaining money. The specific choices depend on whether you inherited the IRA from your spouse or from someone other than your spouse.

Inherited from Spouse

If you inherit a traditional IRA from your spouse, you can basically treat it as your own or treat yourself as the beneficiary. You treat it as your own by designating yourself as the owner or by rolling it over into another IRA you own. If it's treated as owned by the spouse, the rules for owners apply. If you treat yourself as the beneficiary, the rules for beneficiaries apply.

Inherited from Someone Other than Spouse

If you inherit an IRA from someone other than your spouse, you *cannot* treat it as your own. You *cannot* make contributions to it or roll it over into an account in your name. What you can do, *and this is extremely important*, is make a trustee-to-trustee transfer of the IRA and retitle it in the name of the deceased owner but for the benefit of you as the beneficiary. If you do this properly you will be able to stretch the IRA. If you are younger than the deceased, this means that your minimum distributions are smaller, and the IRA lasts longer. You figure your required minimum distributions by dividing the value of your IRA at the end of each year by your life expectancy from the appropriate table in IRS *Publication 590*. Keep in mind that if you inherit a traditional IRA from someone other than your spouse, you *cannot* wait until after 70½ to begin taking distributions. You must begin taking distributions under the rules for beneficiaries. If you don't take the minimum distributions as required, severe financial penalties can be imposed as stated previously.

Letter to Personal Representative/Heirs

An important part of estate planning is providing the people charged with administering your estate with easy access to the information and records they need to properly do their job. The person charged with administering your estate has different titles in different situations and states. The person may be called an executor (will), an administrator (no will), a trustee (trust), or a personal representative.

In any event the person, let's use the title personal representative, has a multitude of tasks to perform. These include handling the probate process if necessary, ensuring that all necessary tax returns are filed, all taxes are paid, and all creditors are paid, and that your remaining property is distributed to your beneficiaries and heirs.

To accomplish the various tasks is no easy job, and it can be time consuming and expensive. Even with all the information, the job can be difficult, particularly if the person has little or no experience. Without the information, it can be a major task. It can also be expensive if significant legal assistance is required. Identifying and finding a dead person's property without records likely would be very frustrating and might be nearly impossible. Additionally, the property must be valued. Legally this is required to be the fair market value; however, there can be legitimate disagreement as to what the fair market value is. It can make a big difference. To minimize any possible estate taxes, you want property values to be as low as legally possible. However, if the property is the type that could subsequently increase in value, your heirs may find it advantageous if it is valued as high as possible, since inherited property currently gets a step up in basis. Identifying and finding creditors can also be difficult. Completing the decedent's final income tax return and estate tax return, if necessary, requires specific information perhaps known only to the deceased.

You can make completion of these tasks as easy and inexpensive as possible by gathering the necessary information while you are alive, and putting it in a place where your personal representative can easily get it after you die. No one knows better than you what you own and what debts you have and where applicable information is located. A good way is to write a letter to your personal representative, identifying important information and where all the records are located. A good source for the type of information that should be in the letter is chapter

44 of the *Encyclopedia of Estate Planning* (Tuozzolo 1998). Some of the information the letter should include are: the location of your latest will, trust, beneficiary documents, and other important documents such as birth certificate, marriage license, and divorce papers, if any; a list of all your assets, how they're owned, and where titles and deeds are located, together with your estimates of the value of these assets; checking accounts, savings accounts, brokerage accounts, IRAs, 401(k)s, and the like should be identified, together with the name of the institution where held; insurance policies should also be similarly identified, together with the location of actual policies; a list of all liabilities you have, including mortgages, equity loans, credit cards, student loans, personal loans, etc., together with identification of the lender and the current values of these liabilities; location of income tax returns of prior years and data you have for preparation of the current year's return; and names and location of your insurance agent, lawyer, accountant, brokers, and other professionals you deal with. Explanatory information that might be helpful should also be included in the letter. If possible, you should review the information with your personal representative to minimize possible misunderstandings later. You may not get all the information in the first draft of the letter, but you can continue to add information. Also, since things change, the letter should be reviewed periodically and updated as necessary. My letter has been updated many times.

Chapter 13

Summary and Recommendations

The previous chapters covered topics about money and personal finance that I believe are important for adults of all ages to understand. This chapter provides a brief summary of the material and some general financial guidance and recommendations.

Money matters. It has a large influence on our lives, and it's much easier to be happy with it than without it. Money creates opportunities and can provide economic security. There's a lot to know about money, and you should take every opportunity to learn about it. Read and study financial books and articles. The citations in the book and documents listed in the reference list are good sources of additional information. Attend lectures you hear about, take formal courses, and speak with knowledgeable people when you get the opportunity.

Money is a medium of exchange and a measure and store of value. Money has earnings power. It can earn more money and when accumulated becomes wealth. The value of money, however, is not constant; it's purchasing power decreases during inflationary times and increases during periods of deflation. Because of its earnings power, money, independent of the purchasing power, has a time value. The money you have now has a potential future value much greater than its present value, and money you expect to receive in the future has a present value less than the amount you expect to receive in the future.

Net worth is a measure of wealth. Household net worth is the value of household assets minus liabilities. All adults should know how to calculate their net worth and should do so periodically. To do this with reasonable accuracy, you need to know how to value assets and liabilities.

Savings and successful investments increase your net worth. Gifts and any inheritance you might receive also add to it. If you are managing your finances properly, your net worth should be increasing over time.

Good management of your money is essential if you are to accumulate any significant amount or preserve what you already have. For most people, money accumulation requires disciplined savings, smart investments, and time. Spending control is key to being able to save, and minimizing taxes and finance charges makes saving much easier. Avoiding financial pitfalls and setbacks allows you to preserve what you have accumulated. Insurance provides protection for many of life's financial risks, and retirement and estate planning make it more likely that you will be able to enjoy your retirement years and to transfer more of your wealth to intended heirs.

Money can be used for consumption spending or saved and invested. Consumption expenditures are generally for near-term needs and enjoyment while savings and investments are for the future, and there should be a balance of the two. Most people, if they manage their money wisely, could save a significant amount, but to do so, spending must be controlled. Track your spending so you know where your money goes.

Don't spend foolishly; buy only what you need and can afford. Live within your means. Minimize the use of credit cards and debt. If you use credit cards, pay the balance off each month to avoid interest charges. If you can't use the card responsibly, destroy it and cancel the account. Don't borrow money for consumption spending.

Prepare a budget and adhere to it. Include savings in your budget. There are many things to save for, and, for many, there are formal savings plans that allow you to defer income and taxes. Save at least 10% of your income, but make every effort to save 20% or more. Be disciplined about it, and put the money away before you spend it.

Minimize the amount of taxes you pay. Some taxes can be legally avoided, and some can be deferred to the distant future by deferring income. The deferred income, if invested wisely, can earn a considerable amount of money. Itemize deductions on your personal income tax return rather than using the standard deduction, if your deductions are large enough. Even if you can't itemize, take full advantage of all deductions to income and tax credits available to you.

To grow your wealth, savings need to be invested. Your money must be put to work or it will lose value because of inflation. The higher your earnings growth, the faster you can accumulate money, but high growth investments can expose you to significant risk. Select your investments carefully. It is important to understand and value what it is you're planning to invest in. If you don't understand it, don't invest in it. Make sure you understand the potential risks as well as the rewards, and don't be fooled by brokers and other salespeople. Learn how to value assets. Interest rates play a key role in economic activity and are a major factor in determining asset values; make sure you understand why. Buy only when you decide an asset is undervalued, and be alert for asset bubbles.

Make sure to diversify your investments; don't put all your eggs in one basket. Invest in different asset classes as well as buying different things within the same asset class, and buy at different times. Have patience, and allow the miracle of compounding and time to work their magic and turn your savings into real wealth. There are many different ways to invest, but regardless of how you do it, don't just buy and forget. The performance of your investments should be monitored frequently. If investments are significantly underperforming expectations, consider making changes. Don't become a frequent trader, but don't be completely passive either.

Buy the insurance you need to protect you and your family from large financial risks. Make sure you and other members of your family have health insurance of some type, and give serious consideration to the purchase of disability coverage. If you own a car, make sure you have adequate auto insurance, and if you own a home, make sure you have adequate home insurance. If you rent, buy a renter's policy. If you have dependents, buy life insurance (term insurance is inexpensive). Also, give serious consideration to a liability umbrella policy to increase liability protection. If you're approaching old age, consider buying long-term care insurance.

Identity theft is a serious and growing crime. The best defense is prevention. If prevention fails, you want to detect it quickly; if you detect or suspect it, you should take immediate action to correct any damage. While it is impossible to totally protect yourself, you can and should take steps to minimize becoming a victim. Most important is to safeguard your personal data. There's likely a lot of it, and many people potentially have access. Know the ways thieves can get your data, how they can use it, and the steps you can take to help prevent these things from happening. Avoid giving out personal information unnecessarily, store personal information in a safe place, secure your computer, and shred documents that contain personal information after you are finished with them. Take particular care to protect your Social Security number, financial information, and passwords. It is important to detect any evidence of possible identity theft as soon as possible. This requires that you be observant. You should monitor and carefully check all the data available to you. Be alert to suspicious or irregular activity involving your personal information and particularly your finances.

Make sure you plan for the future. Plan ahead for your retirement, for education for children and possibly grandchildren, and to ensure that your assets end up in the hands of the people you choose, after your death.

An enjoyable retirement requires advance planning and should begin early in your working life. Think about what you want to do in retirement, when you want to retire, how long you might live after retirement, how much money you'll need, and where this money will come from. A comfortable retirement takes substantial financial resources, and the younger one is at retirement, the more resources one needs. Consider the fact that you might need to work part time in retirement and prepare accordingly. Since things change, retirement planning should continue throughout your working life and even into retirement. Start early, develop a plan, and implement it, making changes as necessary.

Like retirement planning, estate planning requires thought about the future; in this case, about what you want to happen to your assets after your death. Who do you want to get them and do you want to exercise any control or put restrictions on how they're used? To do it right requires specialized knowledge. Before getting professional help, however, you should have a basic understanding of what the process entails and the choices you have.

There are various estate planning tools available to implement your plan, but you should understand what they can and cannot do. Many people have wills, but many mistakenly believe their will controls the disposition of all their property. It doesn't. Beneficiary designations (in beneficiary documents) control the disposition of certain types of property, such as life insurance and IRAs, and neither a will nor a trust can countermand these designations. Keep beneficiary designations up to date. Make sure the way you hold title to property is consistent with your intentions for transferring that property at death. Certain forms of holding title include a right of survivorship, and neither a will nor a trust can override this title right.

Trusts are the most comprehensive of estate planning documents, but not everyone needs a trust. The more money you have and the more control you want to exercise, the more likely you are to benefit from a trust. To be useful, however, a trust must be funded. Trusts are written in legal language, can be complicated, and are not easily understood. If you use a trust, make sure you read it carefully and understand what you're committing to.

Title documents, beneficiary designations, wills, and revocable trusts can be changed during your lifetime. On your death, however, they become irrevocable, so it is of the utmost importance that they accurately reflect your intentions.

Depending on the size of your estate, it might be subject to estate taxes. Both the federal government and many states impose estate taxes, and these taxes can be substantial. There are, however, many things you can do to minimize these taxes. Make sure you understand the potential tax liabilities of your estate, and, if necessary, take steps to minimize any taxes.

Make sure the future executor or personal representative of your estate knows about your assets and liabilities. A good way to do this is with a letter that itemizes them and tells where to get specific information. Your executor should know where the letter is located and have access. Update the letter periodically.

Appendix I

Capitalization of an Income Stream

To capitalize (determine the present lump sum value) an income stream (a series of payments), you basically calculate the present value of each element of the income stream and add all the present values together. The technique is known as discounted cash flow. As discussed in chapter 1 on the time value of money, the present value of an amount to be received sometime in the future is equal to that future amount divided by a discount factor, $(1+D)^N$ where D is the discount rate and N is the number of periods in the future when the funds would be received. If the income amounts $A_1, A_2, A_3 \ldots A_n$, are periodic and are paid at the end of each period, and the discount rate for each period is the same, the present capitalized value is given by the series:

$$V = A_1/(1+D) + A_2/(1+D)^2 + A_3/(1+D)^3 + \ldots \ldots A_n/(1+D)^N.$$

Assuming all the income amounts are constant and equal to A, the above series is a geometric series with first term equal to $A/(1+D)$, common ratio equal to $1/(1+D)$, and last term equal to $A/(1+D)^N$. The sum of a geometric series in terms of the first term, F, the common ratio, C, and the last term, L, is given by the equation below:

$$\text{Sum} = (F-C^*L)/(1-C).$$

Substituting the values for F, C, and L into the sum equation gives the following result for the value of the series:

$$V = (A/D)(1-1/(1+D)^N).$$

This equation provides the present lump sum value of an annuity with N equal periodic payments, each equal to A. As always, the amount A, the number of periods, N, and the discount rate, D, must be consistent.

If the income amounts go on forever, the series is an infinite series. Since the series now has an infinite number of terms, N is equal to infinity, the value of $(1+D)^N$ is infinite, the expression $1/(1+D)^N$ is equal to zero, and the above equation simplifies to:

$$V = A/D.$$

This simple equation provides the present value of a perpetual annuity with periodic payments equal to A.

If the income amounts are periodic and grow at the rate G from period to period such that the value from one period to the next is related by the factor (1+G), the present capitalized value is given by the series:

$$V=A/(1+D)+A(1+G)/(1+D)^2 +A(1+G)^2/(1+D)^3+ \ldots A(1+G)^{N-1}/(1+D)^N.$$

Since the elements in this series are related by a common factor, $(1+G)/(1+D)$, the series is a geometric series and the sum is also given by the sum equation. Substituting the values for first term, F, common ratio, C, and last term, L, into the sum equation gives the following value for the series:

$$V = (A/(D-G)) (1-(1+G)^N/(1+D)^N).$$

This equation provides the present lump sum value of an annuity with N periodic payments but with income amounts growing at the rate G from period to period.

If the income payments go on forever, the series is an infinite series and N is equal to infinity. If D>G, the equation simplifies to:

$$V = A/(D-G).$$

This equation provides the present value of a perpetual annuity with income amounts growing at the rate G from period to period.

Appendix II

Relationships for P/E, P/B, and Business Value

Simple expressions for the price-to-earnings (P/E) ratio, the price-to-book (P/B) ratio, and the value of a business in terms of the amount of its invested capital can be derived by making a number of simplifying assumptions.

If the free cash flow (FCF) belonging to the common equity investors is assumed to grow at a constant rate, G, in perpetuity, and discounted at the rate D, the value of the common equity as given by the continuing value relationship is:

$$V = FCF/(D-G)$$

FCF can be approximated by adding depreciation charges, A, to accounting earnings, E, and subtracting capital expenditures, C, or

$$FCF = E+A-C = E-(C-A).$$

The term (C-A) is net new capital expenditures. Factoring out E gives

$$FCF = E (1-(C-A)/E).$$

The term (C-A)/E is the percentage of earnings invested as net new capital. Assuming the growth in FCF and earnings to be the result of net new capital investment, the term, (C-A)/E can be replaced by G/R, where

R is the rate of return expected on new capital investment. Making the appropriate substitutions into the equation for value and assuming that price is equal to value gives a simple equation for the expected P/E ratio in terms of the major determinants:

$$P/E = (1-G/R)/(D-G).$$

By making some additional assumptions, the above relationship for P/E can be converted into a simple expression for the P/B for a company with no debt. If the company has debt, the relationship is not so simple. A good estimate for the rate of return expected on new capital investment is the return the company currently earns on its existing invested capital or ROIC. If, however, a company has no debt, ROIC is the same as the return on equity (ROE). If a company has debt, ROE is greater than the ROIC. ROE is defined as earnings (E) divided by book equity (B) or E/B. Replacing E with B*ROE, and rearranging terms gives a simple relationship for the P/B ratio.

$$P/B = (ROE-G)/(D-G).$$

A very similar relationship can also be derived for the total value of the operating portion of a company (not just the common equity portion) but now in relation to the value of invested capital. Now, however, the entity free cash flow must be used in the continuing value formulation. As discussed in the book *Valuation*, the entity FCF equals the net operating profit of the entity less adjusted taxes, called NOPLAT, minus net new investment capital. The procedure is essentially the same as above with similar assumptions except now we no longer need to assume the company has no debt. Further R is now the ROIC, D is the weighted cost of capital not the cost of equity capital, and G is the growth in entity FCF. Defining ROIC as NOPLAT/ IC, as in the book *Valuation*, gives the following simple relationship for the value of operations in terms of invested capital (IC):

$$V = IC (ROIC-G)/(D-G).$$

Glossary

accrual accounting. A method of accounting in which income is counted when earned and spending counted when the financial commitment is made.

active management. The process of trying to outperform the market or some market index by buying and selling securities based on some selection criteria.

adjustable rate mortgage. A type of mortgage in which the interest rate varies according to some type of index.

adjusted gross income. The amount of income remaining after subtracting certain allowable deductions (adjustments to income) from total or gross income.

American Depository Receipts (ADRs). Receipts from US banks for shares of foreign stocks that trade on US exchanges like stocks.

annuity. The payment of an amount of money at regular intervals. Also a class of investments sold by insurance companies.

asset. A resource owned by a person or entity, the value of which can be quantified in money terms.

asset allocation. Division of a person's investment assets among different asset classes to achieve diversification.

asset classes. Groups of assets with those having similar characteristics placed in the same group.

bear market. A market characterized by a sustained downward price trend.

beneficiary. A person or entity designated to receive the income or property of another when that person dies.

beneficiary document. A document in which the owner of certain assets designates who or what entity will inherit these assets when the owner dies.

bond. An interest-bearing debt security of a business or government entity.

book value. The monetary value of an item or items recorded in the accounting books. Usually the book value of the common share holder equity.

bull market. A market characterized by a sustained upward price trend.

capital gain. The gain or appreciation in the market value of an asset compared to its cost.

capitalization (cap) rate. A rate used to convert a single year's anticipated income or cash flow from a property directly into a value for that property.

cash accounting. An accounting method in which income is counted only when funds are received and spending counted only when funds are actually disbursed.

collateral. An asset pledged as security for a loan.

compound annual growth rate (CAGR). The annual return that, when compounded, provides the cumulative return over a given time period.

common stock. A proportionate share of the ownership or equity capital of a business or corporation. Owners of the common stock are the owners of the business or corporation.

cost of equity. The return the owners of common equity expect to earn; the implied cost of equity capital.

cost of debt. The interest or interest rate paid to debt holders.

Consumer Price Index (CPI). An index used to measure the increase or decrease in the price consumers pay for a basket of goods representative of what a typical household buys. A measure of inflation.

debt. An amount owed. A financial obligation, usually an interest-bearing obligation, of an individual or entity.

deficit. A shortfall or imbalance of income compared to spending for a period of time, usually a year. Deficits add to debt.

deflation. A general decline in price levels and an increase in the purchasing power of money.

defined benefit retirement plan. A retirement plan in which an earned pension benefit is guaranteed to an employee by a company or government entity.

defined contribution plan. A tax-advantaged retirement savings and investment plan to which both the employee and employer can contribute. Investments are managed by the employee, and the employee has responsibility for the results.

discounting. Reducing the value of money that is expected to be received at some point in the future to obtain its present value; the reverse of compounding.

discounted cash flow (DCF). A method used to determine the present value of a series of future financial inflows.

dividend. A payment made by many corporations or businesses to shareholders.

dividend yield. The annual dividend either paid or expected to be paid, divided by the current price of the asset.

diversification. A way to reduce investment risk by investing in multiple things.

equity. The amount by which the value of a property exceeds the liabilities on it. The owner's claim on the asset.

estate. The assets and liabilities of a dead person.

estate tax. A tax levied on estates valued over a certain amount. Estate taxes are levied by the federal government and some states.

exchange traded fund (ETF). A type of fund that pools money from multiple investors and invests in various securities. ETFs trade on an exchange-like stocks. Like a mutual fund, they generally provide diversification.

Federal Deposit Insurance Corporation (FDIC). A government agency that insures financial deposits of member banks (up to a certain limit), monitors the banks, and manages those that have failed.

fiat currency. A currency that has value by the dictate of a government.

free cash flow (FCF). The amount of funds remaining after capital investments and dividends payable to preferred share holders are subtracted from the cash generated by operations. Money that belongs to the common share holders.

future value. The value of money you have now projected to some point in the future.

gift tax. A tax levied by the government on gifts over a certain amount.

gross domestic product (GDP). The value of all goods and services produced in the country in a given year; a measure of the size of the nation's economy.

gross domestic income (GDI). A measure of the output of the economy in terms of the income accruing to labor, capital, and management (the factors of production) and to government. GDI is equal to GDP.

gross national income (GNI). GNI is equal to GDI plus income payments to the US from other countries of the world (resulting from US investments in these countries) minus income payments from the US to other countries (resulting from foreign investments in the US).

growth stock. A stock that has higher than average earnings growth potential.

hedging. A technique or strategy to reduce risk or the possibility of loss in a bet or investment.

identity theft. Defined by the US Department of Justice as "all types of crime in which someone wrongfully obtains and uses another person's personal data in some way that involves fraud or deception, typically for economic gain."

income tax. A tax levied on income. Income taxes can be imposed by state and local governments as well as the federal government.

index fund. A type of mutual fund or exchange-traded fund that tries to mimic the performance of some market index like the S&P 500 index or the Dow Jones index.

inflation. A general rise in price levels and a loss in the purchasing power of money.

interest. A fee paid for the use of someone else's money or received from others for use of your money.

invested capital. The funds invested in a business or company. Usually the sum of long-term debt (debt capital) and book equity (equity capital). Sometimes the sum of equity and all interest bearing debt.

individual retirement arrangement (IRA). A tax-advantaged personal retirement savings account. Often used to refer to the original or traditional IRA, in which contributions are deductible as an adjustment to income but distributions are taxed as normal income.

intrinsic value. The inherent value of an asset. An estimate of value based on fundamentals.

leverage. The use of debt to buy an asset and increase investment return.

liabilities. Claims others have against the assets of an individual or entity. Debts and other obligations incurred but not yet paid.

liquidity. How readily an asset can be converted to cash.

national income (NI). The income remaining after the capital consumption allowance (economic depreciation) is subtracted from GNI. It is the income from which the various taxes are paid, net new investments made, and available for consumption expenditures.

margin of safety. The amount by which an asset's fundamental or intrinsic value exceeds the current market price. The amount the asset is considered undervalued.

market. The coming together of buyers and sellers of goods and services. In some markets, buyers and sellers meet face to face; in others representatives of buyers and sellers meet, and in others transactions take place electronically.

mutual fund. A company that pools funds from many investors and invests in a portfolio of different stocks, bonds, or other securities. Shares are bought and sold directly from the company or through a broker at a price determined each day after the markets close. Mutual funds generally create new shares to accommodate increased demand of customers.

net worth. The value of assets minus liabilities; also called net asset value. A measure of wealth.

nonrecourse loan. A type of loan in which the lender, in the event of default by the borrower, can take possession of the collateral but has no legal recourse to collect any remaining amounts owed.

owner's equity. The portion of a property or business that belongs to the owner. The owner's claim on assets. The amount by which the value of a property or business exceeds the total amount owed on the property or by the business.

payroll tax. The tax levied on wages of employees and employers to help pay for Social Security and the hospital insurance portion of the Medicare program.

Pension Benefit Guaranty Corporation (PBGC). A government corporation that protects qualified pensions of American workers and retirees.

permanent insurance. A type of insurance that remains in effect as long as premiums are paid and that usually has some type of savings/investment associated with it.

preferred stock. A type of stock that gives the owner a claim on assets of a corporation after bondholders but before common share holders. Owners of preferred stock are also entitled to receive dividend payments before common share holders but have no voting rights.

present value. The value of money you expect to receive at some time in the future discounted back to the present. What you can expect to receive today if you sell your future interest in something. Also what you can expect to pay if you buy a future interest in something.

price-to-book ratio (P/B). The ratio of the current market price of a stock to its book value per share.

price-to-earnings ratio (P/E). The ratio of the current market price of a stock to the annual earnings per share. A popular measure of value.

property tax. A tax levied on property (mostly real estate) by state and local governments.

private mortgage insurance (PMI). Insurance a borrower must buy if the down payment on a mortgage is less than a certain percentage of the property value.

probate court. The court that supervises the passing of property titles that pass through wills and the guardianship of minor children and incompetents.

recourse loan. A type of loan in which the lender can bring legal action to collect the full amount of the loan in the event of default by the borrower.

return on equity. The amount of after-tax earnings (less any dividends payable to preferred share holders) divided by the book value of common equity.

return on invested capital (ROIC). A measure of how well the investment capital of a business is being used. Usually, the after-tax earnings divided by the amount of invested capital.

reverse mortgage. A method of borrowing against the equity in one's home without having to make loan payments.

Roth IRA. An IRA in which after-tax money is contributed and distributions taken according to the rules are exempt from taxes.

sales tax. A tax levied on purchased goods and services. The tax can be levied by the state, county, or local municipality.

secondary market. A market in which investments are traded after their initial sale. The various stock exchanges are examples of secondary markets.

secured loan. A type of loan in which the borrower puts up some type of collateral as security for the loan.

term insurance. Insurance purchased for a limited period of time. Temporary insurance.

total return. The return that includes payments to owners, such as dividends, plus the appreciation in the value of the asset.

trust. A legal document used in estate planning to transfer title to one's property to others, often with restrictions.

underwriting (insurance). The process of determining the amount and acceptability of risk. Also the actual acceptance of this risk.

value investing. Buying stocks or other assets when they are cheap or undervalued.

weighted average cost of capital (WACC). Overall cost of capital determined by combining the costs for each type of capital (common equity, preferred equity, and debt) according to the proportion of each used.

will. A legal statement, usually written, of a person's wishes regarding disposition of his or her property after death.

References

About Identity Theft. n.d. http://www.ftc.gov/bcp/edu/microsites/idtheft/ consumers/about-identity-theft.html.

Anthony, Robert N., and James S. Reece. 1983. *Accounting Principles.* 5th ed. Homewood, IL: Richard D. Irwin Inc.

Avoiding Probate with a Beneficiary Deed. 2008. http://www.co.yavapai. az.us/Content.aspx?id=19530 (accessed November 7).

Banchero, Stephanie. 2010. "Tuition, Pell Grants Rise in Tandem." *Wall Street Journal.* New York: Wall Street Journal, October 28.

Bernanke, Ben S. 2009. *The Federal Reserve's Balance Sheet: An Update.* October 8. http://www.federalreserve.gov/newsevents/speech/ bernanke20091008a.htm#ip1 (accessed August 19, 2010).

Bernstein, William J. 2001. *The Intelligent Asset Allocator.* New York: McGraw-Hill.

Buffett, Warren E. 1984. "Appendix 1-The Superinvestors Of Graham-And-Doddsville." In *The Intelligent Investor*, by Benjamin Graham. Harper Business.

Busch, Glenn. 2010. *Current Tobin's Q Ratio.* April 22. http:// valueinvestingcenter.com/2010/04/22/current-tobins-q-ratio/ (accessed December 21, 2010).

Business valuation. 2010. http://en.wikipedia.org/wiki/Business_valuation (accessed July 4).

CMA Comparative Market Analysis. 2010. http://homebuying.about.com/ od/sellingahouse/qt/062107CMA.htm (accessed July 22).

Copeland, Tom, Tim Koller, Jack Murrin, and McKinsey & Company. 1995. *Valuation.* 2nd ed. New York: John Wiley & Sons Inc.

DiMatteo, Joe. 2005. "H&R Block Income Tax Course-2005 Participants Textbook." Edited by Barbara Herrin. Kansas City: H&R Block Services Inc., April.

Esperti, Robert A., and Renno L. Peterson. 1993. *Protect Your Estate.* New York: McGraw-Hill Inc.

FAQs For Employees About COBRA Continuation Health Coverage. 2009. http://www.dol.gov/ebsa/faq_consumer_cobra.HTML (accessed February 22).

Fed model. 2010. http://en.wikipedia.org/wiki/Fed_model (accessed December 18).

Federal Family Education Loan (FFEL) Program. 2010. http://www2.ed.gov/programs/ffel/index.html (accessed November 16).

Federal Perkins Loan Program. 2010. http://www2.ed.gov/programs/fpl/index.html (accessed November 17).

Fraud Alert. 2008. http:www.transunion.com/corporate/personal/fraudIdentityTheft/pre . . . . (accessed July 13).

Galbraith, John Kenneth. 1975. *Money.* Boston: Houghton Mifflin Company.

Guide to Long-Term Care (LTC) Insurance. 2010. http://www.pueblo.gsa.gov/cic_text/health/ltc/guide.htm#whatis (accessed January 3).

Historical S&P Annual Return & Trading Range 1950-2007 and Volatility Ahead. 2009. http://techfarm.blogspoy.com/2008/02/historical-s-500-annual-return-and.html (accessed October 19).

Holzman, Robert S., and John Tuozzolo. 1998. *Encyclopedia Of Estate Planning.* 16th ed. Greenwich, Ct.: Boardroom Classics.

Homeowners Policy. 1996. State Farm Insurance, August.

How Credit Reports Work. 2008. http://money.howstuffworks.com/credit-report4.htm (accessed July 26).

How the new tax law may affect you. 2010. http://guidance.fidelity.com/viewpoints/new-tax-law (accessed December 26).

Hungelmann, Jack. 2009. *Insurance For Dummies.* 2nd ed. Hoboken, NJ: Wiley Publishing Inc.

ID Theft: What It's All About. 2008. http://www.ftc.gov/bcp/conline/pubs/credit/idtheftmini.shtm (accessed July 24).

Identity Theft and Fraud. 2008. http://www.usdoj.gov/criminal/fraud/websites/idtheft.html (accessed May 17).

Identity Theft Protection Services. n.d. http://www.consumercompare.org/identity_theft_protection_services.

"Instructions for Form 1040." 2009. Internal Revenue Service.

International Investing. 2010. http://www.sec.gov/investor/pubs/invest.htm (accessed December 11).

Invest Wisely: An Introduction to Mutual Funds. 2010. http://www.sec.gov/ investor/pubs/inwsmf.htm (accessed November 29).

Investing Wisely On-Line. 2008. http://onguardonline.gov/investing.html (accessed August 21).

IRS Publication 950-Introduction to Estate and Gift Taxes. 2009. Internal Revenue Service, December 14.

Jackson, Jill, and John Nolen. 2010. *Health Care Reform Bill Summary: A Look at What's in the Bill.* March 23. http:www.cbsnews.com/8301-503544_162-20000846-503544.html (accessed August 11, 2010).

Loomis, Carol. 1999. "Mr. Buffett on the Stock Market." *Fortune.* November 22. http://library.northernlight.com/PN19991109040000127. html?cb=13&sc=0 (accessed January 1, 2001).

Loomis, Carol. 2001. "Warren Buffett on the Stock Market." December 10. http://money.cnn.com/magazines/fortune_ archive/2001/12/10/314691/ (accessed December 18, 2010).

Low Cost Health Insurance For Families & Children. 2010. http://www. cms.hhs.gov/LowCostHealthinsFamChild/ (accessed February 22).

Lynch, Peter. 1990. *One up On Wall Street.* Penguin Books.

Margin: Borrowing Money to Pay for Stocks. 2007. http://www.sec.gov/ investor/pubs/margin.htm (accessed August 3).

Markels, Alex. 2007. *It's Online But Off Price.* April 29. http:www.usnews. com/usnews/biztech/articles/070429/7real.htm (accessed July 22, 2010).

Medicare & You 2011. 2010. U.S. Department of Health and Human Services.

Merrill, Craig B., and David F. Babbel. 2007. "Investing Your Lump Sum at Retirement." Wharton Financial Institutions Center, August 14.

Miller, Theodore J. 1994. *Invest Your Way to Wealth.* Washington DC: Kiplinger Books.

Recourse Loans and Non-recourse Loans. 2009. http://banking.about. com/od/loans/a/recourseloan.htm (accessed September 22, 2009.

Samuelson, Paul A. 1955. "Appendix to Chapter 29." In *Economics,* by Paul A. Samuelson. McGraw-Hill Book Company Inc.

Shea-Joyce, Staephanie, ed. 1992. *The Appraisal of Real Estate.* 10th ed. Chicago: Appraisal Institute.

Shiller, Robert. *CAGR of the Stock Market.* 2009. http://www.moneychimp. com/features/market_cagr.htm (accessed October 9).

Shiller, Robert J. 2009. *Irrational Exuberance.* New York: Broadway Books.

A Shopper's Guide To Long-Term Care Insurance. 1996. Kansas City, MO: National Association of Insurance Commissioners.

Sjuggerud, Steve, PhD. 2004. "Don't Lose Money: The Most Important Law of Lasting Wealth." In *The Book of Money*, edited by Mike Palmer and Ryan Markish. Baltimore: Agora Publishing Inc.

Social Security (United States). 2007. http://en.wikipedia.org/wiki/Social_Security_(United_States) (accessed July 19).

Spitzer, John J., Jeffrey C. Strieter, and Sandeep Singh. 2007. "Guidelines for Withdrawal Rates and Portfolio Safety During Retirement." *Journal of Financial Planning.*

State Balanced Budget Requirements. 2010. http://www.ncsl.org/issuesresearch/budgettax/statebalancedbudgetrequirements/tabid/12660/default.aspx (accessed April 1).

State Estate Taxes. 2009. September 18. http://www.finance.cch.com/text/c50s15d170.asp.

State Farm Car Policy Booklet—Arizona Policy form 9803A. 2009. State Farm Mutual Automobile Insurance Company.

Title (property). 2009. http://en.wikipedia.org/wiki/Title_(property) (accessed September 15).

The U.S. Public Debt. 2010. http://www.publicdebt.treas.gov/ (accessed November 10).

Weston, Liz Pulliam. 2009. "The 'death tax' is far from dead." http://articles.moneycentral.msn.com/RetirementandWills/PlanYourEstate/TheDeathTaxisFarFromDead.aspx (accessed September 18).

What Does Long-Term Care Cost in Your State? 2010. http://www.aarp.org/families/caregiving/state_ltc_costs.html (accessed February 25).

What is a Zestimate? 2010. http:www.zillow.com/wikipages/What-is-a Zestimate/ (accessed July 22).

William D. Ford Federal Direct Loan Program. 2010. http:www2.ed.gov/programs/wdffdl/index.html (accessed November 16).

Wolinsky, Jacob. 2010. *Stock Market Valuation October 31st 2010.* October 31. http://www.gurufocus.com/news.php?id=111092 (accessed December 19, 2010).

Wonnacott, Paul, and Ronald Wonnacott. 1986. *Economics.* 3rd ed. New York: Mc Graw-Hill Inc.

Yardeni, Dr. Edward. 2003. *Stock Valuation Models (4.1)*. Prudential Financial Research.

Your Reverse Mortgage Guide. 2007. Wells Fargo Home Mortgage.

Index

Footnotes are referenced by *italics 'n'* in page numbers

Tables and Illustrations are referenced by *italics 'ill'* in page numbers

CPSIA information can be obtained at www.ICGtesting.com
Printed in the USA
BVOW040351030112

279646BV00002B/4/P